Education in Present Scenario

ABOUT THE AUTHOR

Dr.R.Annadurai is working as Director-in-Charge in Centre for Educational Research at Madurai Kamaraj University in Madurai, Tamil Nadu. He was served Fourteen years in College of Education and University, Experience in field of Education. He is Editor in Chief for International Journal of Educational Research, Development and Extension (IJERDE) at Centre for Educational Research-MKU- He has served as member in the visiting team conducted by NCTE, Bangalore. He was presented the research papers in many National and International conferences and organizing many Conference, Seminar and Workshop related to academic Activities.

ABOUT THE BOOK

"We are living in a regularly evolving world" (Sethy, 2008, p.29) This has changed instructing and adapting especially separate training. The entry of World Wide Web (WWW) has expanded the interest for separation training and ideas like web based learning or e-learning has developed, subsequently. Education is one of the much needed necessities for the development of an individual, and thereby of the society, in today's context. For many, the prospect to get education is often curtailed by several reasons, like poverty, necessity to earn at an early age, geographical constraints and so on. Since it is not viable for every person to avail education in the formal education system, distance education provides an option to many to continue their studies. The aim of educational technology is to improve the effectiveness of teaching-learning process in formal or informal setting and utilizing scientific principles.

❑

Education in Present Scenario

Dr. R. Annadurai
Director-in-Charge in Centre for Educational Research
Madurai Kamaraj University
Madurai, Tamil Nadu

AMIGA PRESS INC.

AMIGA PRESS INC.
H.O:- 28-A, Indra Park, St.No-9
Near-Chander Nagar, Krishna Nagar
Delhi: - 110051 (India)
Tel: - 011-22504028, +91-98736-57000
Email: - amigapress@gmail.com
info@amigapress.co.in
amigaeditorial@gmail.com
amigapub@gmail.com

Website: - www.amigapress.co.in

This edition is published by Amiga Press Inc.

ISBN: 978-93-84533-58-8

First Published 2020

Printed and bound in India by Replika Press Pvt. Ltd.

Contents

❑❑❑

1

Potential Challenges and Strategies of Distance Education in Uzbekistan

In Uzbekistan the processes of internationalization of higher education started in 1991, when this former Soviet republic became politically and economically independent. In 1997, when the new Act on Education and the National program on Personnel Training was approved by the government the international collaboration got its legitimate bases. Even the formal structure of higher education, consisted of 4-year of Bachelor studies and 2-year Master courses which was launched that time underlined the country's endeavours to be implemented in international education. The government decree on development of measures to strengthen material-technical base of higher education institutions and radically improving training highly qualified specialists announced this year is also aims to improve the quality of training specialists with higher education, demanded by industries and sectors of the economy through the strengthening and modernization of the logistics of higher education institutions, equipping them with modern educational and scientific and laboratory equipment, optimization of areas and specialties training of qualified personnel, further develop international collaboration, especially in the areas of academic staffs mobility. Many Uzbek universities are strongly engaged in international educational and scientific collaboration.

Among different international components of higher education distance and e-learning based courses stand for one of the major means of broadening the horizons of the global world. Distance learning is confidently asserting itself, especially in higher education. This is a more flexible and liberal form of education, as any people paying relatively low costs could get a new profession or improve necessary skills and knowledge. First of all, it is important to understand what is meant by distance learning because now you can meet a variety of interpretations of the concept. This includes any form of self-learning and distance education and external studies. Compared with traditional forms of education, distance learning offers more freedom in choosing the learning mode, and is easily adaptable to suit the learner's individual needs and circumstances. One is not limited in distance and learning in higher education regardless of the place of residence. One is also not limited in time and learn when it is convenient and optimal for own pace, instead of attending classes at certain times, as in traditional full-time education. However, one has a well structured curriculum, implementation of which is strictly controlled by the teacher.

The population of Uzbekistan is over 30 million, and it is growing by 0.94%, where urban population is 42%and rural population is 58% (Figure 1). Target population is students of Academic Lyceums and Vocational Colleges and applicants, who are preparing for text exams to enter to universities. Moreover, Target population age varies from 16 to 26; 22.8 percent of whole population (State Committee of Statistics, 2016).

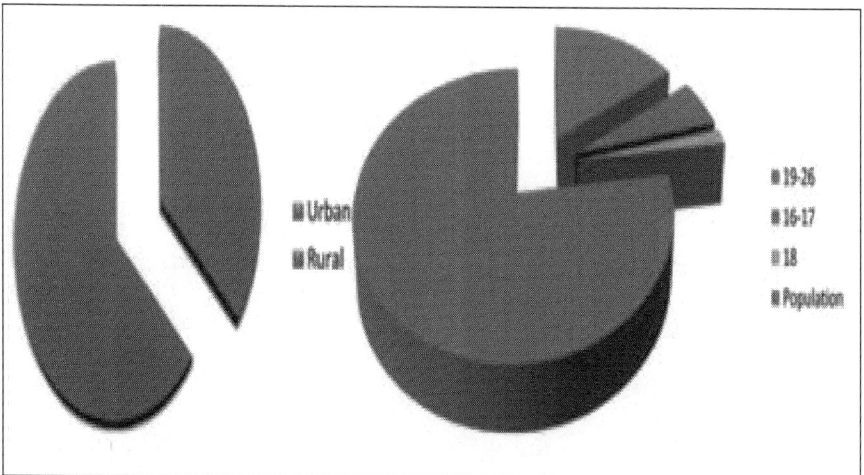

Fig. 1.1: Demographics of Target Segment of Distance Education in Uzbekistan

Source: (State Committee of Statistics, 2016)

According to State Ministry of ICT (2016) Internet users' percentage is 42% and 32% of them PC internet users, the rest are mobile internet users. In addition, 18% of households, whose monthly income is 180 US dollars or less, cannot afford distance education services (Figure 2).

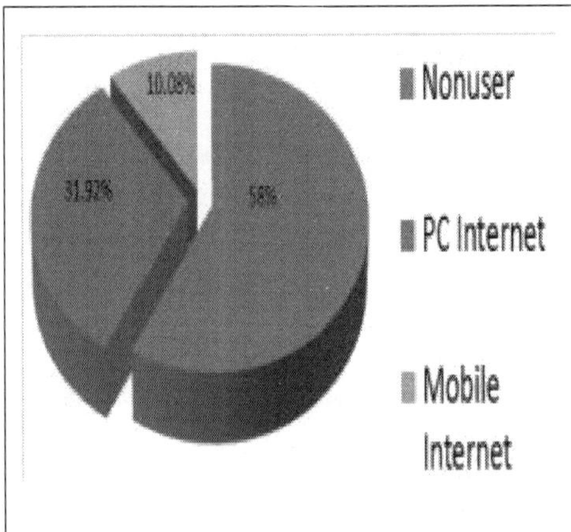

Fig. 1.2

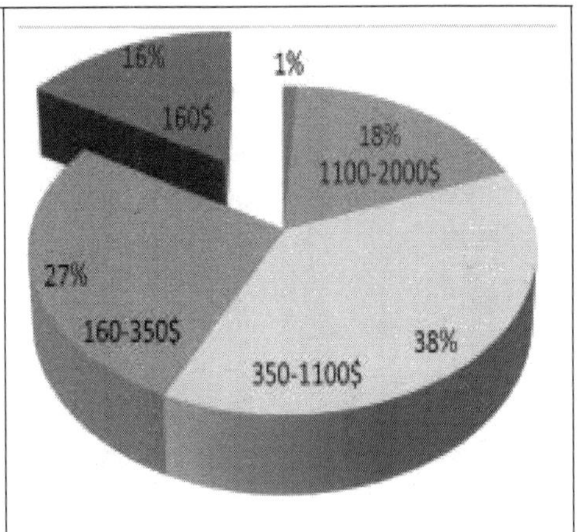

Fig. 1.3

Source: (State Ministry of ICT, 2016) (State Committee of Statistics, 2016)

The Uzbekistan National Education System is divided into following levels (Ministry of Education, 2016)

- Pre-school education
- General secondary education
- Vocational secondary education
- Higher education
- Post-graduate education.

From 1994, the universities of Uzbekistan stared a new way admission practices. Now, it is based on testing system of National Testing Center. Therefore, the entrants are required to pass the State Exams in order to be able to study in any educational organization (Ministry of Education, 2016).

According to Ministry of Education (2016) yearly quotas for admission to institutions of higher education are 62,907 and almost 56,607 of them for undergraduate programs (bachelor degree). Moreover, annual quotas for bachelor degree are divided into grant (scholarship by government) and contract (self-finance) and the total quotas are not changed (no increase in last four years).

The list of the most competitive and high ranked professions:

- Military servants, soldier, officer, etc. (higher education)
- Lawyers, jurists
- Governmental servants

- Tax and Taxation (professions)
- Economist (finance)
- Doctors
- Dentist
- Pharmacy (chemist)

Vocational secondary education is divided into two education institutions, academic lyceum and vocational college. Academic lyceum is a kind of education institution which prepares the students to the State Exams of universities in order to study in undergraduate programs. Academic lyceums divided into two specialization of preparation to the universities, such as exact subjects which includes mathematics, physics etc. and art subjects (humanitarian) which includes history, biology, foreign languages etc.

A vocational college is a sort of institution that gives specialized professional diplomas. In the colleges of Uzbekistan two types of subjects are taught; general subjects (same subjects are taught in academic lyceums), and the subjects related to major specializations of students.

The general subjects are taught only one and a half year in vocational colleges. In fact, the students study major subjects two times more comparing to general subjects. However, you may claim that it is normal standard for colleges but it shows that this tendency may not be effective for the students who are planning to continue their education in higher education. According to the report (Ministry of Higher and Secondary Specialized Education of the Republic of Uzbekistan, 2016) the applicants of the academic lyceum students for undergraduate programs have higher average scores from State Exams comparing to the applicants of vocational college students.

The situation seems to be the same at colleges and academic lyceums but there can be observed difference between them. For instance, the third year students of academic lyceums have fewer classes and they can enjoy this opportunity by taking additional teaching courses. In contrast, the third year students of vocational colleges have a tough, stressful and difficult year of study.

Furthermore, there exists a risk for the students of colleges, if the attendance for the classes is decreased, it may affect to the grade of a student, even it may cause for retaking the exams or revoking from the college. In addition, there is a deficiency of English language teachers all over the country. In order to solve the problem, the ministry of education keeps teaching Dutch in primary and secondary schools, but Dutch is not taught in colleges and academic lyceums anymore. As a result, a teenager faces difficulties after finishing schools, where they have to learn English language from the beginning. And unfortunately, there are not any entrance exams to undergraduate programs with Dutch language except linguistic major. This situation leads students to find good cram schools or private tutors in order to learn the language.

The quality of subjects and the methodology of teaching are inefficient in both institutions of education. As a result, there appear a need for cram schools or private tutors, because, the quality of education of Academic Lyceums and Vocational Colleges does not meet the education standards required for higher education. This situation is obvious and most of the students think that they need additional teaching courses from certain subjects. So, they have only two choices such as finding good and cheap cram school or finding a tutor with good reputation but expensive tuition fees. Cram schools are licensed and official working education centers where the number of students per one-hour class is from 10 to 12 people and each class is held three times in a week (2016).

Private tutors are not licensed and they are not working officially. The number of students per one-hour class is from 5 to 7 people and each class is held three times in a week. According to the report by the State Exam Centre (SEC, 2016) there 558 officially licensed private educational institutions (of all Pre-school education, General secondary education, Vocational secondary education, Higher education and Post-graduate education segments), but the private tutor population is not provided. The recent data by SEC shows an increase in licensing the private educational institutions. According to the Ministry of Public Education of the Republic of Uzbekistan there are 14 big regions and 195 sub-regions, and there are 1 to 3 cram schools in big regions, but cram schools barely exist in other sub-regions. In small 195 sub-regions the common way of private education is private tutoring. In the sub-regions the minimum number of private tutors is 8-12 per subject and maximum number is 30-40 depending on regions. As it is expected, the number of cram schools and private tutors in capital city is quite big comparing to other regions.

The teaching methodology of cram schools is modern and interactive, but sometimes they are inefficient, because teachers are mostly unqualified young graduates or students of universities, even some of them haven't high level of education. In contrast, private tutors are qualified, experienced teachers of academic lyceums, universities, high ranked school teachers and retired teachers of high educational institutions. Moreover, the tuition fee in cram schools is cheaper (25-50%) than private tutors. The prices for private education services differ from each other by areas, whereas the price in urban areas is higher than rural areas.

Currently, the major education service providers are private tutors and cram schools in education market, because, there does not exist distance education service providers in distance education industry. There is a list of web-sites in distance education, which are belonging to cram schools or government authorities, but the goal of these web-sites is to help applicants to check their knowledge. The services are provided only to increase customer awareness and the reputation of the cram schools.

TABLE.1.1: The Non-Profit Web-Sites in Uzbekistan (2016)

The Web-Sites						
Studynet.narod.ru	Testlar.uz	Abcd.uz	Salohiyat.uz	Exam.uz	Itest.uz	Ziyo.uz

According to analysis, middle class people can afford both private educations. For instance, people have advantages in choosing cram schools and tutors in urban areas. Whereas, people may face difficulties in finding cram schools and sometimes it is difficult to them to find qualified tutors in rural areas. Even if it is possible, there are limited vacant places to study.

In contrast, poor class people have difficulties in choosing both private education services. The people hardly can afford cram schools in urban areas. Accordingly, people can't find cram schools and sometimes they face difficulties in finding affordable qualified tutors and they don't have other choice other than choosing unqualified tutors of local areas. Sometimes, they try to study by themselves using reading materials which is considered very tough, time consuming and sometimes inefficient.

The decision making process of teenagers about the future education and specialization usually begin at the age of fifteen and sixteen, in 9th class at a secondary school. Teenagers choose the educational institutions (college or lyceum) and then they choose higher education specialization according to their decisions. As it is clear from the paragraphs above the decisions may differ according to the geographic locations, economic situation, family customs, gender and individual intelligence.

There five causes may influence to the decisions of teenagers about the future education and specialization:

1. The geographic matter may influence to the decision by the location (urban or rural) of institutions.
2. The economic matter (the income and the expenses of families) may influence to the decision.
3. The family customs matter (the family traditions) may influence to the decision. For instance, if the parent is a military soldier, the teenage will choose its parents profession and he may go to Military Academy of Uzbekistan or something related to this. In addition, those military institutions' competition is like a rat race (severe competition), the toughest entrance exam in Uzbekistan. Furthermore, educational majors like juridical, medical, pharmaceutical, dental and governmental management are considered as the most competitive in terms of entrance exams to the institutions.

4. The gender matter may influence to the decision, for instance the professions which are suitable to certain gender.
5. The individual intelligence matter (the skills and mental ability of a person) may influence to the decision.

After the analysis of national education system, analysis of target segment population of distance education industry, and analysis of traditional and distance education service providers following needs were defined:

1. **High Quality:** There is a need for high quality education services. And it is expected to have experienced and qualified teachers who will guaranty high quality education services. In addition, there is a need for good reliable reading materials and books with respected quality.
2. **Affordability:** There is a need for affordable price without additional expenses as transportation etc.
3. **Availability:** There is a need for the service that is available in both rural and urban areas which should be near and in one certain place.
4. **Up to date:** There is a need for up to date education materials and teaching methods.
5. **Guarantee:** There is a need for the guarantee by education service providers for the result of education services and its effectiveness. Online market is still growing, especially in emerging markets the growth rate is high comparing to developed countries. Hence, it means that there is a good opportunity for start-ups to create niche products in specific distance education markets.

The analysis of cases shows that distance education service providers may face a lot of challenges and it is very important to react to them in time. While starting a business project there is essential need for considering the economical and political (governmental) situation, technological infrastructure and demographics of a specific market. Distance education market of Uzbekistan provides opportunities for developing a competitive business. However, there are some drawbacks in the market in terms of technological infrastructure and standards of education.

Distance education service providers may face several challenges and it will not be easy to figure out what kind of strategy could work as a solution. So, there are given some recommendations, and they are about potential challenges and strategies of distance education in Uzbekistan.

Technological infrastructure of the country can be a great challenge, specifically, the internet service coverage, its price and speed is one of the toughest tasks to solve. However, there are a lot of methods that can be a solution for the problem. For instance, Companies can make partnership contracts and work closely with the strategic partners such as internet providers, mobile companies and government as well.

Apparently, the government may be interested in existence of this kind of services, because they can gain benefit from it and in addition it can solve problems related with equal education rights, certification of tutors and taxation. So, the government authorities can be involved in partnership and even they may support the business by giving subsidies and privileges. In addition, the companies can utilize niche market strategy by offering new education services such as offline application and other distance education services.

Online education providers should utilize distance education service properly and they need some additional services. For example, "Educate to educate" service which may consist of tutorials, lessons, tips etc. for potential customers. Moreover, this service also requires training courses for the developers and instructors in order to increase their qualifications regularly. Finally, using cheap online ads and promotion activities on TV and at education institutions helps to increase brand awareness. Also, additional non-profit services can be a good promotion strategy which increases customer trust and emphasizes quality and effectiveness of the services of a company.

Distance education market is growing and distance education service has potential opportunities in global market, especially in emerging markets. The analysis of existing distance education providers proves once more time that businesses do not exist without risks, difficulties and challenges.

❒

2

Distance Education Challenges and Opportunities Overview in India and Afghanistan

Distance Education is playing an important role in India in achieving the objective of higher Education of the Govt. of India. Distance Education ensures higher education for socio-economically and geographically disadvantaged group of population and/or for in-service people. Giving an equal weight age for courses under Distance Mode with Regular Mode courses with offering different courses India government provide further ensured equal opportunity to the students under Distance Mode. I am sure that the valuable deliberations by other resource persons would immensely help all the delegates in having proper perspectives about Distance Education. I congratulate the this opportunity to Bharathidasan University and those who are behind this one day International Conference for taking the initiative approach for improving distance education development.(Discenza et al, 2002).

I am sure that the issues, challenges, suggestion and solutions will be highlight in one day conference and this will be helpful for upgrade policy related to the Distance Education development in India, Afghanistan and broad countries. Evidence clearly demonstrates that Distance Education has changed the life of many people in getting good job especially in the public sector including Higher Learning Institutions. This is a good example before women; working people and socio-economically disadvantaged people to utilize the opportunity of distance mode of education to improve the quality of life. Degrees obtained through Distance Mode of Education have got equivalent status with regular in India more of education in case of recruitment as per the Government of India circular. But still a large number of common people Possess wrong notion and misunderstanding about the value of distance education; given this background.

In Afghanistan, although private colleges teach in-person and provide a lot of facilities for students to continue their education, young people who have not been able to pursue a degree of education for a variety of reasons, they have been eager to work in economics and have become. Outsiders but distance or online studies have provided young people with opportunities to continue their online education through Internet in private and domestic private institutions, and online education through the Internet has been more welcomed by young people because, despite Having a job is also interested in studying and obtaining university documents. (Radiazadi, 2014, February,2).

I am confident that such kind of conferences can help to share the delegates and scholars experience for fulfilling the existing gaps in the future for making proper understanding regarding the distance mode of Education opportunity; specially Afghanistan is one of the country which values and Equality distance mode of education has many doubts and remarks compare with regular courses of educations. A majority of the students still having some idea about correspondence Questions like: What is Distance Education? How is it Different from education through Correspondence Courses? I am sure conducting such international conference in Afghanistan and India can help to address the question of the students in the future.

A Brief Background of Distance Education in India

In India the University of Delhi first established the School of Correspondence Courses in 1962 as a pilot project. Later, Punjabi University, Patiala set up a Directorate of Correspondence Courses in 1968. Government of India constituted an eight member working group on the proposed Open University in 1974. Andhra Pradesh established the first Open University in India as Andhra Pradesh Open University in 1982. Later the name changed to Dr.B.R.Ambedkar Open University. GNOU was established in 1961 and was playing a dual role as an apex body in The country through Distance Education Council (DEC); It was established in1961 under Section 5(2) of IGNOU Act. Responsible for promotion, coordination, and maintenance of standards of Open Distance Learning in the country; Sikkim Manipal University has been ranked 1st in Distance Education. Mention may be made of the School of Distance Education, Madurai Kamraj University, and Symbiosis Centre for Distance

Learning and many more which are engaged to carryout distance education for the pass and needy students particularly those who are deprived of urban-based educational institutions and facilities.(Distance Education in India: Emerging Challenges and Prospects, Pondicherry Central University during Sept 8 – 9, 2016).

The Distance Education Council - a national body overseeing the standards of distance education, earlier a part of IGNOU has now become part of the UGC which is the highest authority mandated to ensure standards and coordination In higher education. (Zawacki-Richter, 2009).

Distance Education Ii Afghanistan

Distance education become a Global collaboration all over the world currently many popular universities offer all sorts of Programmes that might help to improve knowledge those student who are not able to study in regular courses, starting from graduate, post graduate and doctorate Programmes, to short courses to extend higher education in Afghanistan.

Harvard University Extension School

The esteemed Harvard University in America now also offers more than 200 courses online via distance education. These offerings include videos of actual lectures on campus which are available in different formats based on students' needs. Current popular subjects are management, English, environmental management, government courses and computer science.

Boston University Online

Boston University is another respected American university currently offering great courses through distance education. Apart from undergraduate to doctoral level, various non credit professional courses are also available.

Indira Gandhi National Open University

Founded in 1985, the Indira Gandhi National Open University offers 310 degree programmes in science, arts, social sciences, commerce, and information technology through 21 Schools. It is the biggest university in the world with more than four million students in India as well as 36 other countries.

Open University of Catalonia

The Open University of Catalonia in Spain was only founded in 1994 but already boasts somewhat 60 876 students. They offer more than 1000 degree programmes up to doctoral level in three different Schools, including Open Programmes.

University of South Africa (Unisa)

With more than 250 000 students, Unisa has campuses in Pretoria and Florida, Johannesburg, South Africa and numerous contact centers abroad. It also has mega university status. The University was founded in 1873 and in 2004 merged with Technikon Southern Africa to form the new Unisa. It offers internationally recognized qualifications ranging from undergraduate to doctoral studies as well as informal courses in six Colleges.

United Kingdom Open University

Founded in 1969, and with approximately 250 000 students worldwide, the UK Open University, whose academic faculties and research centers are based in Milton Keynes, United Kingdom, offers more than 250 undergraduate and postgraduate qualifications of a high standard.

Open University of the Netherlands

The Open University of the Netherlands was founded in 1984. Students can study academic Programmes or select from almost 300 modular courses. Students have the option to either register for a full-length degree programme or for modular courses, meaning they can register for two modules only if they wish. Programmes in Computer Sciences, Learning Sciences, Environmental Sciences, Law, Management, Cultural Sciences and Psychology are offered.

Open University of Hong Kong

The University offers more than 100 postgraduate, degree, associate degree and sub-degree Programmes to its students, determined to provide only high quality education.

Thomson Rivers University Open Learning.

It has more than 20,000 registrations and offers approximately 55 degrees, diploma and certificate Programmes online, web-based and in printed, formats according to student' own personal requirements.

Osaka University Dec.4,2002-Jan.29,2003

Osaka University Graduate School of Human Sciences, in collaboration with several centers, are organizing a distance education project from Afghanistan. It will be an excellent opportunity for experiencing a practical case of International Collaboration.

What is distance Education?

Distance Education or distance learning is the education of students who may not always be physically present at a school; Wherein students can study in their own time, at the place of their choice (home, workplace or Study centers/learning centre), and without face-to-face contact with teacher. (Wikipedia, https://en.wikipedia.org/wiki/Distance_education). The Distance mode of education is increasing across the world since the facilities for higher education under regular mode is limited compared to the need. Then Distance mode of education is an alternate or second possible option for a large number of students to opt for higher education, especially those who did not get the opportunity for higher education immediately after completion of bachelor degree for various reasons. It is also an opportunity for working people to acquire additional qualification for career growth. Therefore, this is a good opportunity for a large number of students to take up higher education. This opportunity helps an individual in life in fulfilling their thirst and desire for higher education. Thus it leads to higher self-esteem and dignity and finally shapes their future and enables them to gain and enjoy better quality of life. Some of the advantages of distance mode of education are flexible admission Process, no age bar like regular educational programs, flexibility in terms of course completion, timings of class, and less cost. Thus distance education gives an option both for study and gaining the desirable employment for their qualifications. However, evidence clearly demonstrates that some constraints and challenge sexist in the process of running courses in distance mode.

First, obtaining periodic approval from University Second, developing quality educational materials, third, distribution of study materials on time and maintaining overall quality of the programs/courses., Also, updating the curricula from time to time ensuring smooth and effective implementation of the programs.

Distance Education as a learning system where the teaching behaviours are separate from learning behaviours In this, the learner works alone or in the group, guided by study materials or students do have an opportunity to communicate with a tutor with the aid of one or two more media – such as correspondence, telephone, TV, Radio etc. (Moore (1991).

Objectives of Distance Education

- To provide an alternative method of education to enable a large number of persons with necessary aptitude to acquire further knowledge and improve their professional competence.
- To cater for students who had to discontinue their formal education wing to adverse pecuniary and other circumstances.
- To cater for students who cannot find a seat or do not wish to join regular college or university department although they have the necessary qualifications to peruse higher education.
- Few Questions related to Distance mode of Education in Afghanistan
- Are courses under distance mode equally beneficial in imparting knowledge and skills like regular mode education in Afghanistan?
- Do examination and evaluation of answer scripts of courses under distance mode carried out with equal seriousness like regular mode Education?
- How to make sure there is no misuse from the distance mode of education in Afghanistan? And how motivate the students under distance mode in taking their studies seriously?
- Do students with distance educational background enjoy equal opportunity in job selection and career growth both in public and private sectors?
- Are students from rural background benefitted by distance mode of education?

Advantage and Distance Education

Distance education has become platform for delivery of education around the globe. As mentioned elsewhere in this paper, distance education provides anytime anywhere forms of education and bridges the educational gap. At the same time there may be many drop outs from distance education due to various personal reasons and it is important to bring these persons back into the fold of distance education. (AlInfande, 2013).

Advantage

- Ability of combine work with existing commitments
- Cheaper
- No deadlines
- Less pressure
- No set start date
- You can decide your time of and place of study
- Saving transportation challenges for the rural girls

- Avoiding to participate in regular courses due to Traditional restriction in Afghanistan
- Free choice of courses
- No matter where you live you can still achieve and degree from anywhere in the world

Disadvantages

1. Distance learning requires self-motivation
2. Lack of face-to-face time in virtual learning
3. Distance learning does not offer immediate feedback.
4. Distance learning must be accredited by ministry of Higher education (Afghanistan)
5. Distance learning does not always offer all the necessary courses online.
6. Distance learning requires you to have constant, reliable access to technology.
7. Poor connection of Internet access in Afghanistan

COST

Depend entirely on the choice of the course, university and the country. Cost of living in certain cities like New York, Paris and Tokyo is extremely high. Therefore it is quite evident that it will be expensive to study but joining distance learning will save money.

Obstacles And Challenges Through Distance Education Mode

Distance education provides opportunities to gain knowledge but still finding shows that there are some highlighted obstacles and challenges are exist on the way of distance mode. Visser (2012).

- Distance learning is an excellent Method of reaching the adult learner in any place.
- The most important one faced by the Distance Education students is that they are
- notlegible for high level posts. The degree awarded by Distance Education mode is not being recognized by some private and government sectors in India and Afghanistan
- Especially MBA and MCA students are greatly affected for this reason.
- While regular students have a lot of facilities available and people around concerned with their academic activities and growth continuously, open and distant learners are always struggling hard for the same.
- Unfortunately in India most of the distance education universities and institutes do not issue mark sheet and degree timely this is affecting the reputation of the institution and the enrolment of students.

- Some of students require close in-person contact with the instructors some of other students may not be able to take up responsibility for their own learning by themselves.
- There is more stress on sending printing materials in India an Afghanistan.

Conclusion and Suggestion

Majority of the India and Afghanistan people lives in villages the scattered villages suffer from inadequate infrastructural facilities including means of rapid communication. The rural youth can get benefit a lot from distance education because they are deprived of urban facilities. Distance Education program is very beneficial to rural India and Afghanistan.

Distance Education has great potential in India compare to Afghanistan but to realize this potential we have to ensure its standards and quality and equivalence to other modes of Education. That should not be as the purpose of money resource. In this paper, several suggestions has given for improving quality and standard in Distance education and also to know-how to adopt and adaptor rapidly changing technology.

Much of our efforts should be on attracting and retaining good faculty, developing their skills in research and in knowledge acquisition, and provide the faculty opportunities for professional development and making them competent in understanding, assessing and meeting student needs. It is important to give the teachers opportunity also to get trained to make use of new technologies with ease and confidence.

It must be kept in mind that there is no single blueprint solution. The Institutions which provide distance education must develop their own models for integrating the various technologies, modes of imparting knowledge and skills to students and thus increase the quality and outreach of distance Education in both countries India and Afghanistan.

❐

3

Distance Education in India:A Study of Role of Invormation Communication and Tech.

Distance Education Programmes

The distance education programmes are serving wonderfully, especially for the less advantaged segment of people. Distance learning can be availed through various modes such as Postal Correspondence Programmes, Pocket PC or Mobile Learning Programmes, Interactive CD-ROM Programmes, Tele-Courses or Broadcast Courses via Television or Radio and many more.

Defiinition and Characteristic Features of Distance Education

Distance Education or distance learning is the education of students who may not always be physically present at a school. Courses that are conducted (51 percent or more) are either hybrid, blended or 100% whole instruction. wherein students can study in their own time, at the place of their choice (home, work place or Study centers / leaming centre) and without **face-to-face contact with a** teacher.

Moore (1991) defined Distance Education as a learning system where the teaching behaviours are separate from learning behaviours. In this, the learner works alone or in the group, guided by study materials. These students do have an opportunity to communicate with a tutor with the aid of one or two more media - such as correspondence, telephone, TV, Radio etc. Teaching role is shared and different study situations are possible for the learner.

Moore's definition of Distance Education highlights 3 elements: (i) separation of teaching behaviours from learning behaviours (ii) the use of technical media and (iii) the possibility of 2-way communication. While in normal face to face teaching, the teacher's preparation is done apart from the students whom he teaches; in Distance Education both preparation and teaching are done apart from students.

Holmberg (1995) stated the following in regard to distance education:

- All learning concerned with the acquisition of cognitive knowledge and cognitive skills, as well as affective learning and some psychomotor learning, is effectively provided for by distance education.
- Distance education is based on learning as an individual activity. Learning is guided and supported by noncontiguous means.
- Distance education is open to behaviorist, cognitive, constructivist, and other modes of learning.
- Personal relations, study pleasure, and empathy between students and those supporting them (tutors, counselors) are central to learning in distance education. Feelings of empathy and a sense of belongingness promote students' motivation to learn, influencing learning favorably.
- While it is an effective mode of training, distance education runs the risk of leading to mere fact learning and reproduction of accepted 'truths'. However, it can be organized and carried out in such a way that students are encouraged to search, criticize, and identify positions of their own.
- Distance Education is a form of indirect instruction which is imparted by technical media, as for example, printed material, Teaching and Learning Aids, Audio-Visual aids, Radio, TV and computer. Mathews (2002) pointed out that technology based distance education is emerging as an important feature of post-secondary education in the US. The increasing growth of ITC could bring about some of the very profound changes to the ways in which people learn and this is highly applicable to distance education. Distance education is a growth field with the development and spread of the internet. (Bailey, 2007).

It is a multidisciplinary field that has reacted to the many new technological changes that have occurred over time, and as pointed out by Bozkurt et al., (2015), it is still evolving and orienting itself to fulfill the demand for application of new technology to distance education. It is considered to be a hybrid or blended course or program when a physical on-site presence for any reason is required including the appearance of students at examinations.

Information Technology is an amalgam of some wonderful inventions of the 20th Century in Electronics and Communications. During a very short span of time, it has acquired an important place in almost all aspects of human life and particularly in the field of education. India has taken some bold steps to adapt and absorb the advances of Information Technology by constitution of national task force. Having missed the benefits of the industrial revolution as a result of more than two centuries of colonization, the country is overtaken by the information revolution at the same time globalization having opened the doors wide to alien influence, the government has decided to take all steps to make India and Information Technology super power by adoption of it as a national programme so as to enable personal and national growth. The Information Technology Action Plan intends to involve all works of life, i.e. Industry and Commerce, banking and insurance, finance, revenue, communication media, human resource development, defence, etc. The steps taken facilitates in providing effective education in all most all disciplines and particularly for the business schools. herefore, distance education and Information Technology has to develop a mutually supportive relationship for achieving excellence. We in India are using multi technologies in imparting distance education. At the one end some premier institutions are having access to all facilities in terms of education technology such as Multi Media System, LAN, WAN and World Wide Web on the other hand a large number of business schools are still depending only on stereotyped lecture method in imparting knowledge. Therefore, the existence of technology gap provides an opportunity to use Information Technology.

Role of Information Communication and Technologies (ICTs)

Use of ICT in the education sector in India though recent, has picked up fast, and the benefits are already starting to show. In recent years we witnessed many radical changes and rapid growth in the education sector. This is due to several factors, and the one factor that needs to be mentioned first is "India's telecom success story." Thanks to extensive telecom coverage and affordable rates at which bandwidth and Internet access is available due to the participation of corporate sectors in conducting rural training activities. Leading to the higher levels of appreciation for technology tools and creating enthusiasm in rural areas.

Making the IT products at more affordable rates. For instance, projectors, which used to cost upwards of Rs 2 lakh, are now made available for just about Rs 40,000 or less. Resources will be the key competitive advantage that the country has to sustain for its robust growth. Thus, a strong foundation in the form of a robust education system will be the cornerstone to leading India's growth over the next many years. With the Government showing a clear willingness to engage the private sector in accomplishing the daunting task of educating India's 13.5 Crore students the following may be focused. Providing significant opportunities for IT and ICT companies to play a contributory role in the development of education both in the Government and Private schools. Developing the students as the products useful to the industries as well as other businesses. During the Financial Year 2011-12, the Central Government of India has allocated Rs 38,957 crores for the Department of School Education and Literacy which is the main department dealing with primary education in India. Within this allocation, major share of Rs 21,000 crores is for the flagship program 'Sarva Siksha Abhiyan'. However, budgetary allocation of Rs 21,000 cores is considercrores is considered very low in view of the officially appointed Anil Bordia Committee recommendation of Rs 35,659/- for the year 2011-12.

Methodology of Education

With lots of information to gather and more and more books to study, now students are found more burdened with studying, learning and grasping the materials and the lectures. On a contrasting note however, so much efforts are being put into making the learning process an enjoyable one.

Technology Enabled Teaching in Schools

Another major contributor of success and memory is technology enabled teaching in schools nullifying the social and economic boundaries by making teaching in classes highly interactive. The intervention of technology has changed our outlook to life and methods of instruction bringing the abstract and difficult school curriculum concepts to life inside classrooms and makes learning in schools more enjoyable and memorable.

Opportunities Abound: A recent research study predicts that India's Education sector will step up its IT spending from an estimated USD 356 million in 2008 to USD 704 million in 2012, A large number of institutions are opting for networking solutions, storage and ERP implementations to support their functioning by establishing three most popular IT solutions; Wireless LAN (WLAN), Storage Area Network (SAN) and ERP.

The Encouraging Parts of ICT Application in Education Sector are

Commendable job being done and continuing to be done by Governments both at state and national level in providing the networking infra structure to the grassroots levels with connectivity, security for productive usage. Participation of corporate sectors in conducting rural training activities with higher levels of appreciation for technology tools and more enthusiasm in rural areas. Making the IT products at more affordable rates. For instance, projectors, which used to cost upwards of Rs 2 lakh, are now made available for just about Rs 40,000 or less.

The Support of State Governments in Providing Audio-Visual Aids like

Over head projectors, digital infrastructure and campus-wide network and content servers etc.

Challenges

Those concerned with tapping the opportunities in the education sector should also take note of the typical challenges. Experts point out that it is not as simple as installing a PC and running a CBT (Computer Based Training) package; there are many challenges when setting up projects at a state-wide level and in rural areas. One challenge is the consistency in the way teaching is done. The teachers playing multiple roles; as teacher, administrator, principal and one who is highly respected at the local community level lack consistency in the delivery of education and also in evaluation. In that context digital technology ensures standard delivery of education.

Language and Contextualization is Another bigger Challenge

The teachers and students should be able to relate to the content, rather than just mug it up. While the future of education in India looks promising, ICT can certainly elp in disseminating educational content, and facilitate remote learning, in the Indian context. It can overcome challenges like teacher shortage and student dropout—and bridge the digital divide.

Conclusions

Looking at the things that had happened up to (201 (Din education sector it is clear that human resources will be the key competitive advantage that the country has to sustain for its robust growth. Thus, a strong foundation in the form of a robust education system will be the cornerstone to leading India's growth over the next many years. With the Government showing a clear willingness to engage the private sector in accomplishing the daunting task of educating.

India's 13.5 Crore students the following may be focused. Providing significant opportunities for IT and ICT companies to play a contributory role in the development of education both in the Government and Private schools. Developing the students as the products useful to the industries as well as other businesses.

Undertake reforms in the education sector meeting both local and global requirements in the existing and emerging industrial as well as other business opportunities. Offering a wide range of undergraduate, postgraduate and doctoral programs in Engineering, Management, Medicine and Health sciences, and Science and Humanities through the institutions developed to the level of World Class. Develop professionals of varied talent to ensure all round development. High- skilled talent can enable growth of the economy sooner.

Develop conducive environment for learning in our schools at primary, secondary and higher education. It is unfortunate, our political system/ central or state government is inept to build large universities of their own. But, something is better than nothing at all. These foreign universities, who are ready to come and establish themselves in India; will bring requisite knowhow to successfully run a large university and will help create high-skilled talent in various fields. Create 'private sector' autonomous education zones/ townships along the lines of Oxford and University of Cambridge in or near major metro cities. Take steps to reverse the brain drain thus prevent waste of taxpayers' money used for creating prestigious institutions like IITs, IIMs etc.

Education is the groundwork based on which we can definitely progress and develop provided we can master the change by spotting the trends and keeping ourselves flexible enough to get ready for the changes through our enhanced efforts in education sector in making it more purposive and meaningful by getting ready to acclimatize and succeed. Our growth despite the lack of infrastructure, inadequate resources in industries, endemic corruption, lack of consensus in politics, youth unemployment, large uneducated masses, 'difficult to solve' population explosion etc., should provide us the courage to build India as an economic superpower making use of huge potential available with abundant talent.

4

ICT Tends its Access to Distance Education

ICTs are a potentially powerful tool for extending educational opportunities, both formal and non-formal, to previously underserved constituencies – scattered and rural populations, groups traditionally excluded from education due to cultural or social reasons such as ethnic minorities, girls and women, persons with disabilities, and the elderly, as well as all others who for reasons of cost or because of time constraints are unable to enroll on campus.

Any Time, Anywhere

One defining feature of ICTs is their ability to transcend time and space. ICTs make possible asynchronous learning, or learning characterized by a time lag between the delivery of instruction and its reception by learners. Online course materials, for example, may be accessed 24 hours day, 7 days a week. ICT based educational delivery (e.g., educational programming broadcast over radio or television) also dispenses with the need for all learners and the instructor to be in one physical location. Additionally certain types of ICTs, such as teleconferencing technologies, enable instruction to be received simultaneously by multiple, geographically dispersed learners (i.e., synchronous learning).

Access to Remote Learning Resources

Teachers and learners no longer have to rely solely on printed books and other materials in physical media housed in libraries (and available in limited quantities) for their educational needs. With the internet and the World Wide Web, a wealth of learning materials in almost every subject and in a variety of media can now be accessed from anywhere at anytime of the day and by an unlimited number of people. This is particularly significant for many schools in developing countries, and even some in developed countries that have limited and outdated library resources. ICTs also facilitate access to resource persons – mentors, experts, researchers, professionals, business leaders, and peers – all over the world.

ICTs for Preparing Individuals

One of the most commonly cited reasons for using ICTs in the classroom has been to better prepare the current generation of students for a workplace where ICTs, particularly computers, the internet and related technologies, are becoming more and more ubiquitous. Technological literacy, or the ability to use ICTs effectively and efficiently, is thus seen as representing a competitive edge in an increasingly globalizing job market. Technological literacy, however, is not the only skill – well paying jobs in the new global economy will require. EnGauge of the North Central Regional Educational Laboratory (U.S) has identified what it calls "21st Century Skills," which includes digital age literacy, cultural literacy, and global awareness), inventive thinking, higher –order thinking and sound reasoning, effective communication and high productivity.

ICTs and Quality Education

Improving the quality of education and training is a critical issue, particularly at a time of educational expansion. ICTs can enhance the quality of education in several ways; by increasing learner motivation and engagement by facilitating the acquisition of basic skills and by enhancing teacher training. ICTs are also transformational tools which, when used appropriately, can promote the shift to a learner-centered environment.

Motivating to Learn

ICTs such as videos, television and multimedia computer software that combine text, sound and colorful, moving images can be used to provide challenging and authentic content that will engage the student in the learning process. Interactive radio likewise makes use of sound effects, songs, dramatizations, comic skits, and other performance conventions to compel the students to listen and become involved in the lessons being delivered. More so than any other type of ICT, networked computers with internet connectivity can increase learner motivation as it combines the media richness and interactivity of other ICTs with the opportunity to connect with real people and to participate in real world events.

Facilitating the Acquisition of Basic Skills

The transmission of basic skills and concepts that are the foundation of higher order thinking skills and creativity can be facilitated by ICTs through drill and practice. Educational television programs such as Sesame Street use repetition and reinforcement to teach the alphabet, numbers, colors, shapes and other basic concepts. Most of the early uses of computers were for computer-based learning (also called computer-assisted instruction) that focused on mastery of skills and content through repetition and reinforcement. (See section below on Computer-Based Learning).

Enhancing Teacher Training

ICTs have also been used to improve access to and the quality of teacher training. For example, institutions like the Cyber Teacher Training Centre (CTTC) in South Korea are taking advantage of the internet to provide better teacher professional development opportunities to in-service teachers. The government-funded CTTC , established in 1997, offers self-directed, self-paced information society, "Education Reform" and "Future Society and Education". Online tutorials are also offered, with some courses requiring occasional face-to-face meetings. In china, large-scale radio and television based teacher education has for many years been conducted by the China Central Radio and Television University, the Shanghai Radio and Television university and many other RTVUs in the country. At Indira Gandhi National Open University, satellite – based one-way video-and two-way audio-conferencing was held in 1996, supplemented by print-materials and recorded video, to train 910 primary school teachers and facilitators from 20 district training institutes in Karnataka State. The teachers interacted with remote lectures by telephone and fax.

Conclusions

We are living in the digital age. In this digital age knowing / utilizing without information and communication technology is very impossible to run our day to day classroom environment very successfully and effectively. This is the order of the day that every teacher must be given proper exposure and encouragement in learning and utilizing the technological gadgets for the effective teaching of the teachers, inspiring learning of the students and the excellent system of institutional management.

5

Revisiting Curriculum through CDPS & CSR–An Initiative towards S.Sensit. in H.E

One of the foremost challenge in the field of distance education is leadership & institution building. Challenge becomes more serious with present youth found to be inclined more towards use of social media. The present study aims to act as a catalyst among the policy makers in the higher education, the students and community. The desired outcome is sensitizing educated youth towards social problems, inculcating leadership skills and enabling them to contribute towards social issues.

A deep thinking on this issue will reveal that if CSR is aligned with the curriculum of higher education (professional programs), the desired goal of high involvement of corporate world for CSR initiatives may be achieved. The outcome will be sustainable too. Community Development Programs, these days, are forming the peculiar feature of some institutions offering higher education at national and at international level. As part of CDPs (Community Development Programs), both the students and teachers undertake a series of initiatives to address social problems of gravity like female feticide, unemployment, overpopulation, corruption, crime against women, pollution, challenges of construction labor and many others. Participating students are evaluated in terms of social performance as academic task and faculty supervisor get due weightage in appraisal. These projects in groups aim to serve the community in three ways; survey based reports on social problems and possible solution, catalytic role as connect between people and government agencies and, by creating self-help groups at local level for sustained solution of problem. The focus areas revolve around inclusive growth, social entrepreneurship and women empowerment etc. In the absence of policy, a lot of disparity is visible in adoption among educational institutions (as some are highly involved, others are not). But no organized and consistent effort at all is being made presently by any institute offering higher education in professional programs. Here, lies the immense potential (opportunity) to leverage the human energy and channelize it towards social goals in a professional and formal way.

Review of Related Studies

Corporate Social Responsibility has gained attention of both industry as well as academia in last few decades. A wide range of issues pertaining to CSR have been covered by the researchers; Relating CSR with financial performance (Mackey et. al., 2007; Surroca et. al, 2009; Choi et. al. 2010; Yang et. al, 2010; Demacarty, 2009; Sulkowski, 2009; Poddi and Vergalli, 2009), customer perceptions towards CSR (Stanaland et. al., 2011;Smith et. al, 2010), CSR relationship with branding and marketing (Lai, et. al. 2010; Marquina, 2010; Pozniak et. al, 2011), CSR models and theories (Redman, 2005; Hopkins, 2004; Carroll, 1991;Visser, 2005; Holding and Pilling, 2006), strategic CSR (Morsing and Schultz, 2006; Lee, 2011;Helsin and Ochoa, 2008), CSR and shareholder value (Becchetti, et. al, 2009; Freeman & Velamuri, 2005), CSR and Education (Reinhard et. al. (2010); Gorenak,2011; Timane & Tele, 2012). One prominent area in CSR is Community Development Programs. Leading corporate houses like Reliance, Tata & Bharti group have always been found indulged in community development initiatives in one way or the other.

Need & Objectives

The need of the hour is to bring the desired seriousness among the institutes offering professional education for CSR through CDPs. Focus needs to be towards injecting the element of social concern in the mind of youth through CDPs and utilizing the human energy in right direction and for larger interest of society. Youth represent the future managers of developed India and surely, will sensitize towards CSR in times to come.

The proposed study will critically evaluate the existing initiativesof higher education institutions in community development though exploratory research.The present study will assist in sensitizing youth towards social issues by incorporating community development programs in the curriculum of higher education.

Discussion & Implications

Weiss (2016) acknowledges that a number of reputed universities take pride in integrating CSR with mission statement and acknowledge the contribution of higher education to the society. Nanyang Technological University is running 40 overseas community development projects were number of students who participate every year is around 750. Exposure to Higher education enables the students to address problems of the society. Reinhard et. al. (2010) explored the nature of Corporate Social Responsibility(CSR) and its relevance to industry and education. Many organizations are viewing interest in adopting CSR practices. Academic institutions such as the Baden Württemberg Cooperative State University Ravensburg are exploring approaches in which CSR can be included in their curriculum. It has studied selected organizations to determine their current practice related to CSR. It found that it is important to include CSR into their curriculum. Gulavani et. al (2016) opine that higher education institutes perceive CSR as a tool for earning good reputation and gaining competitive advantage. CSR in higher education are not immune to external impact and micro factors like internal capacity organizational performance also affect their contribution . Gupte & Jadav (2014) found that CSR regulations must be clear and surf towards contribution to the society through CSR projects. it is disappointing to find contradiction among implementing agencies towards CSR projects consequently overlap of CSR efforts is found .This results in duplication of activities by Corporate Houses.local ngos should come forward and play a decisive role for contribution to the CSR. Timane & Tele (2012) observed that composition of Corporate Social Responsibility initiatives has undergone a substantial change with passage of time. Indian business organizations have kept their focus towards philanthropic and community programmes. One of the positive aspect of CSR is that business now take pleasure in benefits like lower tax rates, less regulatory interventions, faster approvals, highly motivated workforce, customer loyalty, risk mitigation, enhanced brand image, value-based supplier network and favourable public opinion about company. Mehta (2011) studied the emerging relationship between CSR and Universities and voted for a defined goal for universities to involve themselves with the world outside academics.The research community (as stated above) acknowledges the need for CSR through Community Development Projects (CDPs) by Higher Education Institutes (HEIs) imparting Professional Education . The proposed studycritically evaluatesthe existing initiativesof higher education institutions in community development.

Conclusions

Future Research needsto explore the likely acceptance of senior functionaries (from educational institutions, regulatory machinery, Central and State government) for inclusion of CDPs in curriculum of higher education. Such study will create a platform for a large number of emerging private institutions offering higher education in professional programs to contribute actively towards corporate social responsibility and channelize the human energy in right direction.

❐

6

A Study of Work Environment of Teachers in Pondicherry Region

Role of teachers in the society and in the education can change, but the importance of their position remains same. Every teacher must have the potential and clear intention to discharge their duty with utmost devotion to derive satisfaction from their work. Work environment is one factor that will ensure class performance and productivity of schools. Teachers would perform to maximum capacity, only if they are satisfied with their working environment. So, Work environment is an important phenomenon in every sector especially in the teaching.

Need for the Study

The present study aims to study Work environment of teachers in Pondicherry region. A teacher who is satisfied with their job can perform their work effectively and efficiently. If the teachers work under stress, they cannot be satisfied with their job and it will create a negative impact towards the job. So, it is necessary to identify the factors that influence the teachers to derive satisfaction from their work. Additional energy can be developed when the teachers are satisfied with the environment in which they work.

Hypotheses

1. The level of work environment of teachers is high.
2. There is no significant difference in the mean scores of work environment of government and private school teachers.
3. There is no significant difference in the mean scores of work environment of urban and rural school teachers.

Research Design

The present study is a descriptive research. The main aim of this study is to study the work environment of teachers. A self structured questionnaire has been used to collect the data. The questionnaire was designed on 5 point likert scale ranging from strongly disagree to strongly agree. The questionnaire consisted of two parts. First part was related to the demographic profile of respondents and second part contained study of factors associated with work environment.

Results and Discussion

TABLE. 6.1: Demographic Details

Age	Number	Education	Number	Teaching experience	Number
<25	36	Dted	27	1to10	49
26-45	79	UG Bed	128	11 to 20	60
>46	85	PG Bed	45	21 to30	91
Total	**200**	**Total**	**200**	**Total**	**200**

Age wise classification of the respondents reveals that 18% of teachers are young, that is in the age group of 25 and below and 39.5 % respondents are middle aged(between 26 to 45 years). Other teachers are older (46 and above). With regard to teaching experience, it shows that majority of the teachers had been in their for 21-30 years (30 percent).24.5 percent have teaching experience of one to ten years and the teachers in this study are fairly highly experienced with more than 21 years working in the present school.

TABLE. 6.2: The Level of Work Environment of Teachers is High

Number	Mean	Mode	Standard Deviation
200	56.38	54.46	13.16

From the above table it is found that the mean scores of work environment is56.38. Therefore the work environment of teachers is average. Hence the null hypothesis is rejected.

TABLE. 6.3: There is no Significant Difference in the mean Scores of Work Environment of Government and Private School Teachers.

Categories	Number	Mean	S.D	't' value	Significant level
Government	100	69.93	15.72	12.57	Significant
Private	100	57.55	18.18		

It is evident from the table that the mean score of private school teachers work environment is higher than that of government school teachers work environment. The obtained "t" value is 12.57. It is higher than the table value. Therefore it is significant. Hence the hypothesis is rejected.

TABLE. 6.4: There is no Significant Difference in the mean Scores of Work Environment of Urban and Rural School Teachers.

Categories	Number	Mean	SD	't' value	Significant level
Urban	100	74.54	9.35	14.33	Significant
Rural	100	50.83	14.42		

It is evident from the table that the mean scores of teachers in urban areas have a viable working environment than teachers in rural areas. The calculated 't' value is higher than the table value. Therefore it is significant. Hence, the hypothesis is rejected.

Conclusions

The results of this study show that there exists a significant difference in the level of work environment of teachers in Pondicherry region. There exists a difference between government and private school teachers as well as the urban and rural school teachers with respect to work environment. Thus, the study concludes that organizational support in enhancing work environment of teachers is very important. All efforts should be taken to improve the work environment of teachers which in turn would have a positive outlook in the school.

❐

7

Best Practices for Integrating Technology into the Classroom

Research into the integration of technology in teacher education and professional development consisting primarily of surveys into their opinions and attitudes self-reports, interviews and descriptions of good practices or experimentations of specific technologies as well as case studies (Lawless & Pellegrino, 2007) has enabled scholars to outline various theoretical and practical proposals for pre-service and in-service training (e.g., Fulton, Glenn & Valdez, 2003; Hughes, 2004; Niederhauser & Stoddart, 2001) and to develop theoretical models geared toward group action technologies into teaching (e.g., Angeli & Valanides, 2009; Garrison, Anderson & Archer, 2000; Mishra & Koehler, 2006; Wang, 2008). Of the existing models that Mishra and kochler (2006) seems particularly appropriate for stimulating teachers' reflections on what integrating technology in teaching means. In fact the model represents a theoretical/cognitive framework able to direct personal reflection towards the proper actions to develop professional competence: in our opinion, a basic value in any type of educational innovation.

According to Bozeman (1999) there are five key components of successful technology application. These include having support from the administration, adequate training for the teachers, ready access to both hardware and software, technology support, and appropriate curriculum planning. There exist, in current research, great similarities in the reasons educators do not integrate technology into curriculum. Friedrichsen, et al. (2005), for example, found a survey of science teachers that there were four common reasons the teachers did not use technology. First, they lack adequate training in using the technology. Second, there is finite computer availability. Third, the personality of the teacher, that is, they are reluctant to change. Fourth, the high cost of technology when it comes to budget allocations. In 1995, for example, 69% of all public school districts report funding as the number one barrier to successful technology integration (U.S.D.O.E., 1995).

Similarly Strehle, Whatley, Kurz, and Hausfather (2005) found four recurring themes that transcended their research of teacher educators, one of these themes being obstacles to implementation. This included equipment not arriving, inadequate time to explore software and plan implementation, and inability to adapt the integration to fit personal methodologies

Best Practice in Technology Integration

Studies have shown that, once integrated meaningfully into curriculum and instruction, technology will completely impact student learning and accomplishment. Decades of analysis has shown drill and apply programs to be effective in reinforcing basic skills and boosting student performance in specific areas. (Boster, Meyer, Roberto, & Inge 2002). More recently, research has shown that, when integrated into curriculum-based student-centered classroom activities, tools such as word processors, spreadsheets, databases, modeling and presentation software can promote the development of such twenty first century skills as communication, collaboration, and analytical thinking.

Integration of technology, then, refers to the process of matching the most effective tool with the most effective pedagogy to achieve the learning goals of a particular lesson. Each tool brings totally different opportunities to the educational atmosphere and involves a distinct set of skills on the part of teachers and students. Each can play a unique role in the learning process when used at the appropriate time, under the most appropriate learning conditions. It is simply the degree to which a particular technology's capabilities are matched to the expected learning outcomes and supported by appropriate pedagogy that will determine the impact that technology has on learning and achievement.

Meeting educational goals through authentic, student centered learning activities presents many challenges to traditional instruction. Teaching students correct and effective use of technology tools in this context will be even harder. Current studies recommend, however, that it is in combining the fundamentals of reformed pedagogy and the appropriate integration of technology that students can gain priceless twenty first century learning skills.

Conclusions

The teacher has the responsibility of tending to the needs of the students. Not only does this individual have to understand how technology works, but also must determine the best way to integrate it into the curriculum. Moreover, technology leaders must have the correct personality, understand curriculum, be an effective communicator, this astute individual must also be motivated to go to great lengths to assist educators with finding quality resources and to promote technology use in an effort to enhance learning opportunities.

The last area of concern identified in this research is the need for a refresher course in current technologies available within each building. Educators are also asking for training on emerging technologies such as Web 2.0 tools and electronic whiteboards. As hardware, software and related devices become more prevalent and cost effective; school officials must take the necessary steps to ensure that educators understand how to integrate technology so they can effectively instruct youngsters on how it can be used in society. This paper truly recommended that teachers learn to create student-centered classroom environments that engage students actively in the development of learning, thinking, and real-world technology skills that will serve them as 21st century citizens.

❒

8

Role of Technology in Education at Present Scenario

India is known as one the world's top education destination in the global education industry. With some of the best universities and colleges India has been successful in attracting bright talents all over the world. Indian education system is robust and built on strong foundations. According to Indian Brand Equity Foundation Indian education market is currently pegged at 100 billion with higher education contributing to 59.7%, school education at 38.1%, pre-school at 1.6% and the remainder 0.6% consists of technology and multi-media based education.

India may not be the early adopters of technology in the education sector but with access to high speed broadband internet and low lost computers and mobile devices there has been growth in the use of technology for learning. Today India is one of the fastest growing markets for e-learning based products and services. It is expected that this segment will have a turnover of 40 billion by 2017. There are different ways technology can be used to bring about reformation in the Indian education system. Even government aims to increase digital literacy of the country to 50% from current 15% by bringing out favorable policies to give impetus to technology based learning. Many entrepreneurs and startups have grabbed this opportunity to develop technology based educational products for private and government based schools, colleges and universities.

USES OF TECHNOLOGY IN EDUCATION

Distance Education

Distance education is a way of learning where the students or working professionals can learn the courses remotely through online access and interact with faculty via online classroom. It helps students to interact with their mentors or tutors directly through chat, e-mail or phone call. Indian is a developing country and for many students who are living in remote places or villages getting degree for higher education is still a distant dream. In such instances technology enabled distance education can help them to complete their studies, upgrade their skills and get a degree. This gives the students or working professionals the flexibility to learn at their own time without the compulsion of going to a class.

All India Survey on Higher Education 2014-2015 by Ministry of Human Resource Development the total enrollment of students for Distance education constitute of 11.7% out of which 46% are female students. Availability of broadband and hi-speed internet along with low cost computers to tier 2 and tier 3 cities has made learning seamless without any glitches.

Classroom Based Learning

Nowadays technology has become integral part of classroom based teachings. Today in many schools, colleges and universities in India instead of blackboard projector screens are used for teachings. Hand writings of teachers are replaced by power point presentation. Student experience a different kind of set up in today's technology based classroom. Gadgets like tablets and laptops are used to take down notes. Animated content are created on various subjects and in different languages so that students can have better understanding of a complex subject in a simple way.

Online Learning Management System

Many colleges and universities in India are integrating online Learning Management System or LMS platform into their web portal. Students can remotely login to access course material and also attend live classes with teachers. Pre-recorded lectures, videos can be uploaded on the LMS platform making it easy for students to go through it multiple times. LMS adoption is still poor in many parts of India where students do not have the access to computers or broadband internet. However, government is providing computers to remote areas and creating content that consumes less data and can be easily accessed on internet.

Learning Through Mobile Apps

India has become the second biggest smart phone market in the world after China with more than 220 million active users. This presents a huge opportunity for delivering e-learning content through mobile apps. Today educational mobile apps are available on popular platforms like Android and iOS. Developers are creating educational apps based on particular subjects. They are simplifying complex concepts with easy to understand illustrations and animations, puzzles games etc. There are apps available for grammar, physics, chemistry, mathematics and so on. With the prices of tablets and smart phone coming down people from villages and remote areas can also make use of this apps to learn and update their skills. There are also certain websites like Khan Academy and various YouTube channels that offer video lectures by eminent scholars and teachers in various subjects.

Even though some of the educational institutions in India ranks par with world's best universities and colleges the use of technology is still limited in Indian education sector. With the rising cost of education, technology based learning can come to the rescue of those who wants to go for higher degree but cannot afford it. Government needs to play an active role in encouraging educational institution in adopting latest technology for teachings and delivering course content. With its population of 1.2 billion people the scope for technology based learning can surpass that of many developed and developing nation.

How Technology Can Be Used io Improve Learning

The following are ways that technology could be better leveraged to improve learning:

- With the widespread availability of student databases that are able to track individual progress, teachers are encouraged to identify learning objectives and differentiate instruction based on the needs of their students.
- Whenever teachers attempt to present instruction using technology, they should do so using a channel that is relevant to the objectives, the learning style, mode and the technology selected.
- When evaluating technology-based instruction, there needs to be appropriate evaluation techniques that are in line with the methods of instruction, objectives and the technology.

Role of ICT in Education

ICTs are a potentially powerful tool for extending educational opportunities, both formal and non-formal, to previously underserved constituencies—scattered and rural populations, groups traditionally excluded from education due to cultural or social reasons such as ethnic minorities, girls and women, persons with disabilities, and the elderly, as well as all others who for reasons of cost or because of time constraints are unable to enroll on campus.

Anytime, Anywhere

One defining feature of ICTs is their ability to transcend time and space. ICTs make possible asynchronous learning, or learning characterized by a time lag between the delivery of instruction and its reception by learners. Online course materials, for example, may be accessed 24 hours a day, 7 days a week. ICT-based educational delivery (e.g., educational programming broadcast over radio or television) also dispenses with the need for all learners and the instructor to be in one physical location.

Admittance io Remote Learning Resources

Teachers and learners no longer have to rely solely on printed books and other materials in physical media housed in libraries (and available in limited quantities) for their educational needs. With the Internet and the World Wide Web, a wealth of learning materials in almost every subject and in a variety of media can now be accessed from anywhere at any time of the day and by an unlimited number of people. This is particularly significant for many schools in developing countries, and even some in developed countries, that have limited and outdated library resources. ICTs also facilitate access to resource persons— mentors, experts, researchers, professionals, business leaders, and peers all over the world.

Improving the Quality of Education

Improving the quality of education and training is a critical issue, particularly at a time of educational expansion. ICTs can enhance the quality of education in several ways: by increasing learner motivation and engagement, by facilitating the acquisition of basic skills, and by enhancing teacher training. ICTs are also transformational tools which, when used appropriately, can promote the shift to a learner-centered environment.

Motivating to Learn

ICTs such as videos, television and multimedia computer software that combine text, sound, and colorful, moving images can be used to provide challenging and authentic content that will engage the student in the learning process. Interactive radio likewise makes use of sound effects, songs, dramatizations, comic skits, and other performance conventions to compel the students to listen and become involved in the lessons being delivered. More so than any other type of ICT, networked computers with Internet connectivity can increase learner motivation as it combines the media richness and interactivity of other ICTs with the opportunity to connect with real people and to participate in real world events.

Conclusions

ICTs are potentially a useful tool both for managing education and for teaching. Use in managing educational institutions should be encouraged, as should use by instructors to gain access to educational materials. And, by teaching computer skills to youngsters, they may influence inward investment. Well-designed ICTs can allow educators to reach new groups of prospective students, particularly mature students, lifelong learners, and students with physical disabilities, students in employment and students who are far from education centres. Finally, technology is never a substitute for good teaching. Without skilled instructors, no electronic delivery can achieve good results. But neither can traditional classroom teaching.

❐

9

Development of Distance Education and the Role of Teaching Learning Process

In, American the distance education began in 1874 at Illinois Wesleyan University where bachelor and graduate degrees could be obtained without being actually present in the classes. The Chautauqua movement in the year 1882 gave the much required thrust to correspondence education. Correspondence education became quite famous by 1900 and problems of excellence and fair practice came with the popularity. The National Home Study Council (NHSC) was formed in 1926 in part to deal with such issues.

Distance Learning in India

Distance Learning in India for higher education in India was initiated in the form of Correspondence Courses in 1962, in response to the ever-increasing demand for higher education which could not be met by the conventional system. The Delhi University established a School of Correspondence Courses and Continuing Education in 1962. Encouraged by the success, the Education Commission (1964-66) recommended the expansion of correspondence education for various purposes. Consequently, the University Grants Commission UGC formulated guidelines for introducing correspondence courses in Indian Universities. Three more Institutes of Correspondence Studies were established in the late sixties. Twenty one more universities introduced correspondence programmes during the seventies. In the early eighties seven more universities started institutes of cor-respondences studies. At present there are 45 universities including four deemed universities offering correspondence programmes in the country.

Strong Foundation

The establishment of the Open University in the United Kingdom, in 1969 encouraged several countries to deliberate on the new concept and its potential in making higher education more accessible, flexible and innovative. India was one of those countries which examined the possibility of establishing an open university in the early seventies. This influenced a few universities like University of Mysore and Andhra University to adopt open admission policies in the mid seventies by relaxing formal qualifications for entry to undergraduate and post- graduate courses. This seemingly minor innovation provided impetus to efforts towards greater access to higher education for larger segments of the population especially those adults who could not complete school education.

Concrete Structure

The establishment of IGNOU at New Delhi in 1985 has proved to be a significant milestone in the development of Distance Learning in India. It provides a central Organisation for guiding and coordinating the activities of all distance education institutes and state open universities in the country. It has popularized the concept of open learning system resulting in the establishment of three more state open universities in the late eighties viz. – Kota Open University in Kota (Rajasthan), Yashwant Rao Chavan Maharashtra Open University at Nasik (Maharashtra) and Nalanda Open University at Patna (Bihar). States of Madhya Pradesh and Karnataka have also established Open Universities recently.

Number's Game

From just a handful of students in 1962-63 the enrollment in correspondence courses rose to about 65,000 students in 1975-76. During the last fifteen years the annual growth rate of enrollment in open universities and the institutes of correspondence studies attached to conventional universities has been appreciably higher than in the conventional universities and in 1990-91 it was approximately 600,000. The proportion of students enrolled in distance education has steadily increased from 2.6% of the enrollment in higher education in 1975-76 to 11.5% in 1990-91. During 1992-93 the enrollment for Distance Learning in India programmes was over eight lakhs.

E-learning

E-learning incused numerous types of media that deliver text, audio, images, animation and streaming video and includes technology applications and processes such as audio or video tape, satellite TV, CD-ROM and Computer Based Learning, as well as local intranet/extranet and web-based learning. E-learning can occur in or out of the classroom. It can be self-paced, asynchronous learning or may be instructor-led, synchronous learning. E-learning is suited to distance learning and flexible learning, but it can also be used in conjunction with face-to-face teaching, in which case the term blended learning is commonly used.

Educational Approach

The extent to which e-learning assists or replaces other learning and teaching approaches is variable, ranging on a continuum from none to fully online distance learning. A variety of descriptive terms have been employed (somewhat inconsistently) to categorize the extent to which technology is used. For example, 'hybrid learning' or 'blended learning' may refer to classroom aids and laptops or may refer to approaches in which traditional classroom time is reduced but not eliminated and is reduced but not eliminated and is replaced with some online learning.

INTERACTIVE TOOLS

Asynchronous

- **E-mail**- used for questions and discussion
- **Web forums**- also called discussion forms or bulletin boards. They are probably the most common form of interaction in online courses.
- **News groups**- public forums that use the use net system.
- **BBS** – A computer bulletin board that you dial, the use like a web forum, e-mail, file transfer.

Synchronous

- **Chat Rooms**- can be either moderated by an instructor of un-moderated foe class use.
- **Shared Whiteboards**- allow class members to write on the same digital whiteboard.
- **Application Sharing** - the same program and file can be shared for demonstration or collaboration.
- **Teleconferencing**- could be used to deliver instructor audio or for collaboration.

- **Video conferencing-** either from expensive, high quality, dedicated systems or from less reliable desktop versions.
- **Technology:** Various technologies are used to facilitate e-learning.

Audio

Streaming audio used to deliver the instructions comments over any network. Audio tapes could is mailed to students.

Video

Videos allow teachers to reach students who are visual learners and tend to learn best by seeing the material rather than hearing or reading about it. Teachers can access video clips through the internet instead of relying on DVDs or VHS tapes.

Computers, Tablets and Mobile Devices

Computers and tablets allow students and teacher's access to websites and other programs, such as Microsoft Word, Power Point, PDF Files and images. Many mobile devices support m-learning.

Blogging

Blogs allow students and teachers to post their thoughts, ideas and comments on a website. Blogging allows students and instructors to share their thoughts and comments on the thoughts of others which could create an interactive learning environment.

Virtual Classroom

Virtual Learning Environments (VLE) known as learning platforms, utilize virtual classrooms and meetings which often use a mix of communication technologies. The virtual classroom also provides the opportunity for students to receive direct instruction from a qualified teacher in an interactive environment. Students have direct and immediate access to their instructor for instant feedback and direction. The virtual classroom also provides a structured schedule of classes, which can be helpful for students who may find the freedom of asynchronous learning to be overwhelming.

Computer Aided Assessment

Computer aided assessment (also but less commonly referred to as e-assessment), ranging from automated multiple-choice tests to more sophisticated systems is becoming increasingly common. With some systems, feedback can be geared towards a student's specific mistakes or the computer can navigate the student through a series of questions adapting to what the student appears to have learned or not learned.

E-Learning in Higher Education

In higher education especially, the increasing tendency is to create a virtual learning environment (VLE) (which is sometimes combined with a Management Information System (MIS) to create a Managed Learning Environment) in which all aspects of a course are handled through a consistent user interface standard throughout the institution. A growing number of physical universities, as well as newer online-only college, have begun to offer a select set of academic degree and certificate programs via the internet at a wide range of levels and in a wide range of disciplines. While some programs require students to attend some campus classes or orientations, many are delivered completely online. In addition, several universities offer online student support services, such as online advising and registration, e-counseling, online textbook purchases, student governments and student newspapers.

E-learning can also refer to educational websites such as those offering learning scenarios, worksheets and interactive exercises for children. The term is also used extensively in the business sector where it generally refers to cost-effective online training.

Conclusions

E-learning provides the excellent learning support to the students, which is as good as face-to-face teaching. This support will be available anywhere anytime on the internet. These presentations will offer much better learning effectiveness and quality due to clarity of communication and interaction during discussions or tutorials with real teachers and fellow students. E-learning is highly cost effective, without compromising with quality.

❐

10

Media Technology Trends and Distance Education

Education is one of the much needed necessities for the development of an individual, and thereby of the society, in today's context. For many, the prospect to get education is often curtailed by several reasons, like poverty, necessity to earn at an early age, geographical constraints and so on. Since it is not viable for every person to avail education in the formal education system, distance education provides an option to many to continue their studies. Distance education is a planned learning experience or method of instruction characterized by quasi permanent separation of the instructor and learners. With the advances in the educational technologies, more emphasis is laid on self learning and on the use of effective technologies to access education anywhere, anytime through distance mode.

Media Technologiesand Distance Education

Generally media technology has a strong portability which is replacing books and notes. Their capabilities enhance learning through interaction and collaboration; it creates a learning community, providing access to a variety of online resources, allowing new skills or knowledge to be applied immediately. The emergence of new technologies has almost revolutionized the field of teaching and learning. New media technologies enable collaboration over the Internet. Blogs and wikis offer collaboration among a small or large group, depending upon the nature of the media. Collaboration and interaction between the student-student, teacher-student and student-content are vital for distance education courses. A distance education programme utilizes various media to deliver learning information and to connect teachers with learners at a distance.

(i) Internet

The Internet is a worldwide broadcasting capability, a mechanism for information dissemination, and a medium for collaboration and interaction between individuals and their computers without regard for geographic location.The Internet has created new forums of social interactions and social relations including social networking websites such as Face book and My Space, which could be used as tools of imparting education and information at a distance. Over six million people use blogs and message boardsas a means of communication and for the sharing of ideas. Educational video-clips uploaded on You Tube, blogs and social networking sites, are being successfully adopted into the delivery process of distance education by many institutions around the world. Distance education via the Internet provides learners with a low cost, flexible option to expand into global markets.

(ii) E-Learning

E-learning is commonly referred to the planned use of networked information and communication technology in teaching and learning. A number of other terms are also used to describe this form of teaching and learning, as online learning, virtual learning, distributed learning, networked and web-based learning. The letter "e" in e-learning stands for the word electronic. E-learning would include all educational activities that are carried out by individuals or groups working online or offline, and synchronously or asynchronously via networked or standalone computers and other electronic devices. E-learning not only covers content and instructional methods delivered via CD-ROM, the Internet or the Intranet, but also includes audio and video tape, satellite broadcast and interactive television.

(iii) Electronic Book

An electronic book or e-book is a portable hardware and software system that candisplay large quantities of readable textual information to the user, and that lets the user navigate through this information. An e-book is an integration of the classical print structure with an electronic environment giving additional value added features that paper cannot provide. They can be accessed anywhere, anytime with thetechnological developments, proving to be very handy for a distance learner. The various advantages of e-books are the easy availability and search, customization, portability, multimedia facilities, environment-friendly, cost-efficient, and easy storage. E-ink technology has made reading on a screen comparable to readingfrom paper, and walkmans, cell phones, iPods and iPods have made it comfortable for the people.

(iv) Internet Radio/Web Radio

Radio programmes were being delivered over the Internet. With thetechnological innovations, radio programmes are available not only fromterrestrial networks but also from a large variety of satellite, cable and telecommunications networks. Radio is now assuming the shape of various multimedia-enabled computer devices. Traditional broadcasters could stream their content over the channel ofInternet radio, and brand new broadcasters could reach online audiences generally without requiring any governmental approval. Internet radio services are accessible from anywhere in the world, with the help of a suitable internet connection. One can listen to the Internet radio on a personal computer or similar devices, through an embedded player programme located on the respective station's website. Streaming technology is used to distribute Internet radio.

(iv) Audio/Audio-Visual Materials

In the 1970 and 1980s, audio and video cassettes offered greater flexibilities andmore opportunities for media integration and student-active learning.Audio and video cassettesand CDs possess most of the capabilities of radio and television, and can belistened to and viewed as per the convenience of the learner, and hence, providingthe learner a control over the learning process. The 15 to 20 minutes of discussionor interview on any topic related to the study area of the learner could help incapturing the attention of the learner while providing knowledge. It is sometimesas good as face to face learning. These audio/audio visual study materials couldeffectively help in filling the gap between the teacher and distance learner to agreat extent, at a much lesser cost.

(v) Digital Library

Digital libraries are an organized and focused collection of digital objects, including texts, images, video and audio, with the methods of access and retrieval and for the selection, creation, organization, maintenance and sharing of collection (Smith, 2001). The major benefits of digital libraries are improved access throughinternet and CD-ROM, which can be accessed anywhere, anytime, making the technology suitable for distance learning. Digital libraries have wider access; thus, meet the requirements of large number of users at a time.

(vi) SocialNetworking

Social media toolscan be used to teach students how to collaborate and work with others, which isvery helpful in the distance learning scenario. The students could activelyparticipate in the learning process, rather than being passive recipients oftransmitted knowledge.These tools offersignificant advantages for distance education, in terms of pedagogicalrequirements and student learning outcomes. Social media sites enablecommunication among small or large groups of people, and serve to make theworld a smaller place. The groups of people on these media are able to interactmore regularly and accomplish various tasks through interactions.The most commonly usedsocial media technologies in higher education are blogs, podcasts, social networking,and virtual environments. Various other web technologies which also possess thecharacteristics of social media, like eBay, YouTube, etc., could also be utilized asa platform for creating a learning organization.

(vii) Online Discussion Forums

Today, there are innumerable discussionforums available on the Web on numerous topics and areas, from which anybodycan be benefited. A forum can easily be formed on the Web with the help of someweb space or some hosting providers. Online Discussion Forums can prove to be useful in maintaining a motivationallevel of the learners (Simpson, 2012). These forums can be used by the learnersfor any kind of discussion regarding the course in which the learners are enrolledor on any other related area of study. In some cases, the teachers or experts couldalso be involved in the discussion. A discussion forum enables participants tocommunicate online using text. They can also be used to share viewpoints, createand share thoughts, share information, knowledge and multimedia, and create andshare relations. These forums can prove to be useful in the field of distancelearning as they can provide a platform to the physically distant learners andteachers to interact and share.

(viii) Open Educational Resources in Digital Form

The concept of Open Educational Resources (OER) describes any educational resources (including curriculum maps, course materials, textbooks, streaming videos, multimedia applications, podcasts, any other materials) that have been designed for use by educators and learners, without the need to pay royalties orany fees. OER has emerged as a concept with great potential to support educational transformation. Its transformative power lies in the ease with which such resources, when digitized, can be shared via the Internet. OER is dissimilar from e-learning.The open licensed education materials have tremendous potential to contribute to improve the quality and effectiveness of education. The scope and availability of OER is ever expanding. Inequitable access to learning, especially at the tertiary level has been cited as a reason for OER in the developing nations.

(ix) **Mobile Phones and Mobile Devices**

Mobile learning or m-learninghas been defined as learning that takes place via wireless devices as cell phones, personal digital assistants (PDAs) or laptops.The utilization of new media technologies in the field of learning has led to anew learning paradigm.Keeping in view the increasing number of mobile phone users, its personal andportable nature and rural nature of the learners in distance mode, the mobiletechnology has lot of prospects in bringing improvements in the distanceeducation scenario of the country. The technology can be used for imparting thequick and small messages very easily as well as learning materials, which couldbe received by the learners on their mobile phones. Moreover, mobile technology offers a very hopeful wayto reach the vast population of the developing countries as it does not requirebandwidth connections.

Conclusions

In India, the distance education scenario has changed withthe advent of new media technologies in the recent years, as almost all the distance education universities/institutions possesses and make use of some or the other form ofnew media technologies.Theuniversities offeringeducation through distance mode maintain well-furnished websites, providing almost all necessary information to the learners, along with having other media necessary for delivering education to their distance learners, in the form of multimedia learning materials, open education resources, e-books, educational radio over the internet, information over the social networking sites and blogs of the institutions and so on. Hence, the distance learning system provides an opportunity to the people to avail education for their individual development. By getting education from the distance learning system, an individual prepares himself for better employment opportunities, further promotions and better income generation.

❐

11

Blended Learning in the Classroom

Blended Learning as optimizing achievement of learning objectives by applying the "right" personal learning technologies to watch the "right" personal learning style to transfer the "right" skills to the"right" person at the "right" time. Blended learning as a learning program where more than one delivery mode is being used with the objective of optimizing the learning outcome and cost of program delivery. The concept of blended learning is rooted in the idea that learning is not just a one-time event-learning it is a continuous process. Blending provides various benefits over using any single learning delivery medium alone. Blended learning is a way of meeting the challenges of tailoring learning and development to the needs of individuals by integrating the innovative and technological advances offered by online learning with the interaction and participation offered in the best of traditional learning.

Definition

Blended learning do not use any single learning delivery medium rather incorporates a wide range of learning opportunities like online, face to face.It is the best way of facing the challenges in learning with its innovative technology and regular motivation by teachers in classroom. It's a two way process where teacher acts as facilitator for the students.

Characteristics of Blended Learning

1. Learners have opportunities to interact socially and negotiate meaning.
2. Learners have enough time and feedback.
3. Learners are guided to attend mindfully to the learning process.
4. Learners work in an atmosphere with an ideal stress/anxiety level.

Role of Teachers and Students in Blended Learning Classroom

Teacher should have indepth knowledge about content so that they can teach various subjects. They should also be able to differentiate between various instructions based upon students need. Teachers must not only understand the content that is to be taught within the classroom but they must now have a depth of understanding that allows the content to be morphed into the delivery system allowing the student to take ownership in their learning process. Armes (2012) emphasized on the student ability to integrate online information with their classroom content. Students should also be able to demonstrate through various aids as and when require. The teacher continues to encourage and motivate, guide and monitor progress, give feedback, boost confidence, and maintain motivation. Students must make use of good time management skills as blended courses require them to balance both online and face-to-face course activities. The teacher's role is to encourage each student group to come up with their own answers to the essential question or problem.

Importance of Blended Learning

Blending technique is good to incorporate in teaching method still it is not free of disadvantages being faced by the educators and learners. In this technological era many people are unaware of the new techniques being used in world. Few sections of educators are not ready to change their conventional mode of teaching. Thus before the implementation of blended learning in regular classroom settings few obstacles need to be removed such as

Recruitment of teachers includes looking to effective teachers, who possess the potential to grow into new roles (Jackson, 2014)

1. The fear of loss of control, lower student feedback grades and general uneasiness about the impact of online learning on classroom relationship should be considered (Vaughan,2007)
2. Blended learning requires both the time and a willingness to learn new things (Yonge. 2014)
3. Blended environment also adds additional scheduling and communication challenges as course meet both online and face to face.

Limitation of Blended Learning

1. Before a blended learning scenario can be considered ready for use, the lecture has to do long, detailed and extensive work.
2. Students sometimes feel that they are given more work to do when distance modalities are used.
3. The materials developed by the lecturers cannot simply be the same set that they had developed for handouts.

There is no doubt that the new technology used in teaching and learning process enhances the performance of students. It increases the collaboration among participants. More information can be gathered by using technology and sharing of information can be done not only within the campus but across the world. The flexibility and accessibility of the method make it more interesting and challenging. It provokes students to complete their task in given time. Current generations of students are digital natives, they are born with the Internet network, and now they are experiencing the transition from the old to the new web-based technology, which is more participatory, more collaborative.

Conclusions

The increasing availability of Internet connectivity and interactive Web applications have contributed to the growth in the number of schools implementing Blended Learning. Although implementing Blending Learning is a complex process because educators must determine the perfect blend of face-to-face activities and online learning activities when designing courses, early research indicates students have favorable opinions about participating in Blended Learning courses versus the traditional classroom .In the future, teachers and students will need to work collaboratively and take equal ownership in determining the best principles for an approach that redefines what it means in order to teach and learn.

❐

12

Innovative Practice of ICT Special Reference to Blended Learning

Blended learning is a term increasingly used to describe the way e-learning is being combined with traditional classroom methods and independent study to create a new, hybrid teaching methodology. It represents a much greater change in basic technique than simply adding computers to classrooms; it represents, in many cases, a fundamental change in the way teachers and students approach the learning experience. It has already produced an offshoot – the flipped classroom – that has quickly become a distinct approach of its own.

No single, reliable definition of blended learning exists, or even a universal agreement on the term itself. Many use terms like hybrid, mixed, or integrative to describe the same trend. But the trend is significant. In 2000 an estimated 45,000 K-12 students took an online course, but almost a decade later more than 3 million took courses that way, many of them using computers in the schools themselves.

A learning model in three parts - There is a general consensus among education innovators that blended learning has three primary components:

- In-person classroom activities facilitated by a trained educator.
- Online learning materials, often including pre-recorded lectures given by that same instructor.

- Structured independent study time guided by the material in the lectures and skills developed during the classroom experience.

A course created in a blended learning model uses the classroom time for activities that benefit the most from direct interaction. Traditional education (especially at the college level) tends to place an emphasis on delivering material by way of a lecture, while in a blended learning model lectures can be videotaped ahead of time so the student can watch on their own time. The classroom time is more likely to be for structured exercises that emphasize the application of the curriculum to solve problems or work through tasks.

An individual semester of blended learning may emphasize classroom time at the beginning, then gradually increase the amount of work that students do online or during independent study. Many argue that class discussion boards, for example, are far more useful if the participants have met face-to-face first.

The "flipped" classroom, a more recent coinage, refers to classes that are structured almost exclusively around a reversal of expectations for lectures and homework. Students are expected to watch lectures online at home, and do homework while they are in class.

Blended Learning Redefining Teaching Roles

In some situations, the move to blended learning has inspired educators to redefine traditional roles. The word "**facilitator**" has emerged as an alternative to "teacher," bringing with it a slightly different focus. The facilitator places an emphasis on empowering students with the skills and knowledge required to make the most of the online material and independent study time, guiding students toward the most meaningful experience possible. Facilitators focus on four key areas:

- Development of online and offline course content.
- Facilitation of communication with and among students, including the pedagogy of communicating content online without the contextual clues students would get in person.
- Guiding the learning experience of individual students, and customizing material wherever possible to strengthen the learning experience.
- Assessment and grading, not unlike the expectations for teachers within the traditional framework.
- By putting an emphasis on learning through supervised activities, blended learning has proven to be very adaptable to what some corporations are calling blended training. Trainers can shift their focus from the delivery of knowledge to its application, and companies spend less flying trainers around to oversee all instruction in person.

Blended Learning is not so much an innovation as it is a natural by-product of the digital domain creeping into physical spaces.

Broadly speaking, blended learning just means a mix of learning online and face-to-face, which means it's likely your students are already doing some form of blended learning, and have for years.

As digital and social media become more and more prevalent in the life of learners, it was only a matter of time before learning became 'blended' by necessity.

Obviously, there aren't just 12. It could be argued that there are thousands of types of blended learning varying by content, scale, technology, learning spaces, etc.

The purpose of this post is to A) Explain the most commonly referred to types of blended learning as most educators know them and B) Help you think more about blended learning as a flexible concept that ideally empowers both teachers and students to improve learning outcomes so that you can C) Identify and adapt a blended learning model that's right for your school, classroom, and students.

Types of Blended Learning You've Probably Heard of

Familiar 3 types of Blended Learning

1. **Station Rotation Blended Learning:** Station-Rotation blended learning is a: "...model (that) allows students to rotate through stations on a fixed schedule, where at least one of the stations is an online learning station. This model is most common in elementary schools because teachers are already familiar rotating in "centers" or stations."
   Similar to : Lab Rotation blended learning
   Primarily characterized by: the fixed schedule that guides the 'blending'
2. **Lab Rotation Blended Learning :** 'The Lab Rotation' model of blended learning, similar to "Station Rotation,' works by "allow(ing) students to rotate through stations on a fixed schedule...in a dedicated computer lab allow(ing) for flexible scheduling arrangements with teachers... enabl(ing) schools to make use of existing computer labs."
   Similar to : Station Rotation blended learning
   Primarily characterized by: the use school computer labs in new ways
3. **Remote Blended Learning (also referred to as *Enriched Virtual*)**
   In Enriched Virtual blended learning, the student's focus is on completing online coursework while only meeting with the teacher intermittently/as-needed.

This approach differs from the Flipped Classroom model in the balance of online to face-to-face instructional time. In an Enriched Virtual blended learning model, students wouldn't see/work with/learning from a teacher on a daily basis face-to-face but would in a 'flipped' setting.

Benefits of Blended learning

A blended learning model is undoubtedly a great way to augment the learner's experience, but its advantages go beyond that.Whether you're training employees, partners, customers or planning compliance training, organizations using blended learning will reap many rewards. Let's take a look at some of the benefits for learners and organizations:

Benefits for learners

- Blended learning offers the learner convenience and flexibility; they have the ability to control their learning pace and learn remotely.
- Academic research suggests that blended learning gives learners a more comprehensive understanding of the course content.
- Because blended learning allows learners to interact with instructors and fellow learners, social learning is supported.

Benefits for Organizations

- Blended learning reduces face-to-face training costs, such as travel, accommodation, and printed training materials.
- Companies can use varying eLearning methods, such as webinars, gamification, etc., which result in better learner engagement.
- Because blended learning is a more efficient and cost-effective way to train, you'll see a quicker and greater return on investment.
- It's also easier to track exactly who has, or hasn't, completed training

Blended learning Pitfalls

Now that you know more about what blended learning is, hopefully, we've gotten you excited about what it can offer.Before we let you in on how you can start utilizing it in your training strategy, let's first outline a few major pitfalls to avoid before you begin.

- The most important pitfall you'll need to avoid is using an LMS that doesn't meet your needs. You'll need an LMS like LearnUpon to manage and deliver your blended learning strategy, including the integration of webinar software.
- Keep in mind that what works for in-person training may not necessarily work for online training. You should not automatically assume existing courses are ready for online distribution. Analyze who your learners are, identify what they need to know, review your course content, and use this analysis formulate a blended learning strategy.

- If switching from solely face-to-face learning, take your time when incorporating blended learning into your learning strategy. Starting slow not only enables you to assess what is and is not working from a content perspective, but also gives your learners time to adapt gradually to the blended learning concept.
- Of course, it's important that blended learning isn't used just for the sake of it. Once you have identified your learning goals, you can think about how each goal could be achieved in an online and/or offline setting.

Webinars: An Easy Route to Blended learning

To get started with blended learning, you can utilize webinars in the instructor-led portion of your course. To run a webinar, you'll need a webinar tool. There are many options available; you'll just need to find the one that suits your needs.Things to consider when choosing one include the size of your audience, their requirements, and the learner experience.Some webinar tool options include:Zoom, GoTo Webinar, Cisco WebEx, Adobe Connect, Google Hangouts, Any Meeting

These tools integrate with your LMS to synchronize setup, registration, and attendance reporting. Make sure you record each session so that you can use these recordings at a later date. This is a superb way to generate reusable training content. These videos can then be added to e Learning courses and delivered to your learners.

What are the benefits of integrating a webinar tool with your LMS?

If webinar sessions are part of your blended learning, integrating your chosen tool with your LMS makes sense. This will enable you to:

- Schedule sessions in your LMS that automatically reflect in your webinar tool. This means you'll only have to set up a session once, and there'll be no scheduling conflicts.
- Register your attendees through your LMS, with the data being sent to your webinar tool automatically.
- Monitor attendance data that is automatically transferred back to your LMS, meaning you don't have to waste time by manually updating this information.
- Halt the repetition of tasks, improve reporting, streamline workflows, etc. It's also super easy to set up.

When using blended learning, keep in mind that its aim is to combine the strengths of both traditional and online learning methods in order to give your learners a more engaging learning experience. Through blended learning, you'll take advantage of the best of both worlds, benefitting both learners and instructors. LearnUpon LMS makes it simple to set up blended courses that contain any combination of face-to-face and online training components. To learn more, book a free trial and demo with us today.

Conclusions

If you're familiar with eLearning in any way, there's no doubt you'll have heard about blended learning. It's is a concept that has risen in popularity over the last few years, with its advantages being lauded by eLearning professionals and learners alike.Despite the acceptance of the effectiveness of blended learning, there continues to be some ambiguity around its definition. So, just what is blended learning?In today's post, we'll delve into what blended learning is, and highlight some benefits it offers organizations and learners. We'll also touch on some pitfalls to avoid, and explore how you can use blended learning as part of your eLearning strategy.

❐

13

Socio-Demographics of Test Anxiety among Open School Learners of Kerala

Today's ever-changing, technologically advanced, and competitive environment causes stress and anxiety in children and adult almost alike. Anxiety is the cognitive state related to the inability to control emotional responses to perceived threats in a situation where one's performance is evaluated. Anxiety is common in adolescent life, especially in the school arena where they are under constant pressure to get good grades in examinations. It occurs due to overpowering nature of the symptoms such as difficulty in making decisions, sleeplessness, nervousness, changed physiological status, impaired communication, lowered self-esteem, failure in academic performance etc. of different categories of anxiety, test anxiety is perhaps the most discussed as it is a matter of concern for students, parents, teachers, counsellors, and administrators. Anxiety is a situation-specific anxiety that refers to the anxiety states and worry conditions that are experienced during an examination. It has been found that students consistently perceive examination as a source of increase in anxiety and a situation engulfed with uncertainty and unfairness in letting them demonstrate their true achievements (Zoller & Ben-chain, 1990).

Excessive anxiety is a symptom prevalent in almost all sections of population particularly among school children. Anxiety is a sort of distress that arises when the individual anticipates a threat to his/her self-esteem. No individual is completely free from anxiety, as it is a normal response of psycho-biological system to external or internal threat to one's self. It occurs because of overriding nature of the symptoms like nervousness, altered metabolic status, loss of sleep, difficulty in decision making, blighted communication, poor classroom performance, weakened self-esteem etc. Earlier researches have pointed out that factors like financial difficulties, tough family condition, socio-cultural deprivation, financial difficulties, constrained school atmosphere etc. can also contribute test anxiety that affects the scholastic achievement of adolescents in the school (Zinta, 2008; Mokashi, Gaonkar & Yadav, 2010; Rana & Mahmood, 2010; Yousefi, Redzuan, Mariani, Juhari & Talib 2014; Bogels & Toussaint, 2016).

Open school learners are far separated from the real classroom environment and get minimal teacher support for accomplishing the curricular objectives. The level of achievement motivation in open school learners is at the lowest and they experience less satisfaction in learning situations (Berge & Huang, 2004). Added to this test anxiety is a prevalent problem among open school learners that can handicap their ability to perform well academically. Test anxiety is a major factor contributing to a variety of negative outcomes including psychological distress, academic underachievement, academic failure, and insecurity among open school learners (Hembree, 2008). In addition to the learners' psychological makeup, the nature of open learning, socio-demographic factors is also likely to exert an influence on the test anxiety experienced by open school learners. Keeping this in mind, the present study is a modest attempt to explore the decisive role likely to be played by selected demographic factors on test anxiety of open school learners from Kottayam and Ernakulam districts (Kerala, India).

Hypotheses

The following null hypotheses were tested for the study:

1. There will be no significant difference between boys and girls in open schools with regard to their test anxiety.
2. There will be no significant difference between rural and urban students in open schools with regard to their test anxiety.
3. There will be no significant difference between open school students from joint and nuclear families with regard to their test anxiety.
4. Open school students in different ordinal positions will not differ significantly in their test anxiety.
5. Open school students from high-, average-, and low socio-economic status will not differ significantly in their test anxiety.

6. High-, average-, and low achievers in open schools will not differ significantly in their test anxiety.

Methodology

Normative survey method was used in the present study. The study made use of a convenient sample of 242 open school students (boys = 99; girls = 143) doing their Secondary Course, selected from Kottayam and Ernakulam districts of Kerala. The average age of the subjects were estimated to be 16.23.

Tool used

The test-anxiety of the participants were measured using, the 'Test Anxiety Scale for Open School Students (TASS), developed by Babu Thomas & Panneer Selvam (2019). It is a standardized psychometric instrument used for measuring the physical, mental, emotional and behaviourl apprehensions experienced by students in the age group 13 to 17, before, during, or after an exam or other assessment. The scale contains 50 items covering physical, mental, emotional, and behaviourl responses of fretfulness in test situations, which is sufficient to produce a valuable measure of the test-anxiety of an individual. The scale is designed to produce quantifiable data that may be subjected to statistical analysis to draw scientific inferences. The scale, as claimed by the authors, was developed in line with the Westside Test Anxiety Scale (Driscoll, 2007) and the 'Kerala Examination Anxiety Scale' (Nair, 1976). The external validity of the scale was estimated to be 0.66 and the test-retest reliability (one month interval) was 0.74.

Procedure

The tool was administered on the sample in small group situation under standardized conditions, their responses were collected and the total score on the TASS was found out. A Personal Data Sheet and Socio-Economic Status Scale was also attached with the TASS, so as to collect the required socio-demographic information. The data thus obtained were subjected to appropriate statistical analysis with the help of SPSS and interpreted accordingly.

Result and Discussion

The study was aimed to find out how socio-demographic factors such as gender, residential locale, type of family, birth order, socio-economic status and level of academic achievement affect the test-anxiety of open school students doing their secondary course. The data collected by administering the TASS was analyzed by keeping the hypotheses in mind.

In order to find out the differential effect of gender on test-anxiety, the TASS scores of boys and girls were compared by applying the two-tailed test of significance for difference between means. The data and result of the analysis carried out is given in Table 13.1.

TABLE. 13.1: Comparison of the Test Anxiety of the Sub-samples based on Gender

Groups	Statistical Indices				t-Value	Level of Significance
	N	M	SD	SEM		
Boys	66	128.93	21.329	2.144	6.403	.01 Level
Girls	143	147.39	22.537	1.885		

The t-value obtained on comparing the gender groups is significant (t =6.403; p<0.01), indicating that the boys and girls in open schools differ significantly in their test-anxiety. A closer observation of the data presented in Table 1 makes it clear that the compared to boys, the girls experience greater anxiety in test situation.

The data and result of the comparison of the test-anxiety of open school students living in rural and urban areas is given in Table 13.2.

TABLE. 13.2: Comparison of the Test Anxiety of the Rural and Urban Students

Groups	Statistical Indices				t-Value	Level of Significance
	N	M	SD	SEM		
Boys	130	143.12	23.086	2.025	2.333	.05 Level
Girls	112	136.03	24.174	2.284		

The t-value estimated on comparing the test anxiety of open school students hailing from rural and urban areas is significant at 95% confidence interval (t = 2.333; p<.05). Scrutiny of mean estimates for the groups shows that adolescents residing at rural areas have higher test-anxiety when compared to their urban counterparts.

The differential influence of the type of family on test-anxiety of open school students is find out by comparing the mean test-anxiety scores of students from joint and nuclear families. The data and result of the analysis is given in Table 13.3.

TABLE. 13.3: Comparison of the Test Anxiety of the Students from Joint and Nuclear Families

Groups	Statistical Indices				t-Value	Level of Significance
	N	M	SD	SEM		
Joint Family	117	138.06	22.591	2.089	1.125	Not Significant
Nuclear Family	125	141.50	24.876	2.225		

The result of the t-test carried out for comparing the test-anxiety of open school students from joint and nuclear families produced a t-value which is not large enough to be significant (t = 1.125; p>.05). It shows that the open school students from joint families and nuclear families are almost alike with regard to their test-anxiety.

The sample consisted of three groups with regard to their birth order – first, second and third. In order to find out whether there is any true difference among the first, second and third born students with regard to their test-anxiety, one way ANOVA was carried out. The result of the same is presented in Table 13.4.

TABLE. 13.4: Summary of One Way ANOVA of Test Anxiety of Open School Students with Regard to their Ordinal Position

TA	Sum of Squares	df	Mean Square	F	Sig.
Between Groups	25715.639	2	12857.820	27.701	.000
Within Groups	110935.076	239	464.163		
Total	**136650.715**	**241**			

The F-value obtained is significant at .001 level, indicating that there exists a true difference among the open school studentswith first, second, and the third ordinal positions regarding their test anxiety. To put differently, the test anxiety of open school students varies according to their ordinal position. This makes further analysis indispensable to find out the groups which differ significantly. The Scheffe's post hoc test of intergroup comparison was carried out so as to find out the group-pairs which differ significantly. The data and result of the analysis is given in Table 13.5.

TABLE.13.5: Post Hoc Test of Multiple Comparisons for Test Anxiety of Open School Students in Different Ordinal Positions

(I)Birth Order	(J) Birth Order	Mean Difference (I-J)	Std. Error	Sig.	95% Confidence Interval	
					Lower Bound	Upper Bound
1.	2	21.860*	3.155	.000	14.09	29.63
	3	22.511*	3.952	.000	12.78	32.25
2.	1	-21.860*	3.155	.000	-29.63	-14.09
	3	.652	3.697	.985	-8.46	9.76
3.	1	-22.511*	3.952	.000	-32.25	-12.78
	2	-.652	3.697	.985	-9.76	8.46

*The mean difference is significant at the 0.05 level.

The result of the post-hoc test revealed that significant differences in test anxiety exists between the first born and second born open school students (mean difference = 21.860; p<.001), and between the first born and the third born (Mean Difference = 22.511; p<.001). No true difference, however, is not observed between the second born and third born open school students regarding their test anxiety (Mean Difference = 0.652; p>.05).

The test-anxiety of open school students form high-, average-, and low socio-economic status were compared to find out the differential effect of SES on test-anxiety. The summary of the one way ANOVA carried out in this context is given in Table 13.6.

TABLE.13.6: Summary of One Way ANOVA of Test Anxiety of Open School Students with Regard to their Socio-Economic Status

TA	Sum of Squares	df	Mean Square	F	Sig.
Between Groups	1705.010	2	852.505	1.510	.223
Within Groups	134945.705	239	564.626		
Total	**136650.715**	**241**			

The F-value obtained on comparing the test-anxiety scores of open school students from high-, average-, and low socio-economic status is not significant (F = 1.510; p>.05), showing that socio-economic status is not a decisive factor in discriminating the open school students on the basis of their test-anxiety.

The open school students in different levels of academic achievement were compared to find out the significant difference, in any, in their test-anxiety by applying one way ANOVA. The data and result of the analysis is given in Table 13.7.

TABLE. 13.7: Summary of One Way ANOVA of Test Anxiety of Open School Students with Regard to their Academic Achievement

TA	Sum of Squares	df	Mean Square	F	Sig.
Between Groups	18979.053	2	9489.527	19.274	.000
Within Groups	117671.662	239	492.350		
Total	136650.715	**241**			

The F-value obtained on comparing the test-anxiety scores of open school students from high-, average-, and low levels of academic achievement is significant beyond 99% confidence interval (F = 19.274; p<.001). It shows that test-anxiety exert considerable effect on the academic achievement of the open school students. In view of the observed significant difference, post hoc test of multiple comparison was carried out to find out the group pairs which show true difference. The data and result of the post hoc test is given in Table 13.8.

TABLE. 13.8: Post Hoc Test of Multiple Comparisons for Test Anxiety of Open School Students in Different Levels of Academic Achievement

(I)Birth Order	(J) Birth Order	Mean Difference (I-J)	Std. Error	Sig.	95% Confidence Interval	
					Lower Bound	Upper Bound
Low	Average	-15.520*	3.833	.000	-24.96	-6.08
	High	6.931	5.119	.401	-5.68	19.54
Average	Low	15.520*	3.833	000	6.08	24.96
	High	22.451*	4.177	.000	12.16	32.74
High	Low	-6.931	5.119	.401	-19.54	5.68
	Average	-22.451*	4.177	.000	-32.74	-12.16

*The mean difference is significant at the 0.05 level.

The result of the post hoc test given in Table 13.8 shows that, whereas Low achievers and Average achievers differ significantly regarding the test-anxiety (mean difference = 15.520; $p<.001$), the Low achievers and High achievers are alike in their test-anxiety. The Average achievers, however, differ significantly from the High achievers in test-anxiety. A closer observation of Table 8 reveals that compared to both the High achievers and Low achievers, the Average achievers experience higher anxiety in test situations.

Conclusions

The study revealed a presence of a gender difference in the test-anxiety of open school students ($t = 6.403$; $p<.01$). The girls were found to experience greater anxiety in test situations. The hypothesis formulated in this context, viz., Hypothesis-1 (there will be no significant difference between boys and girls in open schools with regard to their test anxiety) is, hence, rejected. Comparison of sub-samples based on residential locale of open school students exposed the presence of significant rural-urban difference in test-anxiety of the subjects ($t = 2.333$; $p<.05$); wherein the rural students were found to have more test related anxiety. Hypothesis-2, formulated in this context (there will be no significant difference between rural and urban students in open schools with regard to their test anxiety), is, hence rejected. Type of family was found to exert no significant effect on test-anxiety of open school students as no significant difference was found to exist between students coming from joint families and nuclear families ($t = 1.125$; $p>.05$). The Hypothesis-3 (there will be no significant difference between open school students from joint and nuclear families with regard to their test anxiety), is therefore, accepted. The hypothesis formulated in this regard, viz., Hypothesis-4 (open school students in different ordinal positions will not differ significantly in their test anxiety) is, therefore, rejected. Learners from high-, average-, and low socio-economic status was found to be almost alike in their test-anxiety, as there exist no significant difference among the groups ($F = 1.510$; $p>.05$). The Hypothesis-5, formulated in this context (Open school students from high-, average-, and low socio-economic status will not differ significantly in their test anxiety) is, hence, accepted.

❐

14

Concept, Ways and Means of Health Education and Health Promotion

We may think that we are healthy, when we do not fall ill or when we are strong. Health means the total well-being of an individual. Total well-being or complete health is the efficiency provided by physical and mental well-being. Physical and mental well-being helps an individual to be emotionally steady, socially and morally sound, which will lead to a well balanced personality. Our behaviour reveals our personality. Thus we may now realize that health means physical and mental well-being. Let us now consider the inter-relationship of physical, mental, emotional, social and moral development that influences the health of an individual. Complete health is the physical and mental well-being of an individual

Social Fitness

There are two main responsibilities we should fulfil towards society. First, we should improve our own health. Secondly, we should understand the health problems of those around us. This will help us to get adjusted to the society we live in. If we can adjust ourselves to any society and culture, we are socially sound. If we are in perfect harmony physically and mentally we are free from frustration, an understanding and a useful person to the society. Society expects form us qualities of co-operation, helpfulness and good social behaviour.

Moral Development

Home, school and the temple or church influences a lot to mould the morals of the child. This is very important for complete well-being. Constant proper guidance instructions and advice from parents, teachers, religious leaders and adults will develop the co-operation and exemplary conducts are qualities of good health. These qualities will develop in us according to our physical and mental well-being'.

Balance Personality

Personality reveals our physical, mental and social well-being. To be of a balanced personality, we should possess good health habits and try to live a healthy life. Correct posture is a quality of a good personality. Correct posture is a sign of well-being in the child. Physical well-being could be obtained with nutritious food, exercise, rest and recreation. Correct speech is another quality of good personality. This reveals the physical and mental conditions which are influenced by the attitudes, home environment, intellectual development by the attitudes, home environment, intellectual development and the educational background. Our appearance and poise reveals our physical and mental stability, resulting in our correct choices and decisions. If we are not adjusted and suitable to the culture, society, age, we are an upset, dissatisfied and distressed person. Our behaviour reveals our personality. We would now realize that good behaviour is the physical, mental emotional, social and moral well being in action or in other words, the total personality in action.

Objectives Of Health Education

The main objectives of Health Education in its broad outlook, is to make an individual suitable to shoulder the responsibilities of the society. Health Education is generally organised under the following themes. They are Primary Health Care, Mental Health, Sanitation, Diseases and Immunization, Accidents and First Aid, Relationship between the Doctor and the Patient, Education of false beliefs and Environmental Pollution. Highlighted below are a few of the objectives of health education:

1. To cultivate the desirable health practices and health practices and health habits
2. To develop the health attitudes
3. To appreciate the health programmes undertaken by the school and community and to improve the school and community and to improve the necessary materials for the execution of that programme

Ways and Means of Teaching Health Education

This focuses on our work as a health educator. Health education is a very important part of our work and if we do it well it will help us improve the health of the people for whom we are responsible. Teaching methods refers to ways through which health messages are used to help solve problems related to health behaviours. Teaching materials or aids are used to help us and support the communication process in order to bring about desired health changes in the students.

Teaching Methods

There is a wide variety of teaching methods that we will be able to use in our health education work. We will be able to adapt these methods to our own situation, so that we can use the most effective way of communicating our health education messages.

Health talks

The best way of communicating our health messages in certain situations is by using health talks. Talking is often the most natural way of communicating with people to share health knowledge and facts. In the part of our job that involves health education, there will always be many opportunities to talk with people.

Group size is also important. The number of people who we are able to engage in a health talk depends on the group size. However, we will find talks are most effective if conducted with small gatherings (5–10 people), because the larger the group the less chance that each person has to participate.

Lecture

We may have the opportunity to give a lecture, perhaps in our local school or in another formal setting. A **lecture** is usually a spoken, simple, quick and traditional way of presenting our subject matter, but there are strengths and limitations to this approach. The strengths include the efficient introduction of factual material in a direct and logical manner. However, this method is generally ineffective where the audience is passive and learning is difficult to gauge. Experts are not always good teachers and communication in a lecture may be one-way with no feedback from the audience. We may have the opportunity to give a lecture and include a follow-up discussion, perhaps in a local formal setting or during a public meeting. However there are also strengths and limitations to this approach. It is always useful to involve our audience after the lecture in asking questions, seeking clarification and challenging and reflecting on the subject matter. It's important though to make sure discussion does happen and not just points of clarification.

Group Discussion

Group discussion involves the free flow of communication between a facilitator and two or more participants. Often a discussion is used after a slide show or following a more formal presentation. This type of teaching method is characterized by participants having an equal chance to talk freely and exchange ideas with each other. In most group discussions the subject of the discussion can be taken up and shared equally by all the members of the group. In the best group discussions, collective thinking processes can be used to solve problems. These discussions often develop a common goal and are useful in collective planning and implementation of health plans. Group discussions do not always go smoothly and sometimes a few people dominate the discussion and do not allow others to join in. Our job as the facilitator is to establish ground rules and use strategies to prevent this from happening.

Buzz Group

A *buzz group* is a way of coping if a meeting is too large for us. In this situation it is better to divide the group into several small groups, of not more than 10 or 12 people. These are called **buzz groups**. We can then give each small buzz group a certain amount of time to discuss the problem. Then, the whole group comes together again and the reporters from the small groups report their findings and recommendations back to the entire audience. A buzz group is also something we can do after giving a lecture to a large number of people, so we get useful feedback.

Demonstration

In our work as a health educator we will often find ourselves giving a **demonstration**. This form of health education is based on learning through observation. There is a difference between knowing how to do something and actually being able to do it. The aim of a demonstration is to help learners become able to do the skills themselves, not just know how to do them.

There are four steps to a demonstration:

1. Explaining the ideas and skills that we will be demonstrating
2. Giving the actual demonstration
3. Giving an explanation as we go along, doing one step at a time
4. Asking one person to repeat the demonstration and giving everyone a chance to repeat the process.

Role play

In role play, some of the participants take the roles of other people and act accordingly. **Role play** is usually a spontaneous or unrehearsed acting out of real-life situations where others watch and learn by seeing and discussing how people might behave in certain situations. Learning takes place through active experience; it is not passive. It uses situations that the members of the group are likely to find themselves in during their lives. We use role playing because it shows real situations. It is a very direct way of learning; participants are given a role or character and have to think and speak immediately without detailed planning, because there is usually no script. In a role playing situation people volunteer to play the parts in a natural way, while other people watch carefully and may offer suggestions to the players. Some of the people watching may decide to join in with the play.

Traditional means of Communication

Traditional means of communication exploit and develop the local means, materials and methods of communication, such as poems, stories, songs and dances, games, fables and puppet shows. Some of the benefits of traditional means of communication are that they are realistic and based on the daily lives of ordinary people; they can communicate attitudes, beliefs, values and feelings in powerful ways; they do not require understanding that comes with modern education in the majority of instances; they can communicate problems of community life; they can motivate people to change their behaviour and they can show ways to solve problems. Local traditional events are usually very popular and they can be funny, sad, serious or happy. Also, they are easily understood and they usually cost little or no money. All they require is imagination and practice. Remember that effective health education is seldom achieved through the use of one method alone. Therefore, a combination or variety of methods should be used to make sure that people really understand our health education messages.

Health Learning Materials

Health learning materials are those teaching aids that give information and instruction about health specifically directed to a clearly defined group or audience. The health learning materials that can be used in health education and promotion are usually broadly classified into four categories: printed materials, visual materials, audio and audio-visual materials.

Printed materials

Printed health learning materials can be used as a medium in their own right or as support for other kinds of media. Some printed health learning materials that we will already be familiar which include posters, leaflets and flip charts.

Posters - In recent years, the use of posters in communicating health messages has increased dramatically. Since a poster consists of pictures or symbols and words, it communicates health messages both to literate and illiterate people. It has high value to communicate messages to illiterate people because it can serve as a *visual aid.* The main purposes of posters are to reinforce or remind people of a message received through other channels, and to give information and advice. Visual aids like posters explain, enhance, and emphasize key points of our health messages.

Visual Materials

Visuals materials are one of the strongest methods of communicating messages, especially where literacy is low amongst the population. They are good when they are accompanied with interactive methods. It is said that a picture tells a thousand words. Real objects, audio and video do the same. They are immediate and powerful and people can play with them.

Audio and audio-visual materials - Audio material includes anything heard such as the spoken word, a health talk or music. Radio and audio cassettes are good examples of audio aids. As the name implies, **audio-visual materials** includes both seeing and listening. These materials include TV, films or videos which provide a wide range of interest and can convey messages with high motivational appeal. They are good when they are accompanied with interactive methods. Audio-visual health learning materials can arouse interest if they are of high quality and provide a clear mental picture of the message. They may also speed up and enhance understanding or stimulate active thinking and learning and help develop memory.

Conclusions

Health education builds students' knowledge, skills, and positive attitudes about health. Health education teaches about physical, mental, emotional and social health. It motivates students to improve and maintain their health, prevent disease, and reduce risky behaviours. Health education curricula and instruction help students learn skills they will use to make healthy choices throughout their lifetime. Effective curricula result in positive changes in behaviour that lower student risks around. Health education also teaches about the emotional and mental health of the student. A healthy person is the happiest person in the world. A healthy person can enjoy life fully. He can carry out his duties in a responsible manner. He is an asset to the family, the society and to the entire nation. He is always full of energy. He lives a long and happy life.

❐

15

A Review of Distance Learning Influences on Adult Learners: Advantage and Disadv.

Distance Learning (DL) is defined as any type of instruction that takes place in which the student and instructor are not in the same room, and are separated by physical distance. It is one of the greatest advantages offered by modern electronic technology. Technology has the ability to instruct without the teacher's or student's direct presence in the classroom. With the growth of distance-learning programs, many institutions offer more on-line courses, and this has led to a growing interest in learning among adult learners and in continuing education (Verduin & Clark, 1991). Distance learning has become popular in higher institutions because of its flexibility and availability to learners and teachers at anytime, regardless of geographic location. With so many definitions and phases of distance education, this paper only focuses on the delivery mode of distance education (the use of information technology), background, and its disadvantages and advantages for today's adult learners. There were initial concerns that distance learning might lower the quality of instruction; however, studies show that its benefits are clear and demonstrable and it continues to gain acceptance.

Distance Learning Issues

Online technologies have opened up a new array of distance learning opportunities and, as a result, where once students had to drive a short distance or long distance to attend a class, computer-based systems allow those students to remain in their homes or workplaces to participate in learning activities. Students can attend class at a designated time; participate in an audio, video, or text-based chat; can post to bulletin board discussions; and can access information related to course work right from the computer. It is important to identify and examine the main educational issues that were relevant to and influenced the development of the distance learning between students and teachers, as both have an important role to play. Students need to know their roles in distance learning and how to use the technology to communicate with the teacher and with each other. They not only need to know how to operate the microphone or how to post to a bulletin board discussion, but they also need to understand communication etiquette. It was argued that online teachers could not observe students, could not see and interpret their facial expressions or signs of inattention, and could not react immediately to rectify matters that may have gone amiss.

Organizational Issues

First, a decision must be made to determine how much of the course will be online. In other words, is this to be a Web-enhanced course or a Web-only course? The online component may range from occasional electronic assignments that supplement traditional class meetings, to a course that is online with two or three physical class meetings, to a course that is entirely online.

Obviously many factors may be predetermined and out of the instructor's control; for example, if the course is intended for a geographically dispersed audience, then meeting face to face may not be an option. Another organizational determination must be made as to the type of assignments and interactions that are to be included. These may range from group projects, created and delivered online, using process writing and interactions, or completely individual assignments.

Institutional Issues

Institutional issues must be considered and discussed as an educational organization begins tofocus on online education. Foremost must be recognition (perhaps in the promotion and tenure process) for faculty, but others might be by offering release time and assistance. Institutional support for innovative practices is essential, but it requires that time be allowed for design and development. While acceptance of this type of learning experience is growing, the reality is that at many organizations.Other institutional issues concern the amount and type of credit offered for online courses, andthe students' ability to use the credit for postgraduate or graduate degrees, for salary increments, or certification.

Pedagogical Concerns

Before decisions can be made about delivery or models, an instructor must make pedagogical decisions about the fundamental goals of a course. The salient questions when creating an educational experience have always been: "What are the instructional and personal goals of this course for all students?" "What is the purpose of this course?" These are questions that all educators must ask themselves when designing courses, and in general, they have become comfortable and adept at doing this. The structure of the course, the planning for educational and personal needs, and the teacher's role must all be reconceptualized. It is clear that active and independent learning must take place and the designer will have to determine what actions promote this type of learning. The nature of online teaching requires the instructor to rethink the evaluation process as well. The evaluation component must be ongoing and continual; leaving everything to one midterm and a final paper would put everyone at a disadvantage. It is important that the instructor become familiar with each student's work, and the only way to accomplish that is through many instructional activities.

Advantages of Distance Learning

Many students take a distance-learning course with certain expectations about its advantages and its disadvantages. The following are identified as some of the advantages of a distance-learning course compared to a traditional classroom course:

- **Flexibility:** The greatest rationale for the existence of most forms of DL is that students can do much of the work at times and places of their choosing.
- **Self-Tailored Learning:** Within certain limits, distance learning may allow students to learn at their own pace, in their preferred medium, or in a more comfortable environment.
- **More Choices:** Distance learning courses allow student more choices in course offerings and times without fear of class conflicts.
- **Increased Learner Centeredness:** Learners can study tutorials or add-on material at their own pace and at the appropriated time for them. This is particularly important for learners who suffer from not being

able to follow the pace of the lectures, but who have the capabilities of catching up and finding the missing information by studying on their own.

- Instructors are able to combine lecture material with specific modules offering computer learning tools. This permits instructors to devote more time, if required, to covering concepts in class, while letting students learn the hands-on portion of the course on their own.
- Course standardization for courses in which there is a large number of potential learners; computer aided learning tools help achieve a certain level of standardization in the quality and quantity of material received by all learners.
- Lower course development costs. By centralizing the development of some of the learning tools, institutions may free up time for instructors to focus on other important teaching or training matters.

Disadvantages of Distance Learning

It is also important to be aware that there are certain disadvantages to distance learning.

- The most significant disadvantage is that distance learning requires more self-discipline and time management.
- For some people, the expenditures required for computer equipment and Internet hookups
- outweighed the usual expenses of taking a conventional course such as commuting, parking, and perhaps babysitting.
- Some students feel lonely without face-to-face contact with other students, no matter how much they may communicate with others by phone or email and Internet-based distance learning courses in particular rely on lectures as a means of instruction and more on reading and discussion.
- Students who are uncomfortable with their reading and writing skills may find themselves equally uncomfortable with their distance learning course.
- learners who participate in broadcast lessons without talkback capabilities can feel like second-class citizens having little rapport with the rest of the group.
- Students may have difficulty making certain types of online connections as a result of their type of access to the Internet.

Conclusions

Many studies have attempted to find out whether distance education differs from traditional modes of instruction when referring to facilitating student success. The majority of these studies reported no significant differences between the distance and traditional modalities. Most important, the design of such type of research (whether comparative or evaluative) clearly places emphasis on the importance of the method of delivering instruction and is consistent with the instructive (instructor centered) learning theory but inconsistent with the constructivist (learner centered) theory, which is more concerned with the role of the student in learning than with the role of the instructor in teaching. Teaching online courses could be very challenging, time consuming, and a lot of preparation is necessary to ensure that things are done well and students get feedback within 24 hours of posting their responses. It is certainly beneficial for instructors who have adopted online teaching. Finally, distance leaning is seen as a viable alternative for lifelong learning opportunities, including informal courses, professional development tutorials, and full degree programs. The growth of online courses, enhanced by the ease of access, media attention, and interest from the private sector, has increased demand, and efforts are underway to respond with various online learning activities.

❐

16

Online Education in Distance Mode

Separation advanced education is any discovering that happens with the teacher and understudy being topographically remote from one another. Separation training may happen by surface mail, tape, intelligent television, radio, satellite, or any number of Web advances, for example, message sheets, talk rooms and work station conferencing. Online training conveyed over the Web is one type of separation learning.

Tech Tools Utilized in Web Based Learning

- Electronic or online separation courses may utilize a wide range of advancements. Email, nonconcurring PC conferencing (announcement sheets) and live visit are center advances.
- As Americans have grasped link and DSL, spilling video has flooded to the bleeding edge as a conveyance technique. Today, YouTube is being utilized to convey recorded school addresses to students' PCs.
- A separation instruction understudy likewise can "see" their virtual homerooms and genuine teachers through the expanding utilization of virtual conditions, similar to Second Life. Second Life is a case of a multi-client virtual condition framework, where students make vivified renditions of themselves, called symbols, and can travel through grounds, study halls, libraries and different areas made by virtual colleges and an e -learning advantage.

- Second Life is being utilized to show abilities running from nursing care to mold structure, and the sky is the limit from there through "drenching" or "live demonstrating." students in Second Life are some of the time requested to "carry on" explicit circumstances, for example, mock prospective employee meetings or restorative systems.

Online Training an Ongoing Type of Us Separation Learning:

Separation advanced education returns in any event to the extent the primary century A.D., when St. Paul composed writings called epistles (or letters of guidance) that were given to early Christian people group.

In 1840, the primary formal separation course was offered by Sir Isaac Pitman in Britain. He utilized the Holy book to educate shorthand. By 1850, the main separation degree was granted by the College of London.

For the greater part of the 1900s, separate learning was synonymous with the expression «correspondence learning,» since learning used to be conveyed basically by means of sent correspondence exercises. Students would get their books and assignments via the post office, at that point mail finished assignments back to teachers to be evaluated.

Today, the Web has turned into the essential hotspot for conveyance of school level separation learning. The expression «correspondence instruction» is once in a while utilized; «online training» is the more prominent and precise approach to depict a lot of the present separation training.

By 2020, maybe some new innovation will demonstrate more solid and mainstream than the web; assuming this is the case that new innovation will without a doubt be saddled by schools to transmit information.

Uses Separation Advanced Education

The present separation students, utilizing PCs and rapid transmission lines to for all intents and purposes associate with

Educators and different students from around the globe owe an obligation of appreciation to the ranchers of the past.

That is on the grounds that the improvement of separation advanced education came to fruition as an approach to give provincial students better access to advanced education.

It's hard to believe, but it's true - remove learning has a long history. Actually, school level separation training in the USA is over 100 years of age. What's happening about separation realizing isn't the way to go, yet the kind of understudy it serves and the number and sort of advanced education foundations that are utilizing it to achieve new kinds of students.

During the 1880s, freely subsidized land-concede colleges working in provincial territories of the US chose to enable ranchers to ace increasingly logical and proficient cultivating strategies. Notwithstanding, it was difficult or much of the time even conceivable for ranchers to leave their fields to go ponder.

In this way, in 1892, Pennsylvania State College ended up one of the primary universities in the US to dispatch a forceful mail correspondence program. Agrarian laborers read course readings, at that point sent their finished assignments back to Penn State workforce for reviewing.

Online College Educators Utilize Online Classes Innovation

Around 40 percent of full-time U.S. school personnel have instructed a course at an online college school. That is only one outcome from another top to bottom overview of conventional and online classes innovation utilization incorporated by Essential Exploration Gathering. «The Overview of Advanced education Workforce: Utilization of Instructive Innovation» incorporates the aftereffects of a study of in excess of 550 advanced education personnel in the U.S. also, Canada. Results were discharged in January 2010.

Instruction is an expansive field that includes the investigation and down to earth utilization of showing kindergarten through twelfth grade understudies in both open and tuition based schools. School instruction programs are ordered into numerous claim to fame territories of instructing, regularly at the center and secondary school levels, which incorporate subjects like arithmetic, English, science, history, workmanship education, health, and that's just the beginning. Also, the zone of general instruction is adequate to learn pedantic hypothesis and philosophy for educating at the elementary school level, which comprises of kindergarten through fifth grade.

Online training courses get ready students with the information and aptitudes important to oversee and teach a homeroom by concentrating on two fundamental territories of fixation: subjective advancement (the investigation of critical thinking, basic leadership, and data handling capacities in kids and youths) and learning hypotheses (the investigation of how data is gained). The general part of all training courses, in any case, is figuring out how to transmit data through guidance to students.

Need of Taking the Free Online Education Courses

An online training course can show you the speculations and standards of instruction and instructing, partaking in hands-on practicum is fundamental to figure out how to apply instructive hypothesis and in the end become a teacher. Online training classes are compelling for finding out about the point of view of instructors, instructive brain science, inspirational strategies, and assorted variety in the homeroom. Taking these courses can set you up to answer addresses like:

Homeroom guidance procedures and how they vary between various student age gatherings.

- The effect of exhibition and observational instructing techniques.
- The distinction among great and social states of educating.
- Creating exercise intends to suit offspring of various expertise levels.
- Strategies used to show kids with language obstructions.

Separation training can be conveyed in a paced configuration like customary grounds based models in which students begin and complete a course in the meantime. Paced conveyance is right now the most widely recognized method of separation training conveyance. Then again, a few organizations offer self-managed programs that take into account consistent enlistment and the period of time to finish the course is set by the student's time, aptitude and responsibility levels. Paced courses might be offered in either synchronous mode, yet self-managed courses are quite often offered no concurrently. Every conveyance show offers the two points of interest and detriments for students, instructors and organizations.

Advantages

- Separation learning can extend access to training and preparing for both general masses and organizations since its adaptable booking structure decreases the impacts of the many time-imperatives forced by close to home duties and commitments.
- Devolving a few exercises off-site lightens institutional limit limitations emerging from the customary interest on institutional structures and infrastructure.
- Furthermore, there is the potential for expanded access to more specialists in the field and to different students from assorted geological, social, social, monetary, and experiential backgrounds.
- As the populace everywhere turns out to be progressively associated with long lasting learning past the typical tutoring age, foundations can profit monetarily, and grown-up learning business courses might be especially lucrative.
- Distance instruction projects can go about as an impetus for institutional innovation and are in any event as compelling as up close and personal learning programmes, particularly if the educator is proficient and talented.

Disadvantage

Following an education in a traditional class is an activity that happens in a social context. Interacting with other people is not the main goal of an online course. Soe people absolutely need an educator in order to learn a new subject. Having an educator around to answer your questions and solve your problems is only possible in a traditional classroom setting.

"We will hurt our eyes". This is something a lot of parents say to their children when they spend too much time in their computers. Learning from a computer for hours, without any breaks can pause poor vision, strain injuries and back problems? Also, some topics require practice and cannot be taught simply with online lessons.

If our learners don't have self-discipline, it is very unlikely that they will be motivated to complete their online courses. There is no one around to tell them to sit and get started with their studies.

Conclusions

Online certifications for learning are advanced qualifications that are offered instead of customary paper accreditations for an ability or instructive accomplishment. Straightforwardly connected to the quickened improvement of web correspondence advancements, the advancement of computerized identifications, electronic travel papers and enormous open online courses have an extremely immediate bearing on our comprehension of learning, acknowledgment and levels as they represent an immediate test to the norm. It is valuable to recognize three types of online qualifications: Test-based accreditations, online identifications, and online declarations.

❒

17

Effectiveness of Self Learning Soft. Package and Acade. Ach. in His. at the H.S.level

This is the day and age of technology. Educational Technology is a complex, integrated process involving people, procedure, ideas, devices and organization for analyzing problems and devising, implementing, evaluating and managing solution to those problems involved in all aspects of learning. National policy of education assigned an important role to educational technology for improving the quality of education. The aim of educational technology is to improve the effectiveness of teaching-learning process in formal or informal setting and utilizing scientific principles.

Need of the present study

Emerging technologies challenge the traditional process of teaching and learning. Visual aids make the presentation vivid and memorable. Students captivate the vital points. Everyone is aware of the fact that many students who underachieve in regular classes could benefit from special or improved learning environments and need is realized that the software package can be used as a learning tool in learning history at the high school level.

Scope of the study

The study is confined only to high school level students studying at Matriculation school in the Tiruchirappalli District. Self-learning software package is prepared for class IX considering the State Board Syllabi under the uniform system of school education. A sample of 30 students each in experimental and control group is taken for the study.

Objectives of the Study

- To find out the significant difference between the pre test and post test of the control group.
- To find out the significant difference between the pre test and post test of the experimental group.

Hypotheses of the Study

1. There is no significant difference between the pre test and post test of the control group.
2. There is no significant difference between the pre test and post test of the experimental group.

Methodology

The investigator used the experimental method with parallel groups (control and experimental) to study the above mentioned objectives to know the effectiveness of self-learning software package in learning history and academic achievement of the high school students.

Sample for the Study

The investigator has chosen randomly 60 students studying in standard IX at Jegan Matha matriculation school. The researcher divided these students into two groups. A total 30 students were learnt through traditional method, the other 30 students were learning history through self-learning software package using smart classroom. The present study adopts purposive sampling technique.

Tools used for the study

1. Self-learning software package developed and standardized by the investigator.
2. Academic achievement test was developed and standardized by the investigator.

Data Analysis and Interpretation

Hypothesis-1

There is no significant difference between the pre test and post test of the control group.

TABLE. 17.1: Difference Between Pre Test And Post Test Of The Control Group

Test	N	Mean	SD	't'	Remarks
Control Group pre test	30	4. 067	1. 507	0. 118	Not Significant
Control Group post test	30	4. 3	1. 236		

(At 0.05 level of significance)

From the above table, it is found that the calculated 't' value (0.118) is not significant at 0.05 level. On observing the result it is concluded that the pre test and post test achievement of the control group were similar. Hence, the framed null hypothesis is found to be accepted.

Hypothesis-2

There is no significant difference between the pre test and post test of the experimental group.

TABLE. 17.2: Difference Between The Pre Test And Post Test Of The Experimental Group

Test	N	Mean	SD	't'	Remarks
Experimental Group Pre test	30	37.06	9.73	5.31	Significant
Experimental Group Post test	30	58.93	12.60		

(At 0.05 level of significance)

From the above table, it is found that the calculated 't' value (5.31) is significant at 0.05 level. On observing the result it is concluded that the pre test and post test achievement of the experimental group is higher than theoretical value. Hence, the framed null hypothesis is found to be rejected.

Findings of the study

1. There is no significant difference between the mean scores of pre test and post test of the control group.
2. There is a significant difference between the mean scores of pre test and post test of the experimental group.

Research Educational Implications

- Software package instils self confidence, creativity and freeness among the students improves their academic achievement level.
- Visuals speak many times. So, software technology must replace lecture method in the class rooms.

Conclusions

It is noteworthy that the students who used the software package to learn history achieved success in all the academic activities, such as achieving high scores in examinations, performing the class tasks in an effective and efficient way. The findings of the present study shows that software package saves time and creates an interest in learning and leads to self confidence among the students who are studying at high school level.

❐

18

Education and Society Meaning of Society

In general, society means the group of people. But in sociology it means, society as a structure and frame work and society as a function. Society is the system of usages and procedures of authority and mutual aid of many groupings and divisions of controls of human behavior and of liberties. This ever changing complex system is society. It is the web of social relationship and it is always changing.

Definition

Society is any permanent or continuing group of men, women and children, able to carry on independently the process of racial perpetuation and maintenance on their own cultural level.

Society is not a group of people; it is the system of relationship that exist between the individuals of the group-Professor Wright.

Characteristic of Society

- **Abstractness:** Society is nothing concrete. It is a name given to a system which is more abstract. It is like life an abstract thing as well.
- **Interdependence:** Individuals and groups depend on one another. Unless there is an element of inter dependence the society it function properly.
- **Elements of Co-Operation and Conflict:** In society , people co-operate with one another for achievements of certain aims and objects, On the

other hand individuals and groups have conflicts .These conflicts are based on their interest.

- Element of likeness and differences: Some of the members of the society are alike in through, in behavior and many other things. On the other hand many of them are different from one another. This difference is in regard to appearance, behaviour and other aspects.

Relationship between Education and Society

1. **Society Dictates the Type of Education it Requires**
   Education is as old as man. In incident days, there was no systematic formal education institution, Teacher‘s home was the educational institution. In other words he was the institution. As time passed by , society evolved and education was revamped and restructured so as to meet the demands of the society. Thus the content and the structure of education undergo a wholesale transformation and time to time.
2. **Education makes an Impact on the Society**
   Education has become science based and technology oriented. This type of education has made change on the structure and functions of the society, for e.g. more and more industries are established. Rural areas are changed into urban areas, etc.
3. **Education helps in Socializing the child and Prepares them for Socialization**
   Whenever there is a change in society, there is a change in social institutions also. Joint family is now reduced to nuclear family. Nuclear family consists of a father, a mother and a child, Modern society is materialistic and it requires father and mother work to earn their bread. As a result, the child is in the crèche or with the babysitter. Owing to this emerging situation, family has surrendered some of its function to the school. Now preschools and nursery schools are an extended family
4. **Division of Labours**
   Society is the division of labour. It may be sound paradoxical to consider the diversification of occupations as a factor of homogeneity. In fact, diverse occupations make people indepent. Although farmers, doctors, skilled labours, teachers, grocers, bakers, etc. are all individualized in terms of occupations, they are totally interdependent for their survival;this social co-operation is the product of division of labour.

Education contributes to the survival of the society

Emile Durkheim is of the opinion that the society can survive only if there exist among its members a sufficient degree of homogeneity. Homogeneity is quality of being homogenous means different parts are being welded into an organic whole. In this context by homogeneity Emile Durkheim refers to general values, common cultural traits, and the ethos which binds the members of the society together and gives them an identity.

Education as an agency of social control

Any deviations from social norms and values are considered a social taboo. Such deviations are checked by education. In this way education controls an 'Individual way of life and behavior and makes him conformed to the accepted value sand norms.

Conclusions

Education plays a crucial role in the process, of modernisation in various fields and modernisation in these fields really enhances the evolvement of education technically which calls for in great need for imparting modern education and for producing capable and resourceful manpower.It can rightly be concluded that education and society are the two sides of the same coin and these mutually influence each other.

❐

19

Mobile Learning in Distance Education

Educators seem to have more interest in blended learning, for obvious reasons. Because of this, much of the research on blended learning has been based on classroom situations. All levels of distance education have to be included with blended learning. Mobile learning is one of the technological advancement in distance education. Mobile learning is simply means "learning on the move". In this, the learning process takes place anytime, anywhere while we are moving in our environment. Mobile technologies are an attractive and easy means to maintain literacy skills and gain constant access to information. They are affordable, can be easily distributed and thus hold great potential for reaching marginalized groups and providing them with access to further learning and development. Mobile technologies facilitate distance learning in situations where access to education is difficult or interrupted because of geographical location or due to post-conflict or post-disaster situations (Yousef Mehdipour and Hamideh Zerehkafi, 2013). Traxler (2005) defined it as "any educational provision where the sole or dominant technologies are handheld or palmtop devices". Therefore, mobile technologies have great potential for facilitating more innovative educational methods. Simultaneously, these patterns in educational methods will not only help subject content learning, but may also facilitate the development of communication, problem-solving, creativity, and other high-level skills among students (Warschauer, 2007). Another popular definition of m-learning states it as the delivery of teaching by means of mobile devices such as pocket personal computers, mobile phones, personal digital assistants (PDAs) and similar hand held devices.

Mobile Phones

Mobile phones are by nature social devices. Mobile phones are mainly used in the process of interactivity. It is used for creating and maintaining social networks.

Instructional uses

- SMS (short message service) allows users to send / receive messages for interactive learning.
- The learner can view graphics messages with the help of MMS facility.

Smart Phones

A smart phone combines telephone capability with including PDA, camera, video, mp3 player, internet access and networking features in one compact system. It is a mass storage device.

Instructional uses

The learner can download audio and video lectures

- They can play audio, video and flash movies; display and edit text documents ; access e-mail and web-content; and use the phone for mass storage
- Smart phones enable global collaboration and scientific experimentation and research.
- Users also can access information globally. Smart phones thus support interactive learning.

Personal Digital Assistant (PDA)

The PDA combines computing capability, internet access and networking features in one system with note pad, address book and productivity tools. It is programmable, blue – tooth enabled, Wi-Fi equipped device with a pen/ stylus input interface.

Instructional uses

- PDAs plays audio, video and flash movies; displays and permits editing of text documents; lets users access e-mail and web content; supports text messaging; and can be used for mass storage.
- PDAs support collaborative and interactive learning. Students can use them to present projects; conduct research; word process documents; and take notes in class.

Laptop

Laptop is one of the best handheld IT devices. The most complete and functional system of all portable devices, laptops come blue tooth, Wi-Fi, and Ethernet enabled. They are a robust productivity tool.

Instructional uses

- Students can download audio and video lectures ; create and edit course-related assignments; send e-mails and text messages; and log on to the course website at home or while on the road
- Laptop provides high level of interactivity for global collaboration, scientific experimentation and research.

Tablet PCs

A Tablet pc is a note book shaped mobile computer, equipped with a touch screen technology which allows the user to operate the computer with a digital pen, or a finger tip, instead of a keyboard or mouse. Tablet pc is a portable computer that is different from the laptop and desktop computer. It runs all the business applications like word, excel, power point and it provides the high speed internet connectivity. Tablet pc also has the keyboard and mouse to work as the input devices. It has a Liquid crystal display (LCD) screen on which the user can write with a special purpose digital pen. It allows the users to take notes by the natural hand writing.

Instructional uses

- More natural form of input device which is of selecting and hand writing are much more familiar form of input that a key board and mouse, especially for people who are new to computer.
- Taking notes and drawing diagrams, taking hand written notes and drawings at class increases the productivity and retention of information.
- The physically disabled person can utilize the additional features of a tablet pc to be able to interact with the electronic world.

I-Pod

The I-pod is a portable media player. It allows the user to download music, audio books, photos and video. It has an address book and calendar. It can also serve as a mass storage device.

Instructional uses

- Students can download relevant instructional material with audio and video lectures.
- Students can exchange information files, review course work, prepare for exams and share project results.

Usb Drive

The USB drive is a mass storage device that easily attaches to many computers and other devices. It looks like a pen and hence it is also known as pen drive.

Instructional uses

- A USB drive is great for storing course work and audio and video files.
- Learners can share files for collaborative projects.
- Learners can transfer work to and from computer at school.
- USB used to save their work and submit work to the instructor.

E-Book Reader

E-book readers are used to download text based materials. They can store hundreds of e-books, news papers and magazines. Magnification and highlighting feature of an e-book reader facilitates easy reading and text making and full- text search makes it easy to find specific messages.

Instructional uses

- Learners can use an e-book reader to download and store text based instructional materials and text books.
- Sufficient resources are obtained for reading purpose through e-books.
- Instructional materials downloaded from e-book readers utilized to conduct research.

Conclusions

The goal of a blended approach is to join the best aspects of both face to face and distance education. Classroom time can be used to engage students in advanced level of interactive experiences. Meanwhile, the online support to the course material can provide students with multimedia-rich content at anytime; anywhere. This allows for an increase in flexibility of scheduling students' activities. With the help of mobile devices the blend of learning is more efficient than any other mode of teaching and learning in distance education.

❐

20

Role of E-Learning in Distance Education in India

Education plays an important role in development of society. There are two broad categories of education; Social Interactive Education and Distance Education. Social Interactive method of education is the traditional method of learning where instructor teaches learners face to face. Open and distance learning is frequently made with 'conventional' or personally education, which may be described as the form of education which takes place in a classroom or an auditorium. Distance Education is a method of teaching where the instructor and learners are separated by time and or physical distance. The main objective of distance education is, the availability of education- anyone, anyway, anywhere and anytime without social, physical and geographical restrictions. Open and distance education provide flexible learning opportunities to individuals and group of learners.

E-learning and Eistance Education

Electronic learning or E-learning is a type of education where the medium of instruction modern Technology. There is no personal interaction require to communicate people. Earlier, audio tape, Video tape and Compact Disc were used to deliver course material and lectures but later the technological development changed its face. E-learning is used inter randomly in a wide multiplicity of contexts. E-learning is used to define a specific mode to attend a course or program of study where the students rarely, if ever, attend face-to-face for on-campus access to educational facilities, because they study on-line. E-learning is naturally matched to distance learning and bendable learning. Distance Education in the form of E-learning is the only way to stay current. E-learning can also be used in conjunction with face-to-face teaching, in which case the term Blended learning is commonly used. E-learning pioneer Bernard Lusk in argues that the «E» must be understood to have broad meaning if E-learning is to be effective. Lusk in says that the "E" should be interpreted to mean Exciting, Energetic, Enthusiastic, Emotional, Extended, Excellent, and Educational in addition to «Electronic» that is a traditional national interpretation. This broader interpretation allows for contemporary applications and brings learning and media psychology into the equation.

Components of E-Learning

ELearning consists of the following components, which are created with the state of art Internet Technologies for high quality ease of use and effectiveness.

1. The Virtual Classroom

Virtual Classroom Modules (VCMs) are well-prepared high quality lectures from the

Master trainers, with multimedia color presentations. VCM combines distance education instructional Pedagogy with latest interactive multimedia Internet technology. VCM helps the Counselor to efficiently perform his basic job of providing information in less time, without compromising the quality. Thus, he can utilize his time for developing higher-level mental abilities like comprehension, application, analysis etc in students. Smaller time duration of each module ensures better concentration. Streaming media technology ensures simultaneous playing

And downloading of a module from Internet. Thus, Internet can be used as backup media for

1. Delivery of VCMs to provide 'Anywhere Anytime' learning. Use of video is kept to minimum
2. Possible level and normally restricted to imparting of skills. Easy and fast production of good
3. Quality VCMs is possible. Discussion and tutorial in real time, with counselors and fellow students are expected to follow these lectures at each study centre. Thus, VCM ensures better

Learning through distance system in the following ways:

1. Better time utilization through well prepared lectures from master trainers.
2. Clear knowledge communications through the latest multimedia and Internet technology.
3. Development of better understanding through discussion/tutorials in a group of fellow Students with a Counselor
4. Student can repeat the lecture or its part, on computer. University can even dispatch it Through Internet / email.

2. The Discussion Forum

A discussion forum is an interactive web site that lets site visitors discuss topics by reading articles that have been posted, replying to articles, and posting new ones. Visitors can also use a search form to find articles of interest. Discussion forum offers asynchronous mode.

Role of E-Learning in Distance Education in India

For communication, where messages can be prepared with editing. But it allows only text-based Interaction among students, counselors and the university. Any interaction on the discussion
Forum is visible to all. A discussion forum can have the following features:

1. A table of contents that contains hyperlinks to articles related to discussion topics.
2. A search box that allows searching the articles by a word or phrase.
3. An entry form in which a visitor types an article to post.
4. Threaded replies allow the visitor to choose whether the article they are posting is a New top-level topic for discussion, or a reply to another article. This feature creates Well-classified and well-organized knowledge base on any academic or administrative Topic in a short time.
5. A confirmation page which confirms that a visitor's article has been posted.
6. A registration form that lets site visitors log in to the Web site, if the discussion web is Protected.

3. Online Counseling

'Online Counselor' is a well-qualified and experienced person who interacts with the Students, only through use of discussion forum, for clearing their doubts/difficulties. Depending On the number of students, the university can appoint one or more 'Online Counselors' for each Course (subject). Once a week, each 'Online Counselor' will answer all the questions posted on the discussion forum of the respective course (subject). He will also initiate academic interaction by posting:

1. Home Assignment,
2. Quizzes,
3. Critical Thinking Questions or
4. Any other interesting academic information about the course (subject).

Online counseling will be a step forward towards 'Learner Centric' education, as it provides Anywhere anytime counseling for those learners who cannot regularly attend counseling Sessions at study centre due to various reasons. Online counseling cannot replace regular faceto-Face counseling at study centre, but can act like backup for it, as email and discussion forums Offer only text-based communication.

Indian Perspective

There are many initiatives has been taken to enhance distance education through e- learning,
Some of them are discussed as follows;

1. E-GyanKosh

The e-GyanKosh30 is a national digital repository developed by IGNOU for sharing Learning content. It is a learning platform of students to read content or watch videos of lectures. It has over 2200 video programmes in addition to e-content related to different subjects.

2. NPTEL (National Programme on Technology Enhanced Learning)

NPTEL is a project funded by the Ministry of Human Resource Development. It was first conceived in 1999 to pave the way for introducing multimedia and web technology to enhance learning of basic science and engineering concepts. It is collaborative program of seven Indian Institutes of Technology (IIT) and the Indian Institute of Science (IISc). It opened a new way of learning and also for sharing expertise among faculty in different parts of the world. In India, where a huge number of private institutions have settled the field of engineering education with insufficient faculty hold up and training, the project is meant at provided that a standard for scholastic satisfied for both the teacher and the student. It has 129 web courses and 110 video courses in the field of science and technology. Each course consists of 40 video lectures of one hour and text, images, animations and graphics.

3. Medvarsity

Medvarsity is India's first Medical e-learning programme established in April 2000. It is an Initiative by Apollo Hospitals Group, the leader in healthcare in Asia Pacific Region. It is affiliated to Martin Luther Christian University, a university established under Legislative Assembly of Meghalaya.

4. Tamil Virtual Academy

Tamil Virtual Academy (formally as Tamil Virtual University) is an internet based resource

That provides detail on the History, Arts, Literature and Culture of the Tamils. The main Objective of the project was to preserve the cultural identity, traditions and values of the Tamils.

It was setup by the government of Tamil Nadu for emerging needs of the Tamil Communities

And others interested in Tamil studies. The functions of TVA are guided by a Board of Directors

And it is administered by a full time Director. The courses are free for anyone interested.

5. BITS Pilani

Birla Institute of Technology and Sciences has established a virtual university, with DIT sponsorship. BITS have been one of the pioneers in distance education. BITS has been providing Courses for working professionals in distance education mode leveraging technology.

Conclusions

India is an emerging economy and it required skilled people for the development. The education is one of biggest challenge which is India facing. There are not adequate collages, institutes and universities to provide education to all. The distance education can ensure the availability of education without social, physical and geographical restrictions. The implementation of E-learning can reduce the problems related to distance education. Some initiatives have been taken but they are not enough to bridge the problem. It needs a serious effort from planners and government authority to implement such programs. If they use e-learning effectively, it can reach education to a large constituency that would otherwise not have access to it.

❐

21

Education and Society

Society might be seen as an arrangement of interrelated commonly subordinate parts which collaborate (pretty much) to protect a conspicuous entire and to fulfill some reason or objective. Social frameworks alludes to the organized course of action of parts of society and majority of people interfacing with one another. Instruction is a sub – arrangement of the general public. It is identified with other sub – frameworks. Various foundations or sub-frameworks are a social framework since they are interrelated.

EDUCATION	=	KNOWLEDGE
KNOWLEDGE	=	POWER
POWER	=	RESPECT
RESPECT	=	HAPPINESS

Education

- Education is the social institution through which society provides its members with important knowledge ,including basic facts ,job skills , cultural norms and values .
- The great aim of education is not knowledge ,its aim is "Action" .

Society

- Societies are system of relationship between people.
- Societies consists of members that share some sense of common identity and be small like a family or large like a nation –state .

Relationship Between Education and Society

Clarks(1948) observed that a general knowledge and getting of the ideals and aims of our society is important for all its citizens , and it must be achieved through education but in a form , which makes it compatible with freedom.

Ottaway(1980)observed It is logical to imagine that the type education given in each society will change from time to time as the society changes.

Through education an individual knows the structure of the society and the different types of relationship that exist among those structures in the society.

Role of Education for Society

- Through education an individual knows the structure of the society and the different types of relationships that exist among those structures in the society
- The child is taught how to perform different roles within the social structure in the society.
- It could be said that the role of education in society is to raise the level of awareness of as many people capable.

Functions of Education in Society

- Socialization
- Social Control
- Social Placement
- Transmitting Culture
- Promoting Social And Political Integration
- Agent Of Change

Socialization

- Teach students role, specific academic subjects and political socialization.
- Social control : School are responsible for teaching values.

Social Placement

Schools are responsible for identifying the most qualified people to fill available positions in society.

Transmitting culture

- As a social institution education performs a teacher conservable function – transmitting the dominant culture.
- Promoting social and political Integration:
- Education serves the latent function of promoting political and social integration.

Agent of change

Education can stimulate or being about desired social change.

Social Mobility

Social mobility, movement of individuals, families or groups through a system of social hierarchy or stratification. If such mobility involves a change in position, especially in occupation, but no change in social class, it is called horizontal mobility.

Mobility stands for shift, change and movement. The change may be of a place or from one position to another.

Social Stratification

Social stratification refers to a system by which a society ranks categories of people in a hierarchy. Social stratification is a trait of society, not simply a reflection of individual differences.

Social Change

Social change involves alteration of the social order of a society.It may include changes in social institutions, social behaviours or social relations. Social change as "modification in ways of doing and thinking of people.

Education and Development

Granted that education has an assured value of its own ,it must be still asked what role it could be assigned in national development.Educational systems are costly and must be weighted against other possible development projects in drawing up a list of priorities for developing countries.It is necessary, therefore, to set up clearly the relationship between education and development.

Conclusions

Any society requires a good education system. The leaders of tomorrow are formed and inspired today. However, their leadership can only start by acquiring life lessons and having potential.

❐

22

Supporting Inclusive Practices in Distance Mode throguh E-learning

Access to the distance education requires the adaptation of the curriculum content so that it proves meaningful to every student as an equal participant in the learning process. Technology has great potential in providing access for all learners, and the ability to access the distance education curriculum for persons with special needs. Assistive technology has the potential to augment abilities and bypass or compensate for barriers that disabilities create. As educational reforms include the application of technology to support and expand classroom curricula, assistive technology can provide both routine and customized access to the distance education for students with disabilities.

Technology for Students with Mobility Impairment to Access Distance Education

Students having difficulty with fine motor skills may require larger keyboard while using a computer,an on-screen keyboard or speech recognition programs to coordinate with their learning tasks. The use of a standard keyboard in a computer with access to a 'mouth- or head-stick,where the keys can be pressed with the pointing device can help students with mobility impairments;while Track balls, head trackers and touch screens can serve as suitable alternatives to the computer mouse. Software utilities can create 'sticky keys' that electronically latch the SHIFT,CONTROL, and other keys to allow sequential keystrokes to input commands that normally require two or more keys to be pressed simultaneously.

Students with mobility impairments, using a wheel chair, may have their computer desks adjusted to a comfortable height, to pull up to the computer to work. Keyboard guards can be used by individuals with limited motor control, and repositioning the keyboard and monitor may help in enhancing accessibility; like mounting keyboards perpendicular to tables or wheel chair trays at head-height to assist individuals with limited mobility using pointing devices to press keys, and use of disk guides for inserting and removing diskettes. Left-handed and right-handed keyboards available for individuals who need to operate the computer with one hand, have the provision of more efficient key arrangements, than standard keyboards designed for two-handed users.

For users with severe mobility impairments, keyboard emulation, including scanning and Morse code input, can be used with special switches that make use of at least one muscle over which the individual has voluntary control like - head, finger, knee, or mouth. In scanning input, lights or cursors scan letters, and symbols are displayed on computer screens or external devices, where hundreds of switches tailor input devices to individual needs. Speech recognition systems allow users to control computers by speaking words and letters, where a particular system is 'trained' to recognize specific voices. Abbreviation expansion and word prediction software can also help in reducing input demands for commonly used text and keyboard commands; and on-screen help may assist in efficient access to user guides for individuals who are unable to turn pages in books.

Technology for Students with Visual Impairment to Access Distance Education

Visually impaired students have difficulty accessing visual material in printed form or on the computer screen, where standard keyboards can aid in accessing Braille input devices, with Braille key labels assisting with the keyboard use. The OBR (Optical Braille Recognition) software can enable users having visual impairment to read Braille documents on a standard A4 scanner, scan the Braille document, analyze the dot pattern, translate the text, and present it on the computer screen. Refreshable Braille displays allow line-by-line translation of screen text into Braille, which can help in detailed editing. The Braille printers provide the 'hard copy' output for the visually impaired users. Scanners with optical character recognition can read printed material; which can then be stored electronically on computers, and be read using speech synthesis, or printed using Braille translation software and Braille printers. Such systems provide independent access to journals, syllabi, and homework assignments for the visually impaired students. Speech output systems can be used to read screen text, while the screen readers or the text-to-speech software like JAWS (Job Access with Speech) can help the user in adjusting the volume, pitch and speed of reading, and in choosing or adjusting to a male or female voice according to their preference. Audio materials like talking books and audio cassettes of recorded lessons can be used by students with visual impairment.(Petty,2012).

Technology for Students with Low Vision to Access Distance Education

Students with low vision may find the standard size of letters on the computer screen or printed documents too small to read, while some may also not be able to distinguish one color from another. Use of large print key labels, special equipment for the modification of display or printer output, computer-generated symbols, both text and graphics enlarged on the monitor or printer,can prove useful to students with low vision, especially in using standard word processing, electronic mail, spreadsheet, and other software applications. Adjusting the color of the monitor or changing the foreground and background colors, through special software like reversing the screen from black on white to white on black for individuals who are light sensitive, can help improve access and readability. Anti-glare screens can make screens easier to read, while voice output systems can also be used by people with low vision. The printed material can be read by scanners with optical character recognition and stored electronically on computers, where it can be read using speech synthesis or printed in large print. Assistive devices that are suitable for students with low vision may be used to aid in efficient learning like close circuit television,magnifying glasses and hand magnifiers, Braille language, talking calculators and tape recordings(Burgstahler, 1992).

Technology for Students with Specific Learning Disabilities to Access Distance Education

For students having Specific Learning Disabilities, educational software can help in skill building, by offering multisensory experiences, positive reinforcement, individualized instruction, and repetition. Students having difficulty processing written information can complete writing assignments and tutorial lessons with the aid of computers, like the standard word processor may prove a valuable tool for students with Dysgraphia, an inability to write legibly. Quiet work areas and ear protectors may make computer input easier for students who are hypersensitive to background noise and get easily distracted. Adaptive devices like large print displays, alternative colors on the computer screen, and voice output can help in compensating reading problems. 'Electronic Math Sheets' help in the organization, alignment and working of the Math problems on a computer screen, where the numbers appearing can be read aloud through the speech synthesizer, helping students facing difficulty in aligning Math problems using pencil and a paper. Software like 'Abbreviation expanders' can prove helpful with word processing to create, store, and re-use abbreviations for frequently used words or phrases, to ensure proper spellings for students who have difficulty in writing.

Conclusions

Technology has a major role in remediating and compensating the performance deficits experienced by students, enhancing the students' performance; and ensuring effective evaluation as an accommodation during testing, offering adequate solutions when an extended evaluation is needed. Effective technology integration in education can therefore help in addressing the functional barriers experienced by students with disabilities, providing them with equitable learning opportunities and a leveled field to rightly exhibit their differential abilities, through provision of necessary support and an equally accessible learning environment to all.

❐

23

Impact of CAI on the Achievement of Biology Students at Higher Secondary Level

Biology is a natural science that deals with the living world: How the world is structured, how it functions and what these functions are, how it develops, how living things came into existence, and how they react to one another and with their environment (Umar, 2011). Biology is introduced to students at senior secondary school level as a preparatory ground for human development, where career abilities are groomed, and potentials and talents discovered and energized (Federal Republic of Nigeria, 2009).The quality and quantity of science education received by secondary school students are geared toward developing future scientists, technologists, engineers, and related professionals (Kareem, 2003).

Need and Significance of the Study

Biology occupies a unique position in the school curriculum. Biology is central to many science related courses such as medicine, pharmacy, agriculture, nursing, biochemistry and so on. It is obvious that no student intending to study these disciplines can do without biology. With reference to various research studies, Pfefferova (2015) stresses that "use of computer assisted instruction appears to make easier student's conceptual understanding, requires less time as traditional methods, and improves the ability to predict the results of experiments".

Objectives

1. To find out the significant difference between pre and post test scores in CAI in biology at the higher secondary level in the experimental group.
2. To find out the significant difference between pre and post test scores in biology at the higher secondary level in the control group.
3. To find out the effective size for the difference between the means of pre and post test scores means in the CAI in biology at the higher secondary level.
4. Experimental design: Pre test post test control group will be used.

Sample of the study

The investigator chose the XI Standard students of biology group from St. Charles Hr. Sec School, Thiruvalluvar nagar, Madurai. From the 98 students the investigator selected 50 students based on the scores in the performance test. The students who scored average were selected for this study and the homogeneity was established.

Teaching and learning in Experimental and Control Groups

The control group was taught Digestion and Absorptionfrom bio zoology book of STD 11th text book of Tamil Nadu Govt. from page 106 – 111 using traditional method forthe period of three weeks. The experimental group was taught using Computer Assisted Instruction with the same topic of digestion and absorption from https://www.youtube.com/watch?v=ygBY-TkgYbochosen from existing and freely accessible YouTube from the internet.

Digestion and Absorption Diagram from Zoology

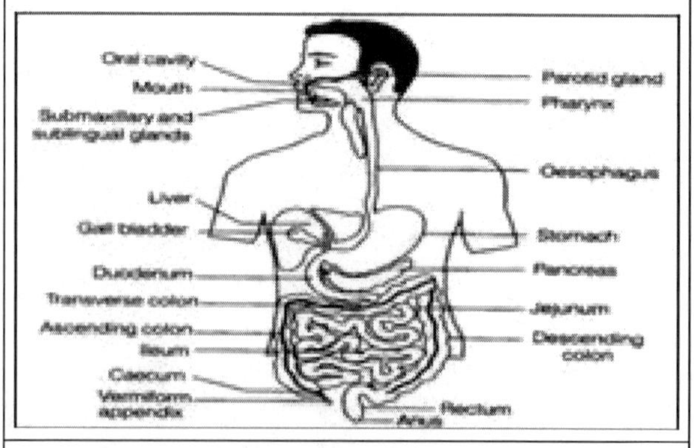

Fig. 23.1: Digestion and Absorption diagram from std XI bio zoology test Book

Digestion and absorption

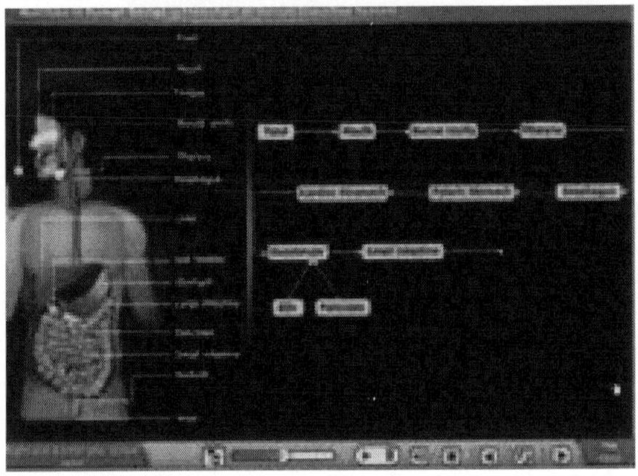

Fig. 23.2: Digestion and absorption from https://www/youtube.com/watch?vuygBY.TkgYb

Research Tool

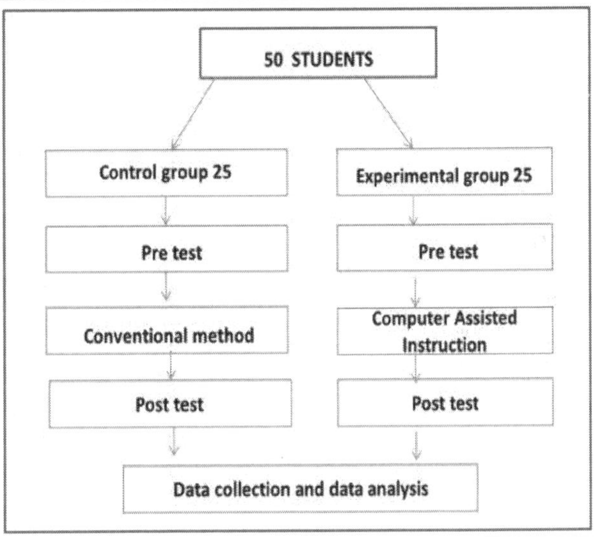

Fig. 23.3

Research tools

The present study used the following tools.

- Computer Assisted Instruction YouTube in biology
- Achievement test

Statiscal used

The sataistiacal techniques used to test the hypothesis were mean, Standard diviation and t test.

Analysis and Interpretation

Hypothesis-1

CAI in biology at the higher secondary level is not effective.

TABLE.23.1: The Post Test Scores of the Experimental Group and Control Group through CAI and Traditional Method do not Differ.

<table>
<tr><th>Variable</th><th>Test</th><th>N</th><th>M</th><th>SD</th><th>Mean Difference</th><th>T Value</th><th>Df</th><th>Level of Significance</th></tr>
<tr><td>Experimental group</td><td>E post</td><td>25</td><td>35.4</td><td>10.39</td><td rowspan="2">10.36</td><td rowspan="2">3.29</td><td rowspan="2">48</td><td rowspan="2">0.01</td></tr>
<tr><td>Control group</td><td>e post</td><td>25</td><td>25.04</td><td>11.83</td></tr>
</table>

The mean of the post test scores of the experimental group thaught through CAI is found to be 35.4 with an SD 10.39. The mean of the post test scores of the control group taught through trational method is found to be 25.04 with an SD 11.83. the mean difference 10.36 is found to be significant at 0.01 level with a 't'of 3.29. therefore the hypothesis is rejected. So it is concluded that the CAI in biology at the higher secondary level is effective is compared to that of the control group.

Hypothesis-2

The Post test means scores will be higher than Pre test scores of the experimental group

TABLE.23.2:

<table>
<tr><th>Variable</th><th>Test</th><th>N</th><th>M</th><th colspan="2">SD</th><th colspan="2">Mean difference</th><th>T Value</th><th>Df</th><th colspan="2">Level of Significance</th></tr>
<tr><td colspan="3" rowspan="2">Experimental group
E pre test</td><td colspan="2">E Post</td><td>25</td><td>35.4</td><td>10.39</td><td rowspan="2">17.2</td><td rowspan="2">5.53</td><td rowspan="2">48</td><td rowspan="2">0.01</td></tr>
<tr><td>25</td><td>18.2</td><td>11.57</td><td></td><td></td></tr>
</table>

In the table 23.2, the mean difference is 17.2 and it is significant for the t value 5.53 which is significant at 0.01 levels therefore the hypothesis is rejected. So it is concluded that there is a significant difference between the post and pre test scores of the experimental group taught through CAI in biology at the higher secondary level.

Hypothesis-3

The post test mean scores will be higher than pre test mean scores of the control group

TABLE. 23.3

Variables	Test	N	M	SD	Mean difference	T value	Df	Level of significance
Control group	e post	25	25.04	11.83	0.84	0.214	48	NS
	e pre test	25	24.2	15.73				

In the table 23.3, the mean difference is 48 is found to be not significant for the t value 0.214 for 48 Df therefore hypothesis is accepted. So it is concluded that there is significant difference between the post and pre test scores of the control group taught through the traditional method in biology at the higher secondary level.

Findings of the Study

1. It is found that there is significant difference between the pre test and post test of the experimental and control group.
2. It is found that there is no significant difference the pretest and post test of the control group.
3. It is found that there is significant difference between the pretest and post test scores of the experimental group.
4. It is found that there is a significant difference between the pretest and post test scores of the experimental group in the CAI in biology at the higher secondary level.

Conclusions

We cannot deny the fact that many technological developments and innovations played a major role in our lives. The kind of life we are currently enjoying because of technology developments. Technology improved our lives and the present things are now better faster, easier, and more convenient. Technology integrated in teaching learning process includes CAI. The study shows that superiority of CAI in relation to traditional method in achievement in biology. Thus efforts can be taken to implement CAI in the biology classes so as to succeed the purpose of achievement in biology at the higher secondary level.

❐

24

Emotional Intelligence and Academic Achievement among High School Students

Education encompasses attitudes and values along with information, concepts and facts. Real education implies in creating a wholesome integrated personality in students who are emotionally intelligent and socially matured. Such student community will be a good achiever in academic performances. On this aspect, the investigators try to find out the relationship among them with respect to back ground variables.

Need and Significance of the Study

Don Bosco(1899) says that in every young person, a point of goodness is accessible, and it is the primary duty of the educator to discover that sensitive cord of the heart so as to draw out the best in the young person. The need of this area of interest is to prepare a student, to live a balanced life style, and to motivate one to respond to others with empathy and compassion. As the significance, a student is able to resolve the conflicts in the society.

Objectives of the Study

- To find out the relationship between emotional Intelligence and academic achievement
- To compare the emotional intelligence between male and female high school students

Title of ihe Study

The title of the study is precisely stated as "Emotional Intelligence and Academic Achievement among High School Students"

Hypotheses

- There is no significant relationship between emotional Intelligence and academic achievement among high school students.
- There is no significant relationship between emotional Intelligence and academic achievement among high school students with respect to gender.

Design of the Study

The present study adopted the survey method. 380 data were collected from IX std from 3 high school from salem district.

Analysis and Interpretation of the Study

Hypothesis-1

There is no significant relationship between emotional Intelligence and academic achievement among high school students.

TABLE. 24.1: Emotional Intelligence and Academic Achievement

Variable	No of students	Mean	S.D	r-value	Degrees of freedom	Level of significance (0.05 level)
Emotional Intelligence	380	69.59	8.32	7.29	378	significant
Academic Achievement	380	497.13	49.85			

The table shows that calculated r- value is 7.29. It is noted that the observed value of r – value is more than the tabulated value at 5% level of significance; therefore the null hypothesis is rejected. So it concludes that there is a significant relationship between emotional intelligence and academic achievement among high school students.

Hypothesis-2

There is no significant relationship between emotional Intelligence and academic achievement among high school students with respect to gender.

TABLE. 24.2: Male and Female Students with Respect of Emotional Intelligence

Variable	No of students	Mean	S.D	r- value	Degrees of freedom	Level of significance (0.05 level)
Male	200	78.23	9.36	0.175	378	No significant
Female	180	77.09	9.03			

The table shows that the Mean value 78.23 is obtained for Male students and Mean value 77.09 is obtained in Female Students. The calculated r- value is 0.175. It is noted that the observed value of r- test is less than the tabulated value at 5% are not significance, therefore the null hypothesis is accepted. So, it concludes that there is no significant relationship between emotional Intelligence and academic achievement among high school students with respect to gender.

Findings of the Study

- There is no significant relationship between emotional Intelligence and academic achievement among high school students.
- There is no significant relationship between emotional Intelligence and academic achievement among high school students with respect to gender

Educational Implications

- The study showed that academic achievement played a significant role. This component can be highlighted and focused at the higher secondary school level also in future.
- Teacher Educators can plan their activities to develop Emotional Intelligence and in turn it can enhance the Academic achievement of the students at all levels.

Delimitation of the Study

- The present study is limited to High school level.
- The present study is conducted only in Salem District.

Conclusions

The high level of emotional intelligence can help to calm the mind and thus to increase the absorption of information received. Thus, it will contribute to students' academic achievement as a result. It is recommended that students' academic achievement may be enhanced with the use of emotional intelligence training. Emotional intelligence could be noted not only for academic interest but also of future success in life.

❐

25

Curriculum Design in Distance Education: An Integrated Approach

The implementation of curriculum is important and is quite a significant stage in the life cycle. The curriculum implementation is an integral part. Institutions are the great laboratories to plan, design, implement and test the impact of innovations in competency-Based curriculum implementation. They can contribute to the curriculum development and Learning Resources Development Centre in a great way.

Curriculum

A curriculum is a carefully planned and well written document that explicitly reflects the knowledge, skills, values and attitudes of societies that are intended to be passed to or mediated to the future generation, comprising both the old and the young. Curriculum depends on and is highly influenced by the knowledge, skills and beliefs of that particular educator as well as the context, milieu, and conditions in which the educator finds himself/herself during the learning mediation. Curriculum comprises the following components: academic programme, practical programme and skills training programme. Curriculum adaptations are modifications that relate specifically to instruction or content of a curriculum. These adjustments or modifications could be to:

Curriculum Design

Identify the needs of the curriculum design process in the distance education. This can be done through needs analysis, which involves the collection and analysis of data related to the learner. This data might include what learners already know and what they need to know to be proficient in a particular area or skill. It may also include information about learner perceptions, strength and weaknesses. It creates a clear list of learning goals and outcomes. Learning outcomes are the measurable knowledge, skills, and attitudes that students should have achieved in the course.

Subject-Centered Curriculum Design

Subject-centered curriculum design revolves around a particular subject matter or discipline. This type of curriculum is standardized.

Learner-Centered Curriculum Design

Learner-centered curriculum design revolves the learner. It takes each individual's needs, interests and goals into consideration.

Problem-Centered Curriculum Design

Problem-centered curriculum design increases the relevance of the curriculum and allows students to get creative and innovate while learning.

Teacher-Centered Curriculum Design

Teachers participate in a variety of curriculum activities at the classroom level selection of specific content, selection teaching approach us of audio-visual aids and so on.

Integrated Curriculum

Integration focuses on making connections with students, allowing them to engage in relevant, meaningful activities that can be connected to real life

Distance Education

Distance education or distance learning is the education of students who may not always be physically present at a school. Traditionally, this usually involved correspondence courses where in the student corresponded with the school. Today it involved online education.

Distance Education and Its Instruction Design

In ancient period the teaching and learning process was done without any additional hardware or software to use. Now-a-days the learning becomes so easy. It is an easiest task when we get it at own time. The number of people felt that we learn our own time and own place, they do not come to learn regularly those who are earning.

The major components of Educational Technology,

- **Methods:** It concerned with the devices such as programmed learning, Team teaching, micro teaching.
- **Media:** The media used audio, visual or audio-visual. Examples: Audio tape recorder, chats , films and computer.
- **Materials:** Instructional materials such as programmed test book, the material of educational technology is soft copy and it may be downloaded.
- **Man Power:** Man power is essential to operate the technologies in education

Benefits of Distance Education

- Distance education can also provide a broader method of communication. With the many tools and programs that technological advancement have offer, communication appears to increase in distance education amongst students and their professors, as well as students and their classmates.
- Distance education programs can act as a institutional innovation and at least as effective as face- to-face learning programs, especially if the instructor is knowledgeable and skilled.
- Distance learning can expand access to education and training for both general populace and businesses. Since its flexible scheduling structure lessons effects of the many time.

Conclusions

The curriculum designed for the distance education should be learner-centered; it should create the self learning and flexible. Distance educational increase in communication, students and their classmates, is an improvement that has been made to provide distance education students with as many of the opportunities.

❐

26

Instructional Technology Module in Chemistry at Higher Secondary Level

The present educational system becomes complex due to lack of individual attention in the classroom. The expansion of education in the form of greater enrolment of learners in schools and colleges makes the systems more rigid and complex. The best answer to this problem is the application of information and communication technology which endeavours to remove monotony, but at the same time, enhances motivation and interest among learners. In the modern educational system, the computers are used extensively and their impact on the social, economic, educational and scientific spheres is greatly recognized.

Need for Study

The prime objective of education is to increase the capabilities and skills of students in order to adapt them to the continual and fast changes in life. It is pointed out that computers are not pressed into the teaching – learning process to a great extent in Indian classrooms. While, students in the developed countries have experienced the dynamics of computers. In order to cope with the education attainment of their western counterparts Indian learners at the school and college level have to be urgently introduced to computer assisted instructional activities.

Objectives

The specific objectives of the study are stated as follows

- To compare the pre – test and post – test mean achievement scores of small experimental group.
- To compare the pre – test attitude score and pot – test attitude scores of a small group.
- To find out whether there is any significant difference between the pre – test and post – test achievement of the large experimental group.
- To find out whether there is any significant difference between the pre – test and post – test attitude scores of the large experimental group.

Research Design of the Study

In this present study, the one – group pre-test, post-test design was employed. Campbell and Stanley (1966) call this design as before – after design. In their design, the control group is not involved. The design has three steps, the first step being administration of a pre - test measuring the treatment for the single group chosen for this purpose, and the final step is the administration of post – test measuring the dependent variable again. The differences due to the application of experimental treatment are then determined by comparing the pre – test and post – test scores. One – group pre – test, post – test is employed for the study.

Research Tools

Achievement test were used to collect relevant data from the subjects. The achievement test where intended to find out the entry behaviour of the learners as well as their exit behaviour. The following research tools were developed validated and used for collecting the data from the experimental groups.

- Pre – test (Achievement test)
- Post – test (Achievement test)
- Computer – Based Module Attitude Scale (CBMAS)

These tools were structured in order to find out the effectiveness of the Computer – Assisted Instructional Technology Module.

Sample

The investigator chose XI Standard Science students from Don Bosco Matriculation Higher Secondary School, Puducherry, for the experimentation. There were 41 learners in the XI Standard Science group. Since, it is a single group design (quasi) al the 41 members from the science group were formed as a large group. With regard to the small group, five first year higher secondary students studying in a school, namely, 'Petit Seminaire' were randomly selected for the try out.

Data Analysis

The following are the statistical techniques used for the analysis of data

- Measure of central tendency – arithmetic mean.
- Measure of variability – standard deviation
- Test of significance – 't' test
- 'r' – Correlation.

Comparison between the Pre-test and the Post-Test mean Achievement Scores of the Small Group

Test	Mean	SD
Pre-Test	54	13.14
Post-Test	72.4	16.4

Comparison between the Pre-Test and the Post-Test mean Attitude Scores of the Small Group

Test	Mean	SD
Pre- Attitude Test	78.13	11
Post-Attitudetest	90.12	5.1

Significance of Different between the Pre-Test and the Post-Test mean Achievement Scores of the Experimental Group

Test	Mean	SD	'r'	't'
Pre-Test	57.9	10.9	0.74	8.1
Post- Test	76.9	10.3		

Significant at 0.01 level

Significance of Different between the Pre-Test mean Attitude and the Post-Test mean Attitude Scores of the Experimental Group

Test	Mean	SD	'r'	't'
Pre-Test	79.9	6.9	0.406	8.69
Post- Test	91.64	5.2		

Significant at 0.01 level

Major Findings of the Study

The following are the major findings of the study:

- **The Computer** – Assisted Instructional Technology Module developed and validated by the investigator proves to be effective in learning chemistry at higher secondary level.
- **The higher secondary learners show a more favourable attitude towards the Computer** – Assisted Instructional Technology Module.

Implications of the Study

The present study reveals the effectiveness of the Computer – Assisted Instructional Technology Module for learning chemistry at the higher secondary level. The learners are able to attain mastery of the subject due to the flexibility of the process at the level of learning. The modules provide them ample freedom to learn chemistry subject at their own speed and ability and reduces stress and anxiety. The modules create interest and motivation by avoiding monotony in the class. Taking into consideration the benefits of technology supported module, there is a need for such module material for the benefit of higher secondary learners. It is, therefore, recommended that there be a greater application of technology modules at all levels of education so as to enable the learners to achieve mastery over the subjects according to their own pace and ability.

The modern world is invaded by the internet. Through networking, learners in different parts of the world know about subjects and they can update their knowledge in a very fast manner. The schools and colleges should take efforts in creating necessary websites for dissemination of knowledge across the world.

Conclusions

The present study was carried out to find the effectiveness of the Computer – Assisted Instructional Technology Module in learning chemistry at the higher secondary level. As the present teaching – learning process at the higher secondary level is rigid, time bound and outmoded, it was planned to device learning tasks in the form of a technology module for the benefit of the learners, so that the learners can attain mastery of the subject according to their own pace and ability and ability and feel motivated through personal involvement in the process of learning. It is pointed out that the technology module is user controlled as the tasks are constructed and offered to each learner through a separate personal computer. The present study clearly demonstrates the effectiveness of the technology based module in learning chemistry at the higher secondary level. As the technology module provides ample scope for learner motivation and user friendliness, it is recommended that this type of technology supported module should be employed in the process of learning for all categories of learners.

❒

27

A Roadmap for Language Education through Neurocognitive Strategies

Language plays a vital role in communication. Every people should try hard to acquire good communication skills which are important for his/her career. The communication skills need a lot of overhauling. To make our India glorious, it is important to create well educated graduates and implement the various methods of education which are one of the best methods is used in this study. English is taught only as a second language in India and there is a great difference between students to acquire the language. The teachers are exposed to a lot of methods to teach English with ample facilities and special training to improve their Listening, Speaking, Reading and Writing skills which are the basic skills for any language whereas students have only limited exposure to learn English. Language learning is a skill that can be perfected only through constant practice and continuous exposure to the target language. This study deals with cognitive functions are linked with the development of the brain and the central nervous system. The basic anatomy and function of brain and learning process are the two important aspects in Neurocognition.

Neurocognition based Language process

The brain is part of the central nervous system, one of several systems that together make up the body. The cerebral hemispheres are great importance for language. It is believed that two hemispheres, right and left are interrelated to puberty and thence begin to lose plasticity; that is what advocates of the critical period hypothesis hold (Nunan, 1999). It is believed that the right hemisphere, which is considered the most creative, is related to art, space, color, rhythm, and musical imagination, among other artistic activities; on the other hand, the left hemisphere is mostly linked to language, to logical operations, numbers, sequencing, and analysis (Fisher, 2005).

Broca and Wernicke are very important areas for language process and link these two areas with the arcuate fasciculus, which has a significant amount of fibers (Lamb, 1999). According to Seldon, it is considered the most extensive sensory area for language. The theory of relational networks emphasizes the fact that there is high connectivity of all the subsystems in the brain. This connectivity can be seen in the different fibers and fiber bundles that make up the white matter and that are under the cortex.

For neurocognitive linguistics, the linguistic system is linked to other subsystems of the total human cognition; and the mind is seen as a system of networks characterized by its connectivity. This cognitive system interprets external symbols resulting from a process of selective activation of neural connections. The activation of these connections strengthens the links between them, thus consolidating the network (Muñoz, 2016). Knowing a language, is knowing how to use it, which implies being able to perform certain processes, which, in the framework of the theory of relational networks in neurocognitive linguistics it means firstly, movements of activation of network connection between node and node, and secondly different operations that alter the shape of the network. These alterations may result either in strengthening connections, or in constructing inhibitory connections; the former causes the strengthening of structures, while the latter results in the weakening of the links between nodes, thus originating defective or erroneous constructions. The language and the system of networks change when in use.

A road map for language Education through Neurocognitive Strategies

Language processing was mostly carried out by repetition and recognition of sentence-level structures, both in the language to which the student was exposed in class and in the evaluation, being a beginner in learning the language. Here the researcher provides four type of Neurocognitive strategies based language teaching and learning.

1. **Neurocognitive Based implicit Learning**
   Implicit learning involves automatic learning mechanisms that are used to extract regularities and patterns distributed across a set of exemplars, typically without conscious awareness of the regularities being learned. Implicit learning is believed to be important for many aspects of skill learning, problem solving, and language processing. Allow more time for students to complete their tasks, such as note-taking, written tests, and copying. Also, allow students to begin written projects earlier than others.
2. **Neurocognitive based Concept Mapping**
   Neurocognitive based concept mapping is an advanced tool for representing knowledge and gathering information by neuronal pathway in human brain. This advanced approach can be inculcated among the learners through keyword repetition techniques, learning by doing method, information processes model, whole brain technique, color coding method, etc. for the enhancement of long term memory.
3. **Neurocognitive based Memory-Related Strategies**
   Memory-related strategies help learner's link one L2 item or concept with another but do not necessarily involve deep understanding. Various memory-related strategies enable learners to learn and retrieve information in an orderly string (e.g., acronyms), while other techniques create learning and retrieval via sounds (e.g., rhyming), images, a combination of sounds and mechanical means (e.g., flashcards), or location. Memory strategies are often used for memorizing vocabulary and structures in initial stages of language learning, but that learners need such strategies much less when their arsenal of vocabulary and structures has become larger.
4. **Neurocognitive based Constructivism Strategies**
   In constructivism, students are encouraged to learn main ideas on their own through discovery learning. Examples include learning about compound words by playing with word strips, learning about addition and subtraction through the use of manipulatives, or learning about capacity through experimentation with different sizes of objects. Students' own ideas about how things work play a large role in constructivism as we attempt to provide activities that clarify and correct misconceptions. Additional constructivist strategies include presenting others' viewpoints, promoting dialogue, and emphasizing conceptual understanding rather than rote learning.

Conclusions

The brain related processes such as, cognitive process, attention, coding, encoding, association, representation etc. are involved in biology of language learning of human through Neurocognitive strategies. The brain interlinks the new learning through various aspects of biology to store the information. The neurocognitive strategies stimulate long term memory and information can be easily retrieved by the brain. So, the researcher involves neurocognitive strategies used to develop the language education.

❒

28

E-Learning in Distance Mode

Education plays an important role in development of society. There are two broad categories of education; Social Interactive Education and Distance Education. Social Interactive method of education is the traditional method of learning where instructor teaches learners face to face. Open and distance learning is usually contrasted with 'conventional' or face-to-face' education, which may be described as the form of education which takes place in a classroom or an auditorium. Distance Education is a method of teaching where the instructor and learners are separated by time and or physical distance. The main objective of distance education is, the availability of education- anyone, anyway, anywhere and anytime without social, physical and geographical restrictions.

E-Learning and Distance Education

Electronic learning or E-learning is a type of education where the medium of instruction modern technology. There is no personal interaction require to communicate people. Earlier, audio tape, video tape and Compact Disc were used to deliver course material and lectures but later the technological development changed its face. E-learning is used interchangeably in a wide variety of contexts. E-learning is used to define a specific mode to attend a course or program of study where the students rarely, if ever, attend face-to-face for on-campus access to educational facilities, because they study on-line.

E-learning is naturally suited to distance learning and flexible learning. Distance Education in the form of E-learning is the only way to stay current. E-learning can also be used in conjunction with face-to-face teaching, in which case the term Blended learning is commonly sed. E-learning pioneer Bernard Luskin argues that the "E" must be understood to have broad meaning if E-learning is to be effective. Luskin says that the "E" should be interpreted to mean Exciting, Energetic, Enthusiastic, Emotional, Extended, Excellent, and Educational in addition to "Electronic" that is a traditional national interpretation

Benefits of E-Learning Assisted Distance Education

The purpose of implementing E-learning assisted Distance Education in India is to take education to the doorsteps of the rural poor, the disadvantaged and marginalized people of the society. The people should be given the opportunity to master the skill to use technology to their advantages without feeling threatened to build a better tomorrow. E-learning assisted distance education enables people to have: 1.Strong academic skills 2.Better thinking 3.Reasoning 4.Teamwork skills 5.Proficiency in using technology 6.Meeting challenges, and 7.Enhance learning .The benefits that can be achieved by the E-learners include: 1.Training facilities at off-hours or from home. 2. Less academic stress 3.Interactivity engages users, pushing them rather than pulling them through training 4.Availability of quick reference materials.

Components of E-Learning

ELearning consists of the following components, which are created with the state of art Internet technologies for high quality, ease of use and effectiveness.

The Virtual Classroom

Virtual Classroom Modules (VCMs) are well-prepared high quality lectures from the master trainers, with multimedia color presentations. VCM combines distance education in-structional pedagogy with latest interactive multimedia Internet technology. VCM helps the counselor to efficiently perform his basic job of providing information in less time, without compromising the quality. Thus, he can utilize his time for developing higher-level mental abili-ties like comprehension, application, analysis etc in students. Smaller time duration of each module ensures better concentration. Streaming media technology ensures simultaneous play-ing and downloading of a module from Internet. Thus, Internet can be used as backup media for delivery of VCMs to provide 'Anywhere Anytime' learning. Use of video is kept to minimum possible level, and normally restricted to imparting of skills. Easy and fast production of good quality VCMs is possible. Discussion and tutorial in real time, with counselors and fellow stu-dents are expected to follow these lectures at each study centre. Thus, VCM ensures bette r learning through distance system in the following ways: 1. Better time utilization through well prepared lectures from master trainers. 2. Clear knowledge communication through the latest multimedia and Internet technol-ogy. 3. Development of better understanding through discussion/tutorials in a group of fellow students with a counselor. 4. Student can repeat the lecture or its part, on computer. University can even dispatch it through Internet/email. 5. Easy Quality Assurance through a) Lectures of master trainers directly reaching the students b) Use of multimedia for enjoyable and worthy learning experience c) Same quality standards ensured at each study centre.

The Discussion Forum

A discussion forum is an interactive web site that lets site visitors discuss topics by reading articles that have been posted, replying to articles, and posting new ones. Visitors can also use a search form to find articles of interest. Discussion forum offers asynchronous mode of communication, where messages can be prepared with editing. But it allows only text-based interaction among students, counselors and the university. Any interaction on the discussion forum is visible to all. A discussion forum can have the following features 1. A table of contents that contains hyperlinks to articles related to discussion topics. 2. A search box that allows searching the articles by a word or phrase.3An entry form in which a visitor types an article to post. 4. Threaded replies allow the visitor to choose whether the article they are posting is anew top-level topic for discussion, or a reply to another article. This feature creates well-classified and well-organized knowledge base on any academic or administrative topic in a short time. 5. A confirmation page which confirms that a visitor's article has been posted.6.A registration form that lets site visitors log in to the Web site, if the discussion web is protected.

Online Counseling

'Online Counselor' is a well-qualified and experienced person who interacts with the students, only through use of discussion forum, for clearing their doubts/difficulties. Depending on the number of students, the university can appoint one or more 'Online Counselors' for each course (subject). Once a week, each 'Online Counselor' will answer all the questions posted on the discussion forum of the respective course (subject).

Indian Perspective

There are many initiatives has been taken to enhance distance education through e-learning, some of them are discussed as follows;

E-Gyankosh

The e-GyanKosh30 is a national digital repository developed by IGNOU for sharing learning content. It is a learning platform of students to read content or watch videos of lectures. It has over 2200 video programmers in addition to e-content related to different subjects.

NPTEL (National Programme on Technology Enhanced Learning)

NPTEL is a project funded by the Ministry of Human Resource Development. It was first conceived in 1999 to pave the way for introducing multimedia and web technology to enhance learning of basic science and engineering concepts. It is collaborative program of seven Indian Institutes of Technology (IIT) and the Indian Institute of Science (IISc). It opened a new way of learning and also for sharing expertise among faculty in different parts of the world. In India, where a large number of private institutions have entered the field of engineering education with inadequate faculty support and training, the project is aimed at pro-viding a standard for academic content for both the teacher and the student. It has 129 web courses and 110 video courses in the field of science and technology. Each course consists of 40 video lectures of one hour and text, images, animations and graphics.

Tamil Virtual Academy

Tamil Virtual Academy (formally as Tamil Virtual University) is an internet based re-source that provides detail on the History, Arts, Literature and Culture of the Tamils. The main objective of the project was to preserve the cultural identity, traditions and values of the Tamils. It was setup by the government of Tamil Nadu for emerging needs of the Tamil Communities and others interested in Tamil studies. The functions of TVA are guided by a Board of Directors and it is administered by a full time Director. The courses are free for anyone interested.

Bits Pilani

Birla Institute of Technology and Sciences has established a virtual university, with DIT sponsorship. BITS has been one of the pioneers in distance education. BITS has been providing courses for working professionals in distance education mode leveraging technology.

Conclusions

India is an emerging economy and it required skilled people for the development. The education is one of biggest challenge which is India facing. There are not adequate collages, institutes and universities to provide education to all. The distance education can ensure the availability of education without social, physical and geographical restrictions. The implementation of E-learning can reduce the problems related to distance education. Some initiative shave been taken but they are not enough to bridge the problem. It needs a serious effort from planners and government authority to implement such programs.

❒

29

Application of Web Based Instruction (WBI) among Teacher Educators

Today the world approaches towards digital revolution and learners have become digital natives and the teacher's role becomes a facilitator, instructor and director to their students in their search for knowledge. The transformation of the society is possible when learners are exposed to a new platform for learning which offers opportunities to pursue knowledge unlimited, independent and proceed at their own interest and pace and also which fosters creative thinking and critical enquiry among the students. The digital devices are capable to gratify the requirements of the learners for ease and comfortable learning in collaborative manner and it facilitates adaptive learning technology.

Need For The Study

The professional development of the teacher is very important and it offers chance equally to the gaining mastery in the subject of specialization and it will be considered an asset, Teachers of today who they possessed with effectiveness and efficiency in using knowledge and application of online source materials and e-packages in classroom instruction and motivating students to follow online facilities and sources for their enhancing learning process will be fruitful and stand with global standard. Lifelong learning is most possible when the learners are digital literates and efficient in adapting to digital learning method and incorporate computers.

Review of Related Literature

The purpose of review is to plan early steps in research work to update information about the literature and to avoid replication. Baytiyeh, Hoda (2018) has investigated on college students' use of Whats App as a communication tool. The results revealed four themes of simplicity for discussion and coordination, cost-effectiveness, immediacy and sense of belonging are the factors contributed for the utilization. Davidovitch, Nitzat Belichennko & Margaita (2018) showed that Facebook groups used to facilitate communication between students, to foster a positive social climate, to create dialogue and to share learning material among group members and improve course quality and students' achievements. Guha, A.S & Isagah Lawrniang (2018) Social site network is connecting and sharing through SSN. It is great advantage for in terms of profession, friendship, research and studies, this can be profitably used for Distance Education. Sociability is accompanied with less wasted resources. Educational institutions offering courses through distance mode used virtual information to reach the unreached and to improve quality of delivery than the education offered in regular mode.

Objectives of the Study

To find out if there is any significant difference exist among teacher educators in their in Application of WBI with reference to some back ground variables of Gender, Locality of Home, Locality of Institution, Department/ Major, facility for Internet accessing and duration of Internet Usage.

Hypotheses of the Study

There is no significant difference exist among teacher educators in their in Application of WBI with reference to some back ground variables of Gender, Locality of Home, Locality of Institution, Department/Major, facility for Internet accessing and duration of Internet Usage.

Method Adopted for the Study

The investigator employed the normative survey method for the present investigation.

Population and Sample

All teacher educators who are working in colleges of education are constituted as the population of the study. The investigator has used the stratified random sampling technique. The sample of the present study contains of 251 teacher educators.

Delimitation of the Study

The tool developed for the purpose of assessing the application of Web Based Instruction has only expressed and this study confined with the sample from teacher educators only.

Tool Used in this Study

The investigator has used the self-constructed questionnaire for assessing the application of WBI among teacher educators in teaching of B.Ed students the present study. The research tool has named as Application of Web Based Instruction scale and which consists of 35 items in it.

Statistical Techniques Adopted

Arithmetic mean, standard Deviation, 't' test, and 'F' test was used to analyze the data and these were done through SPSS packages and the Probability value at 0.05 level of significance has considered to test the hypothesis to reject or accept to arrive the findings and result of the research.

TABLE. 29.1: Significance of Difference Exist among Teacher Educators in their in Application of WBI with Reference to some Background Variables of Gender, Locality of Home, Locality of Institution, Department/Major, Facility for Accessing to Internet and Duration of Internet Usage.

S. No	Variables	Categories	Mean	S.D	't' Value	Level of Sig
1	Gender	Male	30.816	5.050	0.220	NS
		Female	30.950	4.609		
2	Locality of Home	Rural	31.520	4.689	2.097	S
		Urban	30.252	4.910		
3	Locality of Institution	Rural	30.726	4.922	.563	NS
		Urban	31.070	4.962		
4	Department / Major	Arts	1.471	4.906	1.926	NS
		Science	31.388	4.733		

TABLE. 29.2

S. No	Variables	Source of Variation	Sum of Squares	Deg. Freedom	Mean Square	F Value	Level of Sig
1	Facility for Accessing to Internet	Between Groups	191.398	2	95.699	***4.199***	***S***
		Within Groups	5675.031	249	22.791		
		Total	**5866.429**	**251**			
2	Duration of Usage of Internet	Between Groups	261.507	3	87.169	***3.857***	***S***
		Within Groups	5604.921	248	22.600		
		Total	**5866.429**	**251**			

TABLE.29.3: Post Hoc Tests of Duncan Multiple Range Test of Homogeneous Sub Sets Highlights the Specific Group Influence on the Application of Web Based Instruction with reference to Facility for Accessing to Internet and Duration of Usage of Internet.

Variables		Subset for Alpha		
		Num 1	2	
Facility for Internet access	Institution	120	30.008	
	Home	57	31.263	31.263
	Both	75		**31.986**
	Sig.		0.105	0.349
Duration of Internet Usage	1 hour	87	30.0805	
	1 to 2 hour	82	31.0122	
	2 to 3 hour	44	30.2727	
	3 hour above	39		**33.0769**
	Sig.1		0.334	1

Findings of the Study

The results of the study reads as there is no significant difference exists among teacher educators in their application of web based instruction with reference to gender, locality of the institution and the subject of specialization of department or major but they differ significantly in their application of WBI with reference to locality of their home, facility for accessing to internet and the duration of using of internet in their classroom instruction.

Implication of the Study

There is the marked difference prevailed among teacher educators in using WBI due to lack of infrastructure availability and training and which act as the challenges to integrate WBI in teaching and learning in colleges of education. Availability and duration of using internet have highly influenced teacher educators for using web based instruction in their classroom teaching.

Conclusions

Familiar with the language of the digital world will facilitate enormous opportunities for better learning, understanding, application, skill, analysis, synthesis and research in the field of study. The transformation of the country depends upon the development of the structure of knowledge, a teacher in a classroom is not enough to fulfill the needs and expectation of the generation y learners, and they are fast, accurate and authentic in search of knowledge.

❐

30

Blended Learning in Distance Education

"We are living in a regularly evolving world» (Sethy, 2008, p.29) This has changed instructing and adapting especially separate training. The entry of World Wide Web (WWW) has expanded the interest for separation training and ideas like web based learning or e-learning has developed, subsequently. The arrangement of web based learning has been to a great extent utilized in advanced education, and a ton of studies have been done to find the two its qualities and shortcomings (Wang, 2010). Since e-learning conditions present a few disservices, for example, repressing the socialization procedure of people bringing about absence of up close and personal correspondence; another condition has surfaced. This new condition consolidates the e-learning and the traditional learning situations. It has been named as mixed learning, half and half or blended learning. The premier objective of mixed guidance was to overpower downsides of unadulterated online guidance. Since either unadulterated e-learning or conventional learning hold a few shortcomings and qualities, it is smarter to blend the qualities of both learning conditions to build up another technique for conveyance called mixed learning (Azizan, 2010).

What is Blended?

Online Class + Traditional Class = Blended Learning

Driscoll (2002) characterized mixed learning as a blend of instructional strategies. Despite what might be expected, Delialioglu and Yildirim (2007) asserted that orderly and key mix of ICT devices into scholastic courses acquaints another path with methodology instructional objectives. This instructional method has been given many names:

In this respects, the cerebrum needs and anticipates these progressively critical channels of data. In the event that these are not accessible, the mind endures to impart and there is a high plausibility that an error may happen. Lewis (2006) additionally guaranteed that on the off chance that we want to know somebody and grasp this experience through content, we are deluding ourselves. Visual data and unobtrusive feelings, for example, winkles and grins are critical to impart anything remotely and these don't exist in web based learning. He included that there are numerous elements that influence human correspondence that can't be clarified through electronic correspondence and are more persuasive than we understand.

Advantages of Blended Learning

- Blending learning approachcan be contributing tools to complete
- Face to face experiences (Ginns & Ellis, 2009).
- Blended instruction offers an active learning environment with flexibility in using resources for the students.
- Provides more time for faculty members to spend with learners in small groups even individually (Oh & Park, 2009).
- To offer manysources for learners.
- Azizan (2010) presumed that use of innovation in physical study halls offer additional assets for the understudies and this is required to upgrade students' certainty and fitness just as improve the nature of learning.
- Chen and Jones (2007) illustrated different points of interest of mixed adapting, for example, profound comprehension of subjects by utilizing electronic assets just as dynamic investment of understudies in class.
- Online learning commitment gives an intuitive setting to correspondence among instructors and understudies in the study hall and may encourage helpful exercises even past the classrooms(Yuen, 2010).

Distance Education

Distance Education or Distance Learning is a field of training that centers around showing strategies and innovation with the point of conveying instructing, frequently on an individual premise, to understudies who are not physically display in a conventional instructive setting, for example, a study hall. It has been depicted as «a procedure to make and give access to realizing when the wellspring of data and the students are isolated by time and remove, or both.

Advantages of Distance / Online Education

Content is conveyed by means of the Internet, intranet/extranet, sound or video tape, satellite TV, and CD-ROM. It tends to act naturally paced or educator drove and incorporates media as content, picture, movement, gushing video and sound.

Methods of Distance / Online Education

Based on the Learning, the types of available Methods / technologies used in distance / Online education can be broadly divided intothreegroups namely –

1. Synchronous Learning
2. Asynchronous Learning&
3. Hybrid / Blended Learning

Various Approaches in Online (Hybrid) Learning

Though there are too many approaches to Online (Hybrid) learning, based on the software & stream, the following are some of the important approaches in Online learning –

- Computer Based Learning (CBL)
- Computer/web based training(CBT/WBT)
- Computer Supported Collaborative Learning(CSCL)
- Technical Enhanced Learning(TEL)

Conclusions

In a Blended Learning course for example the mix of eye to eye guidance with online stages, understudies and instructors participate in utilizing innovation for dynamic learning. Remembering this view, mixed condition gives a urging circumstance to both the conventional study halls and the online settings. To aggregate up, beneath are the upsides of mixed learning over web based learning situations as Increased correspondence, Engagement of eye to eye correspondence, Sense of network, Improved scholastic execution, Collaborative undertakings, Adequate criticism, interest, Providing help, Fun and functional way of educating and learning, Etc… It can be reasoned that those exercises which are associated with the mixed guidance can encourage the feeling of network having a place and expel the dissatisfaction made by negligible online condition. The up close and personal component ought not be supplanted in view of the huge impact of non-verbal communication, manner of speaking, outward appearances and eye to eye connection on correspondence. These two instructive settings to be specific e-learning and up close and personal learning can supplement each other for educational application. This paper has introduced the fruitful use of mixed learning in separation adapting particularly as far as understudies' learning knowledge, understudy connection and understudy educator collaboration. The blended learning approach is probably going to develop as the transcendent instructional model later on. Colleges or Institutions offering Online Distance Learning can surrender the customary techniques and can take up the Hybrid Learning as an apparatus in their course contributions so as to get the best outcomes. However, on start, usage of Hybrid Learning seems expensive, expenses can undoubtedly be recouped and can without much of a stretch achieve break levels in a brief span.

❐

31

Education and its Role in Societal Change

Societal and natural conditions determine the role and the function of education. The salient feature of education is its communal side. The social context is imperative for education to function well. Society and education are complementary to each other. Society cannot function without education and education cannot exist without society. Education affects not only the person being educated but also the whole community that includes the family too.

Education and Society

Education is regarded as a sub-system of society. The process of education takes place in social settings and society as a whole exercises great control over its process. Education reflects the main features of that societal goals, values, needs and aspirations.

Education as a sub-system executes certain functions for the society as a whole. There are also functional relations between education and other sub-systems. For example, Education trains the individuals in skills that are required by economy. Similarly education is conditioned by the economic institutions. The effectiveness of organized activities of a society depends on the interaction and interrelationships of these institutions which constitute the whole. Now we will examine the role of education for the society and the relationship between education and other sub-system of society in terms of functionalist perspective.

Educational Cntributionto Social Change

Education is a major aspect of development of any modern; society. Education brings awareness in people and keeps them away from superstitious beliefs. It provides best possible settlement not only in India but also in many western countries. Education will direct the person to move in right path at all times in life. A highly educated person can always manage things independently. An educated person can led his life with many comfort. Education makes students physically and mentally strong. Education is the best investment for the people because well educated people have more opportunities to get a job which gives them satisfaction. An educated person will be always respected in any part of world and his talent will be awarded and rewarded. Education also makes the person to be positive. Sometimes people scarify their enjoyment and work hard day and night, because they realize that education is their passport for the further. Literacy rate depend on education. All the advancement in technology is due to education

Education promotes knowledge and understanding in rural communities. Educated person will be health conscious. Education is only pathway to maintain success in life. It increases the ethical values of the person. Education is not only knowledge about books but also learning about life. It rapidly increases one's skill and awareness. Educated person will identify the difference between good and bad. Education provides food for all times. It is best source to raise the economy. The major function of education is the transmission of society's norms and values..

Education is a social concern. It is a social process. Its objective is to develop and awaken in the child those physical, intellectual and moral states which are acquired of the individual by his society as a whole and the milieu for which he is specially destined. It is the significant means of socialization. The function of education is to socialize the young by imparting to them norms and values, culture and heritage, and to provide them with skills and placement. This is traditionally, the accepted role of education

Education and Community

Community development is an overall development. Educational system and economy are two closely related social institutions .Schools as an important componentof educational system provide instruction and personality formation which enables economic progress and community development. Community development and change is particularly related totheeducationand instruction that social problems are identified and citizens are informed about these matters in a democratic way.

Universities also have an obligation to society as torchbearers of social progress. The knowledge they impart has relevance to the great problem of living a purposive life in a changing world. Our universities must now ask themselves how far their work has given a new direction to the thought and action of the younger generation, how far they have shaped the higher intelligence of the nation or prepared it for the major task of our age

Conclusions

Let us not measure the quality of our education by the statistics of pass , failure and wastage, however important these figures maybe as official recordsEducation must provide the nation with good workers and managers. Moreover it should provide thinkers and seekers of light. Education is much more than preparation for a career or a meansof acquiring skills for particular professions. Education is therefore a continuing process from the minute we are born until we die. Education can create a safer, healthier and more prosperous world and enhance the living standards by changing the visions and perspectives of individuals. So it can rightly be concluded that education and modernization are the two sides of the same coin and these mutually influence each other.

❐

32

Developing English Language Proficiency among Rural Areas

English is taught only as a second language in India and there is a great difyference between the city-bred children and the rural children in adapting to English language. The city-bred children are exposed to a lot of methods of learning English with ample facilities and special training in schools to improve their Listening, Speaking, Reading and Writing skills which are the basic skills for learning any language whereas rural students have only limited exposure to learn English.

Status of Rural and Urban Students

The city-bred children are exposed to a lot of modules and they have the privilege of learning English through different methods. Special training is available in the city schools to improve the students' Listening, Speaking, Reading and Writing skills which are the basic skills for learning any language whereas the rural students have only limited exposure to learn English.

The training provided in schools, is purely theoretical and bookish and English is taught only in the exam point of view. Hence, even after twelve years of learning English as a subject the students hesitate to communicate in English.

It is high time to motivate the students, right from their school by creating an awareness regarding the importance of English language. It is necessary that the teachers who teach English in rural areas should be committed and have an honest approach to equip the skills of the students.

The available resources should be completely tapped so as to provide an encouraging atmosphere for learning and practicing the language. This paper deals with the effective methods which can be employed in teaching English to the rural students for their enhancement.

Today, conventional teaching methods are replaced with modern techniques which rely hugely upon media resources and teaching English with the help of such modern techniques fosters a positive attitude among the rural students to learn the language which would enable them to meet the demands of the day in a creative way.

Problems Faced by the Rural Students

To begin with, the first and the foremost factor is the Socio-Cultural and financial background of the family. As most of the parents are illiterate, they are not able to guide their wards as educated parents do.

Hence, the students' performance lacks parental supervision and guidance which is very necessary for education. The illiterate parents are unable to realize the importance of education and also they do not understand the importance of communication skills which plays a vital role in their ward's career.

As there is an increase in the ratio of rural students preferring for professional courses, the above facts should be considered and those students should be trained to meet the need of the hour.

The following activities can be implemented to improve the listening skills.

- Watching English movies on Television
- Watching talk shows on Television
- Listening to speeches of great statesmen & politicians
- Watching headlines
- Listening to recorded speeches, dialogues, interviews and discussions
- Listening to news bulletins, chat shows, commentaries, weather reports

The problems of English language teaching

The problems is the demand for English medium and introduction of English as a medium in some schools in each block in Government schools in many states. In most of the cases English as medium is introduced without ensuring the essential resources for quality teaching through English medium.

Research indicates that learning through mother tongue is ideal for harmonious language and cognitive development To explore, discuss and reflect on the issues and problems relating to the quality of English language teaching-learning in rural schools in terms of teacher inputs, materials and opportunities for learning English and conditions for English language learning in rural schools;

Developing Communication Skill

To explore, discuss and reflect onthe issues and problems relating to the quality of English language teaching-learning in rural schools in terms of teacher inputs, materials and opportunities for learning English and conditions for English language learning in rural schools .

One reason that many English learners have a low opinion of their skills is that they're comparing themselves to native English speakers or other learners who have reached fluency. If you observe that your English is not as good as other peoples', you start to bad about yourself – imperfect, inferior, etc.

The Impact of language in Rural Area

The imposition of English on students belonging to humble background and financially weak background badly affects their performance at the college level. Most of the families of such learners belong to poor farmer, doing petty jobs and have no exposure of outside world, current affairs, educational policies and development of government, politics and world panorama.

Students from such families and background find it difficult to compete with such standards followed in schools and colleges. With little or no English within their rural setting, they are unable to complete their higher education thoroughly. Only few of them dedicated or having a proper guidance complete their higher education.

Conclusions

The main objective of this paper was to provide teachers and stakeholders with an overview of the challenges teachers may face while teaching in rural areas. Some of these encounters were isolation, cultural adaptation, and misconceptions rural families have about education, motivation, infrastructure, and violence. The authors argue that many urban teachers are not willing to take the challenge of facing schools in rural areas because of the previous issues. The text continued by mentioning some alternative ideas to implement in order to help teachers move smoothly into rural settings, inclusion in the syllabus of cultural particularities in rural areas,the proper introduction of teachers to the community, the participation of the community in the planning, local support and the access to learning resource centres. Finally, it indicates that teaching programs should introduce pre-service teachers to the rural context as part of the teaching experiences to avoid misconceptions about rural schooling. This paper ends by calling policy makers to acknowledge teachers working in rural areas. ❒

33

Use of E-Learning in Education

When it comes to online learning in education, the model has been pretty straightforward – up until the early 2000s education was in a classroom of students with a teacher who led the process. Physical presence was a no-brainer, and any other type of learning was questionable at best. Then the internet happened, and the rest is history.

E-learning is a rapidly growing industry, the effects of which we can trace back to the 1980s and even well before that (in the form of distance learning and televised courses). Now that affordable e-learning solutions exist for both computers and internet, it only takes a good e-learning tool for education to be facilitated from virtually anywhere. Technology has advanced so much that the geographical gap is bridged with the use of tools that make you feel as if you are inside the classroom. E-learning **offers the ability toshare material in all kinds of formats** such as videos, slideshows, word documents, and PDFs. Conducting webinars (live online classes) and communicating with professors via chat and message forums is also an option available to users.

Some of the most important developments in education have happened since the launch of the internet. These days learners are well versed in the use of smartphones, text messaging and using the internet so participating in and running an online course has become a simple affair. Message boards, social media and various other means of online communication allow learners to keep in touch and discuss course-related matters, whilst providing for a sense of community.

The History of E-Learning

The term "e-learning" has only been in existence since 1999 when the word was first utilized at a CBT systems seminar. Other words also began to spring up in search of an accurate description such as "online learning" and "virtual learning". However, the principles behind e-learning have been well documented throughout history, and there is even evidence which suggests that early forms of e-learning existed as far back as the 19th century. Long before the internet was launched, distance courses were being offered to provide students with education on particular subjects or skills. In the 1840's Isaac Pitman taught his pupils shorthand via correspondence. This form of symbolic writing was designed to improve writing speed and was popular amongst secretaries, journalists, and other individuals who did a great deal of note taking or writing. Pitman, who was a qualified teacher, was sent completed assignments by mail and he would then send his students more work to be finished using the same system.

In 1924, the first testing machine was invented. This device allowed students to test themselves. Then, in 1954, BF Skinner, a Harvard Professor, invented the "teaching machine", which enabled schools to administer programmed instruction to their students. **It wasn't until 1960 however that the first computer based training program was introduced** to the world. This computer-based training program (or CBT program) was known as PLATO-Programmed Logic for Automated Teaching Operations. It was originally designed for students attending the University of Illinois, but ended up being used in schools throughout the area.

The first online learning systems were really only set up to deliver information to students but as we entered the 70s online learning started to become more interactive. In Britain, the Open University was keen to take advantage of e-learning. Their system of education has always been primarily focused on learning at a distance. In the past, course materials were delivered by post and correspondence with tutors was via mail. With the internet, the Open University began to offer a wider range of interactive educational experiences as well as faster correspondence with students via email etc.

Online Learning Today

By the early 90s, several schools had been set up that delivered courses online only, making the most of the internet and bringing education to people who wouldn't previously have been able to attend a college due to geographical or time constraints. Technological advancements also helped educational establishments reduce the costs of distance learning, a saving that would also be passed on to the students – helping bring education to a wider audience. **In**

the 2000's, businesses began using e-learning to train their employees. New and experienced workers alike now had the opportunity to improve upon their industry knowledge base and expand their skill sets. At home, individuals were granted access to programs that offered them the ability to earn online degrees and enrich their lives through expanded Knowledge.

The Benefits and Drawbacks of Online Learning

Whether you're a high-school teacher looking to engage your students in a more interactive way, or a corporate trainer hired by a large company to design training curricula, e-learning packs a punch when it comes to benefits that make the creation and delivery processes easier and hassle-free. Important benefits are: No Boundaries, No Restrictions; More Fun; Cost Effective and It Just Fits.

Effective Usage of Available Resources

To get the most out of the online learning experience both the teacher and the student should take full advantage of the vast amount of resources that are available online. There are literally **hundreds of online services that offer access to information**, with Wikipedia being a prominent example. Instructors should seize the opportunity to enhance their content with online material or redirect students to additional web resources.

The Future of E-Learning

E-learning is here to stay. As computer ownership grows across the globe e-learning becomes increasingly viable and accessible. Internet connection speeds are increasing, and with that, opportunities for more multimedia training methods arise. With the immense improvement of mobile networks in the past few years and the increase in telecommuting, taking all the awesome features of e-learning on the road is a reality with smartphones and other portable devices. Technologies such as social media are also transforming education constantly.

Micro-learning focuses on the design of micro-learning activities through micro-steps in digital media environments, which already is a daily reality for today's knowledge workers. These activities can be incorporated into a learner's daily routines. Unlike "traditional" e-learning approaches, micro-learning often tends towards push technology through push media, which reduces the cognitive load on the learners. Therefore, the selection of micro-learning objects and also pace and timing of micro-learning activities are of importance for didactical designs. Micro-learning is an important paradigm shift that avoids the need to have separate learning sessions since **the learning process is embedded in the daily routine of the end-user**. It is also perfectly suited for mobile devices where long courses can be overkill. ❐

34

Comparative Curriculum in Distance Education

Deining Distance Learning and its Neighbours

Definitions are important, not merely the espoused definitions but also the enacted definitions, the definitions by denotation and by connotation, what distance learning means to academics but also what it means to managers, students, policy-makers and other stake-holders across the various continents, countries, regions and cities where it seems to take place. A brief discussion of the relevant ones might identify and resolve some of the concepts and confusion around distance learning, its potentials and its possibilities, or perhaps not. One simple definition might be implied by the binary contrast between campus education and distance learning, but similarities with online learning, e-learning and virtual learning now blur the issue, as does, in a different direction, overlap with community learning and adult learning.

We casually referred to campus education and distance learning. This seems a clear distinction, one happens on campus or within campus universities, the other does not. Many campus universities now however exploit digital technologies to reach larger distant markets, and reach out to students who may study entirely remotely and entirely online. So, campus universities can have significant proportions of distance learning students. Online learning, digital learning, e-learning and virtual learning are apparently synonymous and interchangeable and are merely the preferred delivery mechanismformostdistancelearning.

Theyarehoweverneverthesoledeliverymechanismforeither campus universities or distance learning, hence the use of the rather vague term, blended learning, to denote that digital learning is combined in some unspecified proportions with one or more other modalities. We shall see the consequences of this confusion when we look at the global picture.

The Purpose of Distance Learning

Distance learning is education; the possible purposes of distance learning are drawn from those of education. These purposes are now troubled as never before. One purpose of education is to service economies and put learners into employment, specifically the cash economies and paid employment. This has been widely accepted. It is however increasingly problematic. Not only has globalisation over the past two decades meant that employment is a fluid phenomenon as companies pursue changing markets, resources, raw materials and tax and tariff regimes but there is growing talk of the hollowing out of the labour market, meaning the ever-widening chasm between people who manage, create and decide and those who clean toilets and clear trash, and thus an increasing barrier to any social mobility that might have been facilitated by education. On the other hand, any talk of an education for unemployment, for meaningful lives outside the economy, is difficult politically in the public domain. Digital technologies are one of the causes of these trends over our lifetimes and on the near horizon artificial intelligence (AI) and the Internet of Things (IoT) will only accelerate these processes. These factors appear in our later discussion of educational technology trends. This purpose is clearly utilitarian, objective and quantifiable, but even if accepted as the main or sole purpose of education, it is problematic.

There is an increasingly consumerist orientation to higher education, driven by the rhetoric of neo-liberalism and marketization, which responds to a call for job-ready graduates, coming from both employers and the debt-laden graduates but this purpose is potentially at odds with the future-proof graduates (and lifelong learners) depicted in the more utilitarian aspects of digital literacy. Higher education institutions are under continued pressure to produce job-ready graduates and this drives soft skills, digital literacy and problem-based learning inter alia into the curriculum, and some of these may be more challenging to deliver at a distance.

The Global Environment of Distance Learning

Having briefly discussed the various possible purposes of education we can now discuss the pressures and trends, starting with those that make up the environment of the distance learning globally. Technology, the first one, is seemingly the easier to discuss. Any simplistic analysis tells us that digital technology gets smoothly and inexorably better, small, faster and cheaper. In the broadsense, this does seem to be true, but any smooth curves and established paradigms have inevitably been disturbed by each new game-changing innovation, the iPhone being recent and obvious. Both the general trends and the game-changers are however driven by the commercial imperatives of the makers and the vendors of digital technology.

This technology is not only devices and infrastructure but also software, systems and services, and is reflected not only in the shifting balance between say mobile phones and networked desktop computers but also a shifting balance between say web 2.0 applications such as social media and dedicated educational systems such as the learning management system (LMS). These changes not only put more technological power in the hands of learners but also more agency and control. Looking backwards, there was a sea change when the balance of individual digital technology and institutional digital technology tipped away from the institutions but the consequences of this are still to be felt, and we currently live in a world of zombie institutions, dead but still moving, unaware that individuals with personal and social technologies have taken their role, their rationale and their place. These consequences, as and when they happen, will play out differently in different countries, cultures and classes. The general implication, if such an implication is possible, is that learners will expect more choice and control, more respect and more variety, as they import their online experiences and achievements into their distance learning.

General Educational Technology Trends and Distance Learning

The success, survival or transformation of distance learning may depend on its capacity to align, appropriate or co-opt any of the other trends or technologies evolving in the educational technology spaces of practice and policy. Some of these we have already mentioned in trying to define where distance learning fits and is defined in relation to other pedagogies. A recent and much respected UK report [53] highlights some specific developments on the near horizon. These include,

- Spaced learning, a specific regime to improve retention and understanding
- Learners making science, apedagogy to develop a more scientific frame of mindamongst learners.
- Opentextbooks, exploiting technology and the 'open' movement to mix purpose built texts.
- Navigating post-truth, addressing challenges of conflicting perspectives and competing facts and the recent phenomenon of 'fade news'.

- Student led-analytics, the development of learning analytics to empower learners.

Speciic Educational Technology Trends and Distance Learning

We conclude by looking at some specific trends in educational technology and their likely significance for distance learning.

The flipped classroom was originally an American conception and a response to various practical and pedagogic problems and challenges (principally those of encouraging autonomous active learning, discussions about bring-your-own-device and increasing pressure on contact time) and a response to a specific infrastructure and technical environment (namely the widespread availability of cheap connectivity and personal, social and domestic digital technologies). Whilst an underpinning theory of the flipped classroom may have emerged, the idea was nevertheless originally nationally specific and culturally specific, and so are the documented experiences originally from a very specific setting, namely schools in America. The flipped classroom concept should not be interpreted merely as using technology to displace the consumption of content out of the classroom. In fact, the principles of the flipped classroom can be expressed as the following questions,

- How can educators optimise the face-to-face learning experience? What is it that students can only get face-to-face with lecturers?
- How can educators optimise the ways in which students can learn from each other face-to-face? What is it that students can only get face-to-face with each other?
- How can educators optimise the campus experience? What is it that students can only get by coming on campus?
- How can digital technology support addressing these challenges? And what does digital technology do most effectively or uniquely?

We should consider the flipped classroom alongside discussion of personal response systems (PRS) and Problem-based learning (PBL). Whilst the first in carnation of PRS was delivered on dedicated devices, the so-called clickers or zappers, for example in economics and many other disciplines—and thus an unsustainable expense—later incarnations use software or apps, such as Secretive, which run on learners' own devices. They essentially deliver the ability to make the lecture, already highly cost-effective, more interactive and flexible. PBL [62], with its focus on problem-solving, team-work and real-life problems makes learning more authentic and open-ended. These initiatives all potentially separate distance learning from a much clearer articulation of the best of face-to-face learning, namely flexibility, responsiveness and engagement, and distance learning educators must address the implicit critique.

Conclusions

This paper has attempted to put distance learning within the wider context of the global technological and economic trends and pressures and against the context of specific educational technology trends and initiatives. This has not been easy since these trends are characterised by fragmentation and diversification. The abstract conclusion is the need remain open, flexible and aware, to seek and expect change, connection, agency and authenticity. The nature of these wider contexts does however mean there are no simple conclusion, only a more complete understandingof a fluid, partial and complex environment which education, including distance learning, cannot operateinignoranceorisolation. Thepracticalconclusionsmustcomefromtheproviders,thefunders, the managers and the trainers of distance learning, to think through this abstract conclusion to their individual programmes, institutions and responsibilities.

❒

35

Social Interaction and Pro-Social Behaviour through Media

Much public attention has been paid to potential negative effects of the media on students that parents and researchers alike have scarcely acknowledged the positive. Yet if television and movies can teach students antisocial behaviours such as aggression, and then it makes sense that these media also teach beneficial behaviours as well. The chal¬lenge is to differentiate the media messages that are potentially harmful from those that are positive or prosocial in nature.

Prosocialbehaviour can be broadly defined as any voluntary behaviour intended to benefit another person. Altruism is the most com¬mon example of prosocialbehaviour. Some of other behaviours are friendliness, sharing, co-operation, sym¬pathy, and even acceptance of others from different groups.

Social Interaction and Prosocialbehaviour through Media

Another concern often voiced about screen media is that they may interfere with student's social interaction. Indeed, student and their parents spend less time talking and looking at each other, when the television set is turned on and off.On the positive side, families engage in more physi¬cal contact and cuddling when they watch television together and doing other activities.

Although the sheer amount of time spent in front of a TV or computer screen may have detrimental effects on social interac¬tion, in viewing particular types of programs that can teach students social skills.

The effect is con¬sistent with the notion that prosocial lessons may be difficult for very young person to understand, especially lessons conveyed with words instead of action. Prosocial film clips had a greater effect on students

Movies and television have a powerful influence in developing value systems and shaping behaviour. Movies exert a far more subtle and insidious effect by shaping viewers attitude and perception of social norms. Movies and television have positive effect on social behaviour of students. Enhance prosocial value based activities among college students through movies clip or videos.

NCTE Commission Recommends Media Education

The Media Commission of The National Council of Teachers of English conducted the

NCTE conference (1991) following recommendations to encourage:

1. Portfolios of student work that include a wide variety of media forms, as a welcome and healthy trend in teaching and evaluation.
2. Materials to help teachers address, evaluate, discuss and monitor representations of gender, class, race, age, ethnic backgrounds, etc. in classroom media.
3. The NCTE to provide teachers with materials to support the high quality analysis of television commercials, their messages and effects.
4. Those NCTE teacher accreditation standards require teachers to be knowledgeable in critical analysis of media and this requirement is treated seriously through teacher workshops, training, materials and guidelines for media education.
5. The increased uses of non-print media within school systems (laser discs, interactive media, etc.) should be understood as a wave of the future and that uses of these media need to be incorporated intelligently within curriculum.
6. Materials and methods that alert students to the perspectives and limitations of televisions constructed presentations of people and events.
7. Media education must clearly be recognized as "teaching about" the media, not simply as inclusion of an occasional film or tape within a class lesson.
8. The clarification of "rulings" regarding copyright so that teachers will fully understand how to incorporate media literacy materials into their curriculum.
9. The empowerment of teachers through networking and work toward the creation of a network of teaches and professionals nationally and internationally, will enrich and enliven media education.

10. Media production in schools is an absolute necessity.Wherever possible, students need to develop essential critical thinking skills that work with in a medium. Students also need to tell their own stories in their own voices and through their own eyes, whether in print or in any of a host of other media.

Enhancing Prosocialvalues through Television Media

Television media play a key role on the development and acquisition of values which should be recognized. Some authors have stated that television is one's our most important narrative reference and, in some cases, the centre of one's lives. Nevertheless, a review of existing literature on the impact of television on the formation of values shows that research is scarce and there are several major gaps in knowledge. In addition to entertaining and amusing, television should also educate. Television transmits as many materialistic as prosocial values and one can believe that this ambiguity is harmful from the point of view of moral education.

Discussion and Conclusion

Multimedia technology presents a new venue for teaching social skills because emerging evidence indicates that media (e.g. television, movies, magazines, and the internet) may be one of the key forces contributing to hoe young viewers' beliefs and behaviors are shaped (ward.20050. The multimedia involves teaching social skills through television, movies, computers, and virtual reality. The use of positive social, language, and academic outcomes from children with a variety of disability (sturmay, 2003). Researchers only have began to tap the potential of multimedia technology as a means to social skills intervention, Based on recent literature, it appears that the prospects of gaining greater knowledge of multimedia techniques are extremely high.

Multimedia techniques may be used for developing social skills training programs and interventions, measuring outcomes of such interventions, and generalizing and maintaining treatments, thus, it is proposed that multimedia enhanced social skill interventions be used with students who have emotional and behavioral disorders to increase their adaptive behavior and decrease competing non-desired behaviors, transfer role play to the real world, behaviors, transfer role play to the real world, increase low-frequency skills, and enhance learning by observation.

❐

36

Gender Inequalities Issues in Education

The genesis of RMSA can be traced to the Secondary Education Commission (1952-53) that focuses on development of democratic citizenship, improvement of vocational efficiency, promotion of leadership and development of personality. The significance of this stage of education was touched upon by the National Policy on Education 1986. The policy mentions "Secondary education begins to expose students to the differentiated roles of science, the humanities and social sciences. This is also an appropriate stage to provide children with a sense of history and national perspective and give them opportunities to understand their constitutional duties and rights as citizens. Conscious internalization of a healthy work ethos and of the values of a humane and composite culture will be brought about through appropriately formulates curricula" (Experts from National Policy on Education (1986). In the context of gender, this policy mentions that sex stereotyping in vocational and professional courses will be eliminated and women's participation in non-traditional occupations, and emergent technologies would be encouraged.

Textbooks and Gender

In the Indian context textbooks are important repository of knowledge. It is an important teaching and learning material that teachers and students rely upon across the country. Implicit and explicit knowledge woven in textual materials pertain to the domain of social science, science, mathematics, languages and other emerging & applied fields of knowledge. The content of all disciplines are determined by experts, who de-limit it as per age, ability and level of understanding of children. In addition, books are part of the social milieu and they attempt to mirror social realities

Teaching and Learning Process

Textual materials at the secondary stage have sharper contours related to science, social science, languages and mathematics. It is important that at this stage, children are able to acquire knowledge embedded in different subjects, apply the knowledge to understand their lived realities, and are skilled enough to communicate, negotiate and critically understand their surroundings from a gender lens. While teaching subjects at the secondary stage, the pedagogical processes have to be well designed for making classrooms, in multiple settings, genders sensitive. Classroom transactions have an important bearing on the personality of children. The methodology followed in delivering the content, related to various domains of knowledge, not only promotes learning and understanding but also overall personality of children. In the context of gender, engaging children in discussions, problem solving, multifarious activities and voicing their doubts and experiences are ways of breaking gender barriers related to caste, class, region and location.

Curriculum and Gender

Science is based on hands – on – and inquiry based approach. It is hoped that after going through the content of Science at the secondary stage, children's spirit of inquiry would be ignited. They would become curious to know the natural phenomena existing around them and continue their journey of exploration, invention and application. The boundary or discipline in Sciences gets carved at secondary stage like Physics, Chemistry, and Biology under the broader rubric of Science.

Classroom Organization and Management

In India school and classrooms vary in many contexts. There are large and small size classrooms in the urban, semi-urban, and rural contexts. The classroom organization and management goes a long way in shaping gender relations. Several research studies over the years have clearly shown how the classroom environment can facilitate students learning and remove gender bias and stereotype. In fact, a gender friendly environment can easily be created by a teacher in any context. It just requires sensitivity and positive intent. A gender friendly classroom environment and its overall management can build harmonious relations between boys and girls at different stages of education.

Conclusions

Gender worries in instruction should be tended to genuinely with regards to globalization, advancement and blast in the field of data innovation. These progressions have affected the lives and states of individuals from all areas of society. With regards to sexual orientation, ladies and young ladies keep on possessing an optional status in the public eye, in spite of their support in various limits in all divisions of the economy. Further, they face the brunt of physical and passionate brutality and their bodies get commoditized in print and broad media. Likewise, statistic markers, similar to the marvels of declining sex proportion, sexual orientation aberrations at auxiliary and senior optional phases of instruction, has made sex an imperative zone of worry for strategy creators, 26 educationists, organizers and all individuals from the common society. While the past Focus Group Paper has concentrated on these issues, yet there is a need to relook at these rising contemporary difficulties looked by young ladies and ladies from varying backgrounds. Endeavors ought to be made to coordinate sexual orientation worries with all the standard controls. Parcel of research in the field of sexual orientation considers propose an interdisciplinary methodology should be energized wherein sex issues can be looked in from a comprehensive focal point by embracing diverse research techniques from the field of Social Science, Sciences and Education.

❒

37

Educational Innovations in Distance Education

Today most of the people are improved in various activity in the view of revolutions in technology. In ancient period, we faced more difficulties in basic activities also. Such as to pass the message, to travel, to learning, etc. But today we moved to the new world with lot of New innovations. In this chapter we are going to see about the educational innovations in distance education.

Educational Innovations

Educational innovations is the process of delivering the New ideas, introducing new devices or creating new methods with regarding to education.

Distance Learning

Distance learning is a mode of delivering education and instructions, often on an individual basis, to students who are not physically present in a traditional setting such as a classroom. Traditionally, this usually involved correspondence courses wherein the student corresponded with the school via post. Today it involves online education. Courses that are conducted are either hybrid, blended or 100% distance learning.Distance education technologies delivered in two modes. They are synchronous learning and asynchronous learning.

Synchronous Learning

In synchronous learning, all participants are "present" at the same time. In this regard, it resembles traditional classroom teaching methods despite the participants being located remotely. It requires a timetable to be organised.

Examples of synchronous learning,

Asynchronous Learning

In asynchronous learning, participants access course materials flexibility on their own schedules. Students are not required to be together at the same time. Mail correspondence, which is oldest form of distance education, is an asynchronous delivery technology.

Examples of asynchronous learning,

Educational Revolution

The educational revolution is nothing but "the revolution of education among students or children. The educational revolution focused on the whole children through both academic and social or environmental aspects of learning."

Big data, artificial intelligence and robotics will fundamentally change the way products are designed and built and how services are provided. They are already changing how we live and communicate. Although it is difficult to accurately predict the future, it is clear that jobs in 2030 will be very different from the other jobs of today. The technological changes in the workplace mean that education will have to change too, to take advantage of the possibilities of the technology for education and to provide a workforce capable of exploiting rapidly evolving technologies.

Graduates will need good digital skills and strong digital capabilities and they will also need well-developed critical thinking, creativity and problem-solving abilities so they can adapt and make sense of their changing world. Moreover, students expect an education experience that reflects the way they live, communicate and learn – that is, driven and enhanced by digital tech.

Digital Textbooks

A digital text books is a digital book or e-book intended to serve as the text for a class. Digital text books may also be known as e-textbooks or e-texts. Digital textbooks are major component of technology-based education reform. They may serve as the text for a traditional face to face classes, an online courses or degree.

Remote Learning

Remote learning or distance learning is a form of education in which the main elements include physical separation of teachers and students during instruction and the use of various technologies to facilitate student-teachers and student-student communication. Distance learning traditionally has focused on non-traditional students, such as full time workers, military personnel, and nonresidents or individuals in remote regions who unable to attend classroom lectures.

MOOC's

A Moon's or Massive Open Online Courses is an online course aimed at unlimited participation and open access via the web. In addition to traditional course materials, such as filmed lectures, readings, and problem sees, many MOOC's provide interactive courses with user forums' to support community interactions among students, professors, and teaching assistance as well as immediate feedback to quick quizzes and assignments. MOOC's are a resent or widely researched development in distance education, first introduced in 2006 and emerged as a popular mode of learning in 2012."Asia's first MOOC" given by the Hong Kong University of Science and Technology in April 2013 registered 17,000 Students.

Conclusions

By this article, I addressed about the educational innovations in distance education and the various innovations and also about their benefits and their drawbacks.

❐

38

Role of E-Learning in Distance Education in India

Social Interactive method of education is the traditional method of learning where instructor teaches learners face to face. Open and distance learning is usually contrasted with 'conventional' or face-to-face' education, which may be described as the form of education which takes place in a classroom or an auditorium. Distance Education is a method of teaching where the instructor and learners are separated by time and or physical distance. The main objective of distance education is, the availability of education- anyone, anyway, anywhere and anytime without social, physical and geographical restrictions. Open and distance education provide flexible learning opportunities to individuals and group of learners.

Historical Background

Today the concept of distance education is fairly well-understood and the importance of distance education in the future of education is also acknowledged. The history of distance education can be traced back to the 18th century, to the beginning of print-based correspondence study in the US. In the mid-19th century correspondence education started to develop and to spread in Europe (Great Britain, France and Germany) and the United States. Isaac Pitman, the English inventor of shorthand, is generally recognized as the first person to use correspondence courses. The advancement in technology has given new life to distance education. It may regard1922, when Thomas Edison invented motion picture and boldly predicted that motion picture would replace textbooks in education, as the starting point of the history of media technologies for learning. Although Edison's prediction has not exactly come to pass, video tapes were used by the US army during World War II for the training of soldiers. Television broadcasting became one of the pioneering technologies for distance education. By the late 1960's and early 1970's significant changes in distance learning occurred due to development of new media technologies and delivery systems. The Open University (OU) in Great Britain became the first autonomous institution to offer college degrees through distance education. The OU now uses all possible forms of technology to deliver learning to students. Distance learning in India started in the 1960s. In the 1980s there were 34 universities offering correspondence education through departments designed for that purpose. The first single mode Open University was established in Andhra Pradesh in 1982, followed by the Indira Gandhi National Open University (IGNOU). Some states like, Bihar, Rajasthan, and Maharashtra, Madhya Pradesh, Gujarat, Karnataka, West Bengal, and Utter Pradesh also established open universities during 1980s and 1990s. The aim behind establishment of these universities was to ensure availability of education to the each person of society. These initiatives encourage people towards distance education and the year 1995 witnessed the enrolment of 200,000 students in open and distance learning, accounting for 3% of total higher education enrolment. The most of open and distance universities in India follow the UK model of open university as like formal education model.

E-learning and Distance education

Electronic learning or E-learning is a type of education where the medium of instruction modern technology. There is no personal interaction require to communicate people. Earlier, audio tape, video tape and Compact Disc were used to deliver course material and lectures but later the technological development changed its face. E-learning is used interchangeably in a wide variety of contexts. E-learning is used to define a specific mode to attend a course or program of study where the students rarely, if ever, attend face-to-face for on-campus access to educational facilities, because they study on-line. E-learning is naturally suited to distance learning and flexible learning. Distance Education in the form of E-learning is the only way to stay current. E-learning can also be used in conjunction with face-to-face teaching, in which case the term Blended learning is commonly used. E-learning pioneer Bernard Luskin argues that the "E" must be understood to have broad meaning if E-learning is to be effective. Luskin says that the "E" should be interpreted to mean Exciting,

Energetic, Enthusiastic, Emotional, Extended, Excellent, and Educational in addition to "Electronic" that is a traditional national interpretation. This broader interpretation allows for contemporary applications and brings learning and media psychology into the equation.

Benefits of E-Learning Assisted Distance Education

The purpose of implementing E-learning assisted Distance Education in India is to take education to the doorsteps of the rural poor, the disadvantaged and marginalized people of the society. The people should be given the opportunity to master the skill to use technology to their advantages without feeling threatened to build a better tomorrow. E-learning assisted distance education enables people to have: 3 Interactivity engages users, pushing them rather than pulling them through training. 4 Availability of quick reference materials.

Components of E-Learning

ELearning consists of the following components, which are created with the state of art Internettechnologies for high quality, ease of use and effectiveness.

1. The Virtual Classroom

Virtual Classroom Modules (VCMs) are well-prepared high quality lectures from the master trainers, with multimedia colour presentations. VCM combines distance education instructional pedagogy with latest interactive multimedia Internet technology. VCM helps the counsellor to efficiently perform his basic job of providing information in less time, without compromising the quality. Thus, he can utilize his time for developing higher-level mental abilities like comprehension, application, analysis etc in students. Smaller time duration of each module ensures better concentration. Streaming media technology ensures simultaneous playing and downloading of a module from Internet. Thus, Internet can be used as backup media for delivery of VCMs to provide 'Anywhere Anytime' learning. Use of video is kept to minimum possible level, and normally restricted to imparting of skills. Easy and fast production of good quality VCMs is possible. Discussion and tutorial in real time, with counsellors and fellow stu-dents are expected to follow these lectures at each study centre. Thus, VCM ensures better learning through distance system in the following ways:

1. Better time utilization through well prepared lectures from master trainers.
2. Clear knowledge communication through the latest multimedia and Internet technology.

3. Development of better understanding through discussion/tutorials in a group of fellow
4. Students with a counselor. Student can repeat the lecture or its part, on computer. University can even dispatch it through Internet / email.
5. Easy Quality Assurance through Lectures of master trainers directly reaching the students Use of multimedia for enjoyable and worthy learning experience Same quality standards ensured at each study centre.

2. The Discussion Forum

A discussion forum is an interactive web site that lets site visitors discuss topics by reading articles that have been posted, replying to articles, and posting new ones. Visitors can also use a search form to find articles of interest. Discussion forum offers asynchronous mode of communication, where messages can be prepared with editing. But it allows only text-based interaction among students, counsellors and the university. Any interaction on the discussion forum is visible to all. A discussion forum can have the following features:

- This feature creates well-classified and well-organized knowledge base on any academic or administrative topic in a short time.

3. Online Counseling

'Online Counselor' is a well-qualified and experienced person who interacts with the students, only through use of discussion forum, for clearing their doubts/difficulties. Depending on the number of students, the university can appoint one or more 'Online Counselors' for each course (subject). Once a week, each 'Online Counselor' will answer all the questions posted on the discussion forum of the respective course (subject). He will also initiate academic interaction information about the course (subject). Online counselling will be a step forward towards 'Learner Centric' education, as it provides anywhere anytime counselling for those learners who cannot regularly attend counselling sessions at study centre due to various reasons. Online counselling cannot replace regular face-to-face counselling at study centre, but can act like backup for it, as email and discussion forums offer only text-based communication.

Indian Perspective

There are many initiatives has been taken to enhance distance education through e-learning, some of them are discussed as follows;

1. **E-GyanKosh**
   The e-GyanKosh30 is a national digital repository developed by IGNOU for sharinglearning content. It is a learning platform of students to read

content or watch videos of lectures.It has over 2200 video programmes in addition to e-content related to different subjects.

2. **NPTEL (National Programme on Technology Enhanced Learning)** NPTEL is a project funded by the Ministry of Human Resource Development. It was first conceived in 1999 to pave the way for introducing multimedia and web technology to enhance learning of basic science and engineering concepts. It is collaborative program of seven Indian Institutes of Technology (IIT) and the Indian Institute of Science (IISc).It opened a new way of learning and also for sharing expertise among faculty in different parts of the world. In India, where a large number of private institutions have entered the field of engineering education with inadequate faculty support and training, the project is aimed at providing a standard for academic content for both the teacher and the student. It has 129 web courses and 110 video courses in the field of science and technology. Each course consists of 40 video lectures of one hour and text, images, animations and graphics.

❒

39

Analysis of Distance Education and E-Learning

E - Learning is considered to be a method of education, in which there is no physical contact between the student and the lecturer. Distance learning has won sympathy of those students who for various reasons do not have the opportunity to participate in the traditional form of classes. Nevertheless, the validity of this training is being questioned by some people. According to them, it is a computer that assesses the knowledge of students and tutors. Such considerations contradict the concept of e - learning, in which the computer is just a tool used for the exchange of messages.

During free on - line classes it is possible to make video conferencing, post entries, transmit voice and images. Study materials can be sent in the form of files which students can later print. The duration of courses at distance is determined by the university authorities and the lectures. Only students of a particular school may take part in this kind of classes. They receive their individual passwords and are able to log on an educational platform. This platform is open 365 days a year. The lecturer, who has control over the content of classes, requires from students to log on to the platform and take active part in the training. The student may contact and exchange notes not only with the teacher but also with other participants of the classes.

In e – learning, the vast part of the duties of the teacher falls on the course takers. Some people believe this is a positive factor as it requires from students not only to effectively search for sources of knowledge but also to develop their skills and use of content remarks to form and express their beliefs over discussed issues. E-learning courses predominate in higher education, but they are also used in secondary schools. Some educational websites also offer a wide range of online training and by participating in them students can obtain certificates.

Strenghts and Weaknesses of E-Learning

Positive and negative sides of distance learning are analyzed according to the position and situation of the judging person. While, certain criteria are not evaluated similarly by the student and the lecturer, some obtain consistent review by the representatives of both sides: students and teachers.

E-learning is recommended by lecturers due to possibility of better monitoring of the progress made by their students. On the other hand, students, who can feel stressed under time pressure, appreciate the fact that they are not required to answer questions immediately. Online learning enables students' development. The students can respond with reserve to the interpretation of the presented material and they may also become more direct in their learning process. Students point out that the main advantages of e-learning are the use of multimedia, no need for visiting the school every day, the prospect of a joint communication with other course takers, elimination of the anxiety created by the prospect of public oral expression, convenient deadline for completion of tasks placed on the learning platform, own learning pace, reduction of anxiety created by direct contact with the lecturer.

Both the course takers and the teachers agree that one basic disadvantage of distance learning is the lack of 'face to face' interaction. Another drawback is that the time given for the completion of tasks online prolongs significantly in comparison to amount of timespent on completing them in traditional teaching. Character and disposition of each of the students contribute to this fact. Each student is required to become acquainted with the mission and teaching tools used in the given school, and think if he wants to study at school in which learning at distance takes place.

Analysis of the Research

The study was conducted with the use of a survey, which was sent to a group of 150 students, who had already dealt with e-learning. The first task in the survey checked whether students dealt with the total loss of data while using the learning platform. The result is surprising, because according to the interpretation, up to 102 people lost data which could not be recovered and all work of students was in vain. The remaining group of respondents did not encounter the problem of data loss. Therefore, the suggestion would be to put more work and effort in improving the eLearning platform, so in the future students could avoid problem with data loss. Another task of respondents was to tell which method of teaching and learning they recognize to be better: e - learning or traditional methods. 99 people identified the traditional teaching methods as the better, and 46 people would prefer to have classes in the form of e- learning. Five respondents were not able to point out which method is better. The result might be different if more respondents took part in the study.

The last question required answer why students had chosen only the activities in the form of e-learning and was asked only to those students, who in the previous question, were in favor of online learning. Proponents of distance learning (18 people) decided that one of the main advantages of distance learning was studying at home, at any time. 13 students named working as the reason why they had chosen online learning. 11 respondents named saving of time as the main factor which helped them decide on online education. 3 students had chosen the distance learning because of doing two degrees at the same time, whereas one person named another cause.

Conclusions

E-learning is not an easy form of education, therefore it is introduced gradually. It requires proper adoption from both students and teachers. Contrary to appearances, e – learning classes do not reduce the work effort of the lecturer. It all depends on the curriculum, a group of students, the degree of their mobilization as well as on the use of creative forms of teaching. Unfortunately, in this form of education, students do not show up too much commitment, do not complete their homework assignments and also reluctantly take part in various discussions on the online forum. This situation usually changes just before the exam. Through the use of distance learning schools of higher education increase their chances to participate in not only domestic but also in international research projects, many of which are financed by the European Union.

❐

40

Role and Challenges of E-Governance in Distance Education

E-governance involves the use of information and communication technologies (ICTs) to transact the business of government. At the level of service, e-governance promises a full service available 24 hours a day and seven days a week. At all level of basic factors such as government accountability and general acceptance of state institutions, e-governance contributes to the functioning of democracy by online provision of government information which would otherwise be difficult to obtain or unavailable, and through online debates and plebiscites (Saxena, 2005; Teicher et al., 2002). At the same time, e-learning seems to have taken the world by blizzard and is fast becoming a major form of learning. It is an approach to teaching and learning that is now used widely by schools, colleges, universities and distance learning cells, and academic institutions. In this regard, if e-learning is a process, e-governance is a means. However, all forms of e-learning do not come under the purview of e-governance. Though 'e-learning' and 'e-governance' have different connotations, they are just two pictures on the same paper. Nevertheless, successful implementation of e-learning and e-governance policy helps in bridging the digital divide through a wide-ranging approach to digital environment across the world.

Importance of E- Governance

According to the World Bank (2002) E-Governance has the following benefits;

- It greatly simplifies the process of information accumulation for citizens and businesses.
- It empowers people to gather information regarding any department of government and get involved in the process of decision making.
- E-Governance strengthens the very fabric of democracy by ensuring greater citizen participation at all levels of governance
- E-Governance leads to automation of services, ensuring that information regarding every work of public welfare is easily available to all citizens, eliminating corruption.

Challenges to Implementation of e-Governance

E-governance helps people, businesses and the government to interact with one another by bringing them closer. Cognizant of the importance of e-governance, the Government of India has taken several positive measures in this regard. The objective of National e-Governance Plan (NeGP), as stated, is to "make all Government services accessible to the common man in his locality, through common service delivery outlets, and ensure efficiency, transparency & reliability of such services at affordable costs to realize the basic needs of the common man."

However, in India, there are large differentials in terms of skewed income and wealth distribution, median income, functional literacy, lack of basic infrastructure. All these combine to pose major challenges to the effective implementation of e-governance.

Low per Capita Income

A large number of the people in India are poor, with low disposable personal income, which is an obstacle for economic progress. The required infrastructure, such as telephone lines, etc. required for Internet, email access, is too costly for the poor. This creates a formidable challenge to realize the fruits of the e-governance measures.

Technical challenges

Despite six decades of independent political existence, the differentials with respect to technical skills and accessibility across different sections of people still remain unaddressed. Access to Internet is not easy in rural areas, as well as in small towns. Therefore, there are no political incentives for spending time and money on measures that benefit people. Further, there is little education and awareness of the benefits of using technology.

Lack of Awareness of Benefits of E-Governance

This is yet another harsh reality. People are not aware of e-governance and its projects, such as G2C, G2G or G2B, let alone their benefits.

Inadequate Infrastructure

The speed of government websites and their user-friendliness are not very good, even in urban areas. If the websites are not designed well, visitors will not find them of much use. Often, there is an absence of uninterrupted electricity, Internet access and fast communication, which becomes a major challenge to e-governance implementation.

Security Issues

Technology keeps on changing at a fast pace, which most government departments and agencies are unable to keep pace with. This makes security vulnerable. With hackers using new technologies, ensuring security for online transactions is absolutely essential. There have been many instances of government websites being defaced/ hacked.

Need for Restructuring

Implementing e-governance norms necessitates a number of administrative changes, which require streamlining of administered norms. This involves doing away with modules that are no longer relevant and create obstacles to E-governance.

Conclusions

Governments' initiatives for e-governance and academic implementation of e-learning are two hot issues which have been prioritized these days for the benefit of the general public and students respectively. E-government has the potential to greatly improve how government operates internally and how it serves its customers. E-government is much more than a tool for improving cost-quality ratios in public services. It is an instrument of reform and a tool to transform government. Thus, e- Government is not primarily about automation of existing procedures (which may or may not be effective), but about changing the way in which government conducts business and delivers services. E-Governance is an innovative initiative by the government to ensure that government services are easily accessible to people and they are able to accrue its benefits.

❐

41

Effective Communications in Digital Libraries of Distance Edu. through E-Learning

Tubbs and Moss (2006), state, "Communication is effective when the stimulus as initiated and intended by the sender, or source, corresponds closely to the stimulus as it is perceived and responded to by the receiver". In distance education, effective communication is particularly important because students may never or infrequently come to campus. Hence, there may be limited or no face-to-face communication and interaction throughout a student's enrollment. Therefore, it is important that administrators integrate communication theory and methods into training and professional development for faculty. At the same time, e-learning seems to have taken the world by blizzard and is fast becoming a major form of learning. It is an approach to teaching and learning that is now used widely by schools, colleges, universities and distance learning cells, and academic institutions. Nevertheless, successful implementation of e-learning helps in bridging the digital divide through a wide-ranging approach to digital environment across the world. For that the effective communication is a vital challenge in distance education through e-learning.

E-Learning

The Concept Different terminologies have been used for e-learning, a fact that makes it difficult to develop a generic definition. E-learning is defined as instructional content or learning experiences delivered or enabled by electronic technology (Aydin & Tasci, 2005). Terms that are commonly used include "online learning", "internet learning", "distributed learning", "networked learning", "tele-learning", "virtual learning", "computer-assisted learning", "web-based-learning", and "distance learning". All of these terms imply that the learner is at a distance from the tutor or instructor and other learners and that some form of support is provided to learners (Sharifabadi, 2006). Therefore, in brief, e-learning can be redefined as a type of learning for off-site learners by means of electronic technology.

Digital Libraries and E-Learning

One of the natural responses to the challenges of e-learning environment is the introduction of the digital library to support e-learning with resources network, designed to meet the needs of the learners, in both individual and collaborative settings, constructed to enable the dynamic use of a broad array of materials for learning primarily in digital format, and managed actively to promote reliable access anytime and anywhere to quality collections and services, available both within and outside the network (Lippincot, 2002). The introduction of digital libraries into the education process was made easier by distance education, which has developed over the years. With the internet and the World Wide Web, distance education programs can mount sets of materials on web servers to support online courses. One of the basic ideas is to aggregate learning materials on various topics, written by many educators, in a digital library of courseware. Digital libraries have the potential to significantly change fundamental aspects of the classroom in ways that could have an enormous impact on teaching and learning. New pedagogical methods should accompany digital libraries as an emerging technology for education to reach the compelling vision of education (Sharifabadi, 2006). Therefore, for an ideal e-learning situation, digital libraries are regarded as the hub of the library collections and services that function together in the real e-learning environment.

E-Learners' Expectations from Librarians

Communication is not just important to break the isolation of students in an e-learning environment but also for a much more basic reason: Whatever one person says or writes, the receiver of the information will always interpret the information in the receiver's personal context, created through upbringing, culture, language, etc. This does often lead to deep misunderstandings. The only way to make sure that information is properly understood is not by reading, hearing, or seeing, but by being able to check or ask if things have been understood. This is why an e-learning system that ignores the importance of communication will not work. What do e-learners need from librarians? Suggestions advocating changes in librarians' role in support of e-learning in the information age appear throughout the literature. Librarians must assert themselves as key players in the learning process, thereby changing their roles from information providers to educators (Cooper & Dempsey, 1998), and they have been transferred from 'information gatekeepers" to information gateways (Sharifabadi, 2006; Haricombe, 1998). Lippincot (2002) advocates librarian involvement in teaching communities so as to shift the focus from explaining library resources to meeting the ongoing information needs of the students in the broad information environment. In responding to the need to provide ongoing digital library support, librarians have worked at translating what they do in a traditional library into virtual or digital environments while customizing their services and resources for e-learners. The traditional role of academic library services has always been to provide information resources for the teaching and learning activities within the academic sphere. Its role in supporting the virtual learning environment is no different. The linking of digital libraries and virtual library environments is required to provide a meaningful connection between learning activities and learning resources. The digital libraries can help provide information content to teaching staff who are engaged in e-learning. Traditionally, libraries offer circulation services, interlibrary loans, course reserves, an information desk, a reference desk, and library instruction. To serve learners connected to their institutional libraries primarily through a computer network or internet, librarians are providing remote access to, and delivery of, library resources and are using communication technologies to deliver electronic reference services and instructional support. As the literature suggests, e-learners are a wider community of learners than "students". An academic library's learners may include students, faculty, staff, teachers, etc. The library is seen as a source of training and guidance to a community of learners who are concerned with navigating the complexities of locating and using digital resources and services. Moreover, the move towards a digital environment has resulted in a shift from the systematic one-to-one information flow of the past to a new model in which the users and the providers of information are able to relate in a many-to-many, dynamic relationship. For example, in the traditional model, a librarian provides a bridge between learners and information providers by selecting and cataloguing resources and by providing assistance with these resources. In the new model, the library serves as a facilitator by offering ongoing support, enabling learners to interact and exchange knowledge with others, to communicate directly with the publishers and vendors of information resources, and to participate in a collaborative endeavor to make available rich collections of online scholarly information resources.

CONCLUSION

Effective communication is a vital issue of distance education through e-learning which have been prioritized these days for the benefit of the general public and students respectively. In this regard, institutions are gradually building up their e-resources, digitizing their contents, and subscribing to online databases for providing truly qualitative and cost effective online services to the students. Therefore, it is deduced that effective communication of e-learning will shortly bring about an absolutely saturated global electronic world to bridge the gap of digital divide.

❐

42

School Health Education for National Development-A Sociological Perspective

"Health is Wealth" is a well known saying. In simple words health means the physical well-being of an individual. Health education aims at bringing about behavioural changes in the individuals attitude toward health. . "A child's growth rate reflects, better than any other single index, his state of health and nutrition, and often indeed his psychological situation also. Similarly, the average value of children's heights and weights reflect accurately the state of a nation's public health and average nutritional status of its citizens, when appropriate allowance is made for differences, if any, in genetic potential. This is especially true in developing and disintegrating countries." (Eveleth, P.G. and J.M. Tanne). National Health Policy (2002) focuses on the need for enhanced funding and an organizational restructuring of the national public health initiatives in order to facilitate more equitable access to the health facilities.

Concept of Health Education

Health education is a social science that includes biological, psychological, environmental and medical science to promote health and prevent disease through the educational activities. Health education influences the health behavior of the individuals and communities. This education improves the quality of life of all people and reduces the premature deaths. Health education reduces the costs that individuals, families, insurance companies, medical facilities, the state and the nation would spend on medical treatment. Through the health education programs, students learn how to improve their health and prevent disease through developing skills.

World Health Organization defines it thus: "Health education is the part of health care that is concerned with promoting healthy behaviour". Health education is the translation of what is known about health into desirable individual and community behaviour patterns by means of an educational process. John M Last defines health communication as "the process by which individuals and groups of people learn to behave in a manner conducive to the promotion, maintenance or restoration of health". Green L W observes: "Any combination of learning opportunities and teaching activities designed to facilitate voluntary adaptation of behaviour that are conducive to health". The definition adapted by the National Conference on Preventive Medicine in USA reads: "Health education is a process that informs, motivates and helps people to adopt and maintain healthy practices and lifestyles, advocates environmental changes as needed to facilitate this goal and conducts professional training and research to the same end".

Importance of School Health Education

The knowledge and awareness about health and personal hygiene among school children could be empowered to be the flag bearers in the family, community and national development. In developing countries, the success of primary health care programs depends on effective delivery of health education, which is one of the World Health Organization's eight essential activities of primary health care programs (World Health Organization, 1983). Some barriers, like failure to triangulate data from epidemiological sources and behavioral sciences as well as poor organizational and communication skills of health educators, have been identified in health education efforts (Hubley, 1986). Meanwhile, it has been noted that only 47 percent of published articles provide a sufficiently detailed description of educational interventions to allow replication (Loevinsohn, 1990). Recently, in India, similar weaknesses in health education approaches have been reported, such as poor involvement of target audiences in planning and implementation of health education interventions, lack of theory-based behavior change strategies, lack of quality assurance systems, excess use of newspapers, pamphlets and posters and poor organization of the workforce of health educators (Sharma, 2005).

Kothari Commission said that destiny of a nation is shaped in her classrooms. Schools can play an important role in promoting society's health. Much effort has been invested over recent years in health education techniques for schools in low-income communities, including child-to-child methods, curriculum development and the production of locally appropriate education materials. Health Education as a means to improve the quality of life by helping people to acquire health by their own efforts within available resources has been accepted by all. For this reason it has been duly emphasized in both the National Health Policy and National Education Policy. In developing countries, school-age children form a sizable portion of the total population of these countries. School health would promote family and social health as the children would act change agents.

Biswas et al. (1990) reported that health knowledge of the student significantly improved after education. Attitude of the students towards personal hygiene also improved significantly after education. The practice of personal hygiene also revealed improvement. Moreover, Dongre et al. (2006). also ascertained that after giving an intervention of school health programme there was significant improvement in the personal hygiene of the students.

Conclusion

School Health Education Programme is one of the important components of total Health Care Delivery System in the State, which helps in keeping close watch on the health of school going children. It is an admitted fact that the children are the future of the Nation. If the children are healthy, the Nation is bound to be strong. It has been important agents of change in addressing risk factors for non-communicable diseases, as well as improving mental health and reducing alcohol and drug use and injuries. Building evidence health and development is effective in promoting and protecting health and improving academic achievement. Students enhance the relationship between the school, parents and local community. Media and mass communication are influencing lifestyle and shaping our modern culture. The standards for school health education can help students make better decisions about their health. School Health education must emerge as a critical factor in the process of health development in particular and national development in general.

❐

43

Blended Learning in Distance Education

With digital transformation sweeping throughout the education system today, it'smore crucial for educational organizations to utilize them in the teaching process. At present a smart approach to teach students with diverse needs is using blended learning in the classrooms. Blended learning, also called "flipped classroom," "hybrid learning" or "mixed learning," is an approach that mixes the traditional classroom teaching with online content, so that learners can learn and review at their own pace.

Meaning of Blended learning

In Blended learning teachers use technology, frequently in the form of Web-Based instruction, in concert with and as a supplement to live instruction that needs the mentor presence and guidance. The strength of this approach is that it provides a means to ensure learners as they undertake independent learning tasks and provides many affordances for the teacher and students in the form of communication channels, information sources and management tools.

Blended learning commonly refers to a learning that combines traditional teaching and learning approaches with information and communication technologies.It is anticipated that blended learning will enhance the student learning experience, at the same time it also demands that the teachers should be trained as online facilitator. This can be done using e- learning materials, Virtual labs, webinars, roleplay in classroom teaching.

Distance education

Distance Education "is a process to create and provide access to learning when the source of information and the learners are separated by time and distance, or both". In other words, distance learning is the process of creating an educational experience of equal qualitative value for the learner to best suit their needs outside the classroom.

Distance education courses require a physical and online mode it can be done using the present day ICT Tools. This emerging technology is becoming widely used in universities and institutions around the globe. With the recent trend of technological advance, distance learning is becoming more recognized for its potential in providing individualized attention and communication with students internationally.

Benefits of Blended Learning

Blended learning represents a fundamental shift in instructional methods which has the potential to optimize outcomes for individual students rather than the traditional instruction.Extensively studied and practiced in distance education, blended learning also offers an ideal solution for improving training, especially when it comes to up skilling students to achieve digital economy. And with digital assets such as videos and recordings and eBooks, the potential for re-use is huge, reinforces engagement, learning and retention. The benefits of blended learningare discussed below

1. **Different People learn Different things in Different Ways**
   With so many different learning styles to address, a blended learning solution makes sense. For people who learn visually or through reading and ideally alone, online self-paced video delivery would be the best mode. Social and aural learners would gain most from live instructor-led classrooms. Meanwhile, hands-on practice from engaging in applied learning projects would satisfy kinesthetic and logical learners.
2. **Reinforces Engagement, learning and Retention**
   Numerous studies show how for most people, learning is improved by combining different activities alongside more passive study. Ideally, these could include the "human" element of interaction, such as threaded discussions, video conferencing and internal social media forums to share and compare knowledge and to encourage and demonstrate the effective application of newly learned skills to the workplace. By utilizing as many learning delivery methods as possible (video, live instructor, social and practical), we can fill in any knowledge gaps left by modes that were less than optimal for the specific topic or learner.

3. **Learners can Control the Pace of their Learning**

   People learn best when they have some control over their learning. Choice reduces learner apathy, relieves some of the stress of the learning process and motivates people to engage with the material. It makes the learners to come to the table with a wide range of knowledge and experience with the course topic.

   This "flipped" blended approach enables learners to start with the knowledge they gained on their own and then supplement it with the personal attention of instructor-led classroom training (either virtual or on-premises), plus the group interaction of social learning and finally, the hands-on practice of applied learning projects

4. **Blended learning saves Money**

   Organizations of any size can optimize return on investment by saving costs while increasing engagement and retention by integrating eLearning into instructor-led programs. Blended learning reduces instructor fees, expenses on training materials; enables distance learning at a global scale.

5. **Blended learning is Modular and Scalable**

   Dedicated classroom training takes a lot of time to set up and participate in, making it not economical on an ad hoc basis.However, online learning libraries alone lack the engagement, practical exercise and personal feedback that optimize learning. In contrast, by providing easily accessible training, a blended learning program enables students to upskill quickly in a specific technology or subject.

6. **Flexibility and Effectiveness**

   A blended learning approach provides ultimate flexibility in presenting content, potential to enhance both the effectiveness and efficiency of meaningful learning experiences. Complex topics can be presented in the classroom, while other subject matter can be available online with an convenience over how and when the learners participate in learning.

7. **Cost-Effectiveness**

   Mostly blended learning is cost effective method when educational institutions telecast online events to the learners.

8. **Personalization**

   A well-crafted blended learning can provide a seamless transition from classroom to computer or vice-versa through designing the ways of continuing discussion themes and personalizing content to learners interests.

9. Extended Reach

A blended learning strategy reduces classroom teaching time,by digitizing the expertise of talented instructors or subject-matter experts, reach more people with high-quality content at a fraction of the cost. That frees up knowledgeable instructors to offer more classes, or create more training content, or work on other things.

10. Covers all learning Styles

Effective blended learning is a best way to cater to different learning styles of varied learners community through distance mode.

Disadvantages of Blended learning

1. Relies heavily on technology to deliver online learning experiences.
2. The digital tools and online assets need to be reliable, easy to use and up-to-date.
3. Technical issues can be a significant barrier

Strategies of Blended learning towards Distance Education

Virtual Labs

To emerge as a knowledge super power in the world India has to convert our demographic advantage into knowledge powerhouse by nurturing and honing our working population into knowledge enabled working population. Human Resource Development would certainly be the key for it to happen through the virtual labs where Knowledge modules, E-learning contents, and Blogs depending on the personalized needs of the learner would need to be delivered to him /her at the right time with the right content interactively to take care of his / her aspirations. The gravitational attraction of the present generation learners towards teachnological gadgets can be used to make them as part of the blended learning process in distance education system.

Conclusion

Blended learning combines the best of traditional teaching techniques with new ones. Technological innovation in higher education has a significant impact on the formation of the future society whoare going to be the makers of the future. Technological integration has a major influence on learning and teaching process but will not the online blended learning tools cannot replace teachers but aids in increasing the effectiveness of the teaching process in distance education mode.

❒

44

A Bird View of the Program Evaluation Strategies in Distance Education

Distance learning is a method of conveying education and instructions, generally on an individual basis, to the students who are not physically available in a usual setting such as a classroom. Distance learning is rapidly becoming an alternative to traditional classrooms.Distance education is designed to give people options. It makes learning attainable for people from all walks of life. A great alternative to traditional, campus based classes, distance education allows students to study on a more flexible basis.

Program evaluation is defined as "a process used to determine whether the design and delivery of a program were effective and whether the proposed outcomes were met" (Caffarella, 2002, 225). Generally, evaluation is used to determine the degree to which program objectives are met through the procedures used by the program. The evaluation determines whether or not the outcomes or results predicted by the program occurred and if their occurrence was due to the project. It is essential that evaluation and feedback be part of all distance learning programs. Evaluation in distance education must be carefully balanced between a traditional view that allows for program justification/development and a new view that has the potential for empowering. Also, evaluation in distance education is undertaken to guide decision makers program leaders, program coordinators with an overall objective to improve service delivery

12. **Humanistic Evaluation Strategy:** These strategies are: scientific and humanistic strategy is applying standard tests to evaluation of scientific approach indicators and in fact, this approach goes back approach is the ruling on education.
13. **Academic Evaluation Strategy:** This strategy has partially returned in recent times – Emphasis is placed on understanding how knowledge is constructed, deconstructed and reconstructed. Also, this strategy was very concerned with presenting a broad variety foundational issues related to the topic, such as historical, philosophical , social and political.

Conclusion

It is essential that evaluation and evaluation strategies should be part of all distance education programs. In current and related literature there are only a few study on the program evaluation strategies in distance education. In this study, Usun's(2016) thirteen evaluation strategies that are frequently used to collect data for educational program evaluations were reviewed in point of suitabilities and utilities to distance education; The objectives-oriented evaluation strategy focuses on specifying the goals and objectives of a given program attained. This strategy is highly suited to distance education programs that have highly defined objectives, and the purpose of the evaluation is to determine if, and to what extent, these objectives have been met. Major weaknesses often cited regarding this strategy include the difficulty of evaluators of distance education to operate in a program environment with ill-defined objectives, to identify unintended program outcomes, and to measure learning. Systems-based evaluation strategy is very helpful to understanding distance education and that "the systems model provides a tool that not only helps us recognize many of the issues that separate distance education from conventional education, but also helps us distinguish good distance education from bad." Consequently, it is important to evaluate distance education programs by how they work as a whole rather than by evaluating individual components without regard to overall program effectiveness. Potential weakness of the systems based (management oriented) strategy may occur from evaluators giving partiality to top management, from evaluators' occasional inability to respond to questions, from costly evaluation processes, and from the assumption that important decisions can be clearly identified in advance.

❐

45

Gender Inequalities Issues in Education

Gender Inequality in India

It refers to health, education, economic and political inequalities between men and women in India. Various international gender inequality indices rank India differently on each of these factors, as well as on a composite basis, and these indices are controversial.

Gender inequalities, and their social causes, impact India's sex ratio, women's health over their lifetimes, their educational attainment, and economic conditions. Gender inequality in India is a multifaceted issue that concerns men and women. Some argue that various gender equality indices place men at a disadvantage. However, when India's population is examined as a whole, women are at a disadvantage in several important ways. In India, discriminatory attitudes towards either sex have existed for generations and affect the lives of both sexes. Although the constitution of India grants men and women equal rights, gender disparities remain.

Definition and Concept of Gender Inequality

'Gender' is a socio-cultural term referring socially defined roles and behaviors assigned to 'males' and 'females' in a given society; whereas, the term 'sex' is a biological and physiological phenomenon which defines man and woman. In its social, historical and cultural aspects, gender is a function of power relationship between men and women where men are considered superior to women. Therefore, gender may be understood as a man-made concept, while 'sex' is natural or biological characteristics of human beings.

Gender Inequality, in simple words, may be defined as discrimination against women based on their sex. Women are traditionally considered by the society as weaker sex. She has been accorded a subordinate position to men. She is exploited, degraded, violated and discriminated both in our homes and in outside world. This peculiar type of discrimination against women is prevalent everywhere in the world and more so in Indian society.

Causes and Types of Gender Inequality in India

The root cause of gender inequality in Indian society lies in its patriarchy system. According to the famous sociologists Sylvia Walby, patriarchy is "a system of social structure and practices in which men dominate, oppress and exploit women". Women's exploitation is an age old cultural phenomenon of Indian society. The system of patriarchy finds its validity and sanction in our religious beliefs, whether it is Hindu, Muslim or any other religion.

For instance, as per ancient Hindu law giver Manu: "Women are supposed to be in the custody of their father when they are children, they must be under the custody of their husband when married and under the custody of her son in old age or as widows. In no circumstances she should be allowed to assert herself independently".

Extreme poverty and lack of education are also some of the reasons for women's low status in society. Poverty and lack of education derives countless women to work in low paying domestic service, organized prostitution or as migrant laborers. Women are not only getting unequal pay for equal or more work but also they are being offered only low skill jobs for which lower wages are paid. This has become a major form of inequality on the basis of gender.

Educating girl child is still seen as a bad investment because she is bound to get married and leave her paternal home one day. Thus, without having good education women are found lacking in present day's demanding job skills; whereas, each year's High School and 10+2 standard results show that girls are always doing better than boys. This shows that parents are not spending much after 10+2 standard on girl child and that's why they lack in job market.

Gender Inequality in India: Important Data

Global Indices

Gender Inequality is also reflected in India's poor ranking in various global gender indices.

UNDP's Gender Inequality Index- 2014:

India's ranking is 127 out of 152 countries in the List. This ranking is only above Afghanistan as far as SAARC countries are concerned.

World Economic Forum's Global Gender Gap Index- 2014:

India's ranks at 114 in the list of 142 countries of the world. This Index examines gender gap in four major areas:

- Economic participation and opportunity.
- Educational achievements.
- Health and life expectancy.
- Political empowerment.
- India's position on these indicators was as follows:
- Economic participation and opportunity: 134th
- Educational achievements: 126th
- Health and Life expectancy: 141st
- Political empowerment: 15th

These two important Global Indices show the sorry state of affairs in India as far as gender equality is concerned. Only in case of 'Political Empowerment' India is doing fine which is a welcome sign. But other indices are very poor and a lot need to be done to improve the same.

Legal and Constitutional Safeguards Against Gender Inequality

Indian Constitution provides for positive efforts to eliminate gender inequality; the Preamble to the Constitution talks about goals of achieving social, economic and political justice to everyone and to provide equality of status and of opportunity to all its citizens. Further, women have equal right to vote in our political system. Article 15 of the Constitution provides for prohibition of discrimination on grounds of sex also apart from other grounds such as religion, race, caste or place of birth. Article 15(3) authorizes the Sate to make any special provision for women and children. Moreover, the Directive Principles of State Policy also provides various provisions which are for the benefit of women and provides safeguards against discrimination.

Other than these Constitutional safeguards, various protective Legislations have also been passed by the Parliament to eliminate exploitation of women and to give them equal status in society. For instance, the Sati (Prevention) Act, 1987 was enacted to abolish and make punishable the inhuman custom of Sati; the Dowry Prohibition Act, 1961 to eliminate the practice of dowry; the Special Marriage Act, 1954 to give rightful status to married couples who marry inter-caste or inter-religion; Pre-Natal Diagnostic Techniques (Regulation and Prevention of Misuse) Bill (introduced in Parliament in 1991, passed in

1994 to stop female infanticide and many more such Acts. So there are varied legislative safeguards and protection mechanisms for women but the ground reality is very different.

Does Education Promote Equality

The education provider is responsible for promoting equality in educational institutions and preventing discrimination based on gender identity and In this study of gender inequality and declining sex ratio in north India it was found that, India's social stmcture, social norms, caste system, tradition etc. have made women vulnerable for centuries. They have been subjected to discrimination, oppression and deprivation which leads to considerable violence against women in the fonn of rape, molestation, harassment, dowry death, bride burning etc.

However the violence against the unborn female is the worst form of discrimination, which women are subjected to. Thus the female in the womb is as vulnerable as the women out side. The only difference is that those who would have given life to her i.e. her parents bent on taking her life. She is punished for a crime that she is not responsible for....of not being a male.. gender expression according to each educational institutions own equality plan.

Need

Gender equality means that the different behaviour, aspirations and needs ofwomen and men are considered, valued and favoured equally. It does not mean that women and men have to become the same, but that their rights, responsibilities and opportunities will not depend on whether they are born male or female.

Conclusion

Gender inequality in education is one of the major issue faced by the students as well as the education administration..these above passages are elaborately discussed about the gender inequality problems and also has a solution for this problem.

❐

46

Decision Making Skills among College Students Based on Gender

Education is the process through which the experiences of the race, comprising knowledge, skills and attitudes are transmitted to individuals who are the members of the race, concepts change, attitudes and skills undergo alternations, appreciations, interests and values face revisions and life itself involves a continuous modification of experience. In this context, education is the process of assisting the learner to adjust to the ever-changing word.

Decision Making

Definition

Decision making is about deciding what action to take; it usually involves choice between options. A leader who aspires to excellence obviously has a vested interest in seeing that the best decisions are taken.

Decision Making Process (Five-Steps)

Adapt the familiar five-step decision making process (outlined below) to decide which program or service to assess.

Step 1: Identifying/clarifying the decision to be made. If the decision has not yet been isolated, it should be identified as a first step. Sometimes the decision to be made will have been presented to the decision maker. In those situations, Step 1 calls for the clarification of what the decision actually entails.

Step 2: Identifying possible decision options. The next step requires the decision maker to spell out, as clearly as possible, just what the decision alternatives really are. For instance, if one were attempting to buy a bicycle, do the decision options only consist of the different types of bicycles, or is another option to refrain from buying a bicycle altogether?

Step 3: Gathering/processing information. Next, the decision maker collects or processes information that can help guide the decision. If such information is already at hand, then it simply needs to be processed; that is, studied and understood by the decision maker. If there is no relevant information available, or if there is insufficient information, then such information must be collected so it can be processed. The more significant the decision, the more rigorous the information-gathering process.

Step 4: Making/implementing the decision. After the information has been considered according to its relevance and significance, a decision based on that information should be made and, thereafter, implemented.

Step 5: Evaluating the decision. In recognition of the fact that not all of one's decisions are likely to be defensible, the final step in the five-step decision making process is to determine whether the decision was appropriate. Ordinarily, this will be done by ascertaining the decision's consequences.

Impact of Decision Making in The Life of College Students

Decision making is an important life skill at a lst ages in life. More importantly, learning is a part of the decision-making process (Sproles,1990). Appropriate is in making involves logical steps: determin-ing the problem, considering multiple alternatives, and choosing the best alternative based on the particular situation (Garman, 2002) appropriate skills in decision making require abstractt hinking (Baxter Magolda, 1988)which involves considering multipl ealternatives. However, initially, students may enter college without prior education attaining in decision-making and problem solving. And, they may not be able to think abstractly (Baxter Magolda, 1988).

Objectives of te Study

1. To find out the level of decision making skills of college students.
2. To find out the significance difference between male and female college students with respect to decision making skills.

Hypotheses of the Study

1. The level of decision making skills of college students is average.
2. There is no significance difference between male and female college students with respect to decision making skills.

Methodology of the Study

The investigator has adopted normative method and has been survey technique to find out the "Decision Making Skills among College Students". The investigator has used random sampling technique for selecting the sample from the population.

Statistical Techniques Used

The level of decision making skills of college students is average.

TABLE. 46.1: Level of Decision Making Skills of College Students

Decision Making Score	N	Mean	Percentage	Level
37-50	128	21.08	50.60	High
24-36	111	31.82	44.22	Average
10-23	12	40.60	4.78	Low
Total	**251**	**35.78**		**Average**

It is inferred from the above table that, 50.6% of them have scored 37-50, 44.22% of them have scored 23-36 and 4.78% of college students have scored 10-23. Therefore it is interpreted, 50.60% belongs to high level, 44.22% belongs to average level and 4.78% belongs to low level. For the whole respondents, the mean level of decision making skills of college students is average. There is no significance difference between male and female college students with respect to decision making skills.

TABLE. 46.2: Difference Between Male and Female College Students with Respect to Decision Making Skills

Skill	Gender	N	Mean	SD	Calculated 't' Value	Remarks at 5% Level
Decision Making	Male	189	35.40	6.598	0.089	NS
	Female	62	36.94	4.573	0.043	NS

(At 5% level of significance the table value of 't' is 1.960)

(At 1% level of significance the table value of 't' is 2.576)

It is inferred from the above table that there is no significant difference between male and female college students with respect to decision making skills at 5% and also significant at 1% level. While comparing the mean scores of male (mean = 35.40) and female college students (mean 36.94) in their decision making skills, the female college students are better than the male college students.

Conclusion

Decision-making are the important skills for business and life. Decision-making is especially important for management and leadership. There are processes and techniques to improve decision-making and the quality of decisions. Since today's students are tomorrow's leaders and successful leaders are energetic. They exert a great deal of effort in order to communicate effectively, solve problems, make decisions, to set goals, execute plans, and supervise/evaluate. These are a leader's directional (or thinking) and implementing skills. As a leader, he cannot expect positive results from subordinates unless work equally hard at solving problems, making plans and decision into actions. Successful leaders are also work hard at accomplishing their missions and objectives while maintaining only the highest possible standards of performance. This type of leadership standard should be expected from our college students. India is a developing county, improving develop college student's decision making skills will help very shortly India to become one of the developed countries in the world.

❐

47

Impact of Modern Technologies on Education

Technology is a gift of God. It is the mother of civilizations, of arts and of sciences. Technology has certainly changed the way we live. It has impacted different facets of life and redefined living. Undoubtedly, technology plays an important role in every sphere of life. Several manual tasks can be automated, thanks to technology. Also, many complex and critical processes can be carried out at ease and greater efficiency with the help of modern technology. Technology has revolutionized the field of education.

Education and Modern Technologies

According to the latest insights as to how exactly modern students of today prefer to use technology and how does their learning get an impact if they use technology, it was revealed that the use of modern equipment technology and tools, the learning and interactivity of students increases. They also find it much more interactive, as well as full of interesting areas, when aided by technology. The transfer of knowledge becomes very easy and convenient as well as effective. What this means is, that our minds now tend to work faster when assisted with the use of modern technology, be it any part of life, here we talk about education.

1. **Internet Connection and Round the Clock Connectivity**
   The internet has grown in importance by many folds, over the process of decade. Its importance in the education world can now never be

undermined. Despite the chances of fraud and drawbacks, the use of the internet is a blessing for students. Today, the internet is something that is present in almost everything we use. From television to gaming consoles, and our phones, the internet is literally everywhere. The use of the internet allows students to find amazing convenience, they can find various kinds of help, tutorials and other kinds of assisting material which could be used to academically improve and enhance their learning.

3. **Using Projectors and Visuals**

   Visual images always have a strong appeal compared to words. Using projectors and visuals to aid in learning is another form of great technological use. Top institutions around the world, now rely on the use of amazing power point presentations and projections in order to keep the learning interactive and interesting. Technological use such as projectors within the schools and colleges can take the interaction and interest levels right up and also improve motivation. Students like to see appealing visuals and something that entices them to think rather than just reading words. The learning part also has become pretty efficient when it comes to technology.

5. **Digital Footprints in the Education Sector**

   If one talks about digital and education, then the penetration of digital media within the education sector has now grown. This penetration has resulted in round the clock connectivity with students and different forums that are available for different kinds of assignments or help. As the power of digital presentations increases, there are and there will be more applications that will assist students in development and learning.

7. **Online Degrees**

   Online degrees now have become a very common phenomenon. People wish to take up online courses for their learning and certifications. Top institutions offer amazing online programs with the use of various applications and the internet. This is a concept that will continue to rise as it gets more support and awareness. The online degree scenario around the world is more famous among students who work and look for flexible studying programs.

Factors Affecting Technology in Education

The modern technologies are demanding that teachers learn how to use these technologies in their teaching. Hence these new technologies increase the teachers' training needs. Gressard and Loyd (1985) asserted that teacher's attitudes toward computers are a key factor in the successful implementation of ICT in education. They pointed out that teachers do not always have positive attitudes towards computers and their poor attitudes may lead to a failure of the computer- based projects. Also the most commonly cited barriers are: (i) Lack of time, (ii) Lack of access, (iii) Lack of resources, (iv) Lack of expertise and (v) Lack of support.

Impact of ICTs on Education

In educational context, ICT has the potential to increase access to education and improve its relevance and quality. Tinio (2002) asserted that ICTs have a tremendous impact on education in terms of acquisition and absorption of knowledge to both teachers and students through the promotion of:

Active Learning: ICT tools help for the calculation and analysis of information obtained for examination and also students' performance report are all being computerized and made easily available for inquiry. In contrast to memorization-based or rote learning, ICT promotes learner engagement as learners choose what to learn at their own pace and work on real life situations' problems.

Collaborative and Cooperative Learning: ICT encourages interaction and cooperation among students, teachers regardless of distance which is between them. It also provides students the chance to work with people from different cultures and working together in groups, hence helps students to enhance their communicative skills as well as their global awareness. Researchers have found that typically the use of ICT leads to more cooperation among learners within and beyond school and there exists a more interactive relationship between students and teachers (Grégoire et al. 1996).

Creative Learning: ICT promotes the manipulation of existing information and to create one's own knowledge to produce a tangible product or a given instructional purpose.

Integrative Learning: ICT promotes an integrative approach to teaching and learning, by eliminating the synthetic separation between theory and practice unlike in the traditional classroom where emphasis encloses just a particular aspect.

Evaluative Learning: Use of ICT for learning is student-centered and provides useful feedback through various interactive features. ICT allow students to discover and learn through new ways of teaching and learning which are sustained by constructivist theories of learning rather than students do memorization and rote learning.

Positive Impacts

1. **Enhanced Teaching and Learning**
   - Technological developments like digital cameras, projectors, mind training software, computers, Power point presentations, 3D visualization tools; all these have become great sources for teachers to help students grasp a concept easily.
   - It has to be understood that visual explanation of concepts makes learning fun and enjoyable for students. They're able to participate more in the classroom and even teachers get a chance to make their classes more interactive and interesting.
2. **Globalization**
   - The students can "meet" their counterparts through video conferencing without leaving the classroom, when schools are in different parts of the state.
   - Some sites, such as www.glovico.com are used to help students learn foreign languages online by pairing a group of students with a teacher from another country.
3. **No Geographical Limitations**
   - With the introduction of online degree programs there is hardly any need of being present physically in the classroom. Even several foreign universities have started online degree courses that student can join.
   - Distance learning and online education have become very important part of the education system now a day.

Negative Impacts

1. **Declining of Writing Skills**
   - Due to the excessive usage of online chatting and shortcuts, the writing skills of today's young generation have declined quite tremendously.
   - These days, children are relying more and more on digital communication that they have totally forgot about improving their writing skills.
   - They don't know the spelling of different words, how to use grammar properly or how to do cursive writing.
2. **Increasing Incidents of Cheating**
   - Technological developments like graphical calculators, high tech watches, mini cameras and similar equipments have become great sources to cheat in examinations.

- It is easier for students to write formulae and notes on graphing calculators with least chances of being caught.

3. **Lack of Focus**

- SMS or text messaging has become a favorite pastime of many students. Students are seen playing with their cell phone, i Phones during day and night or driving and very often even between lectures.
- Being ever-connected to the online world has resulted in lack of focus and concentration in academics and to some extent, even in sports and extracurricular activities.

Conclusion

Technology has a positive impact on education and at the same time, it may also prove negative effects. The role of technology in the field of education is four fold: it is included as a part of curriculum, as an instructional delivery system, as a means of aiding instructions and also as a tool to enhance the entire learning process. Teachers and students should take advantage of this in the good light and eliminate the drawbacks which are pulling back many of students as well as schools from achieving excellence.

❐

48

E-Learning in Distance Mode

E-learning is a piece of the new elements that attributes the instructive framework. It has turned into a vital piece of the general public, containing a broad exhibit of digitalization methodologies, segments and conveyance strategies. The utilization of data and correspondence advances (ICT) for instructive reason has increased, & the spread of system innovations has caused e-learning practices to develop essentially. Training through web, arrange is e-learning. It is the system based exchange of aptitudes and information. Separation learning gives "access to realizing when the wellspring of data and the students are isolated by time and remove, or both". Separation training is characterized by the relationship for instructive correspondences and innovation as: Institution-based, formal instruction where the learning bunch is isolated, and where intuitive media communications frameworks are utilized to interface students, assets and teachers.

E-Learning

Understanding e-learning is basic. E-learning will be getting the hang of using electronic innovations to get to instructive educational modules outside of conventional study hall. Much of the time, it alludes to a course, program or degree conveyed totally on the web. There are numerous terms used to portray discovering that is conveyed on the web, by means of the web, running from separation instruction, to automated electronic learning, web based learning web learning and numerous others.

Distance Education

Distance education or long-distance learning is the education of students who may not always be physically present at a school. Traditionally, this usually involved correspondence courses where in the student corresponded with the school via post. Today it involves online education. Courses that are conducted are either hybrid, blender or 100% distance learning. A number of other terms (distributed learning, e-learning, online learning, virtual classroom etc.) are use roughly synonymously with distance education.

E-Learning a Boon to Distance Education System

The utilization of e-learning is seen at all dimensions of instructive framework. E-learning is pictured as the India's permit for boosting up separation instruction framework. The expanding combination of the online training organizations and associations, it is unequivocally trusted that India will at last adapt to the slack in its advanced education framework. The best way to connect the developing division out in the open and private schooling in India can be handled by using e-learning and internet learning. A site named Coursera, furnishes such online courses through coordinated efforts with different all around perceived and national dimension colleges and establishments the whole way across. E-learning/showing covers a wide arrangement of utilizations of PC helped guidance, PC based learning, electronic learning, virtual homeroom and web based learning. E-getting the hang of/instructing is an intelligent learning background with the entrance to online coaches which can made accessible from any PC, when the client has the entrance through internet browsers.

It allows the conveyance of learning and data to students at a quickened pace, opening up new vistas of information exchange. The greatest favorable circumstances of e-getting the hang of/showing lie in its capacity to cover separations. It is self-guided, and learning is done at the student's pace. E-getting the hang of/instructing includes conveyance of substance and assets for educating and learning by means of various correspondence conventions. The one such extremely mainstream open online course in Indian is MOOCs which teams up with National dimension Institutes as IITs and gets these online courses. The courses are largely free and give free declarations of consummation who are done and have finished all the tests and companion assessment assignments in the separate courses. One can discover online courses for different fields like proficient showcasing, Digital instructional methods, International Business, Forensic Sciences and a few MBA courses as separation training. Additionally even the state colleges in India have begun their wing of alumni and post-graduate projects as online training.

Advantages of E-Learning in Distance Education

- Class work can be booked around close to home and expert work, bringing about adaptable learning.
- Reduces make a trip cost and time to and from school.
- Learners may have the alternative to choose learning materials that meets their dimension of information and web.
- Learners can ponder wherever they approach a PC and Internet.
- Self-paced learning modules enable students to work at their own pace.
- Flexibilities to join dialogs in the notice board strung exchange regions at any hour, or visit with cohorts and educators remotely in talk rooms.
- Different learning styles are tended to and help of learning happens through differed exercises.
- Development of PC and web abilities that are transferable to different features of student's lives.
- Successfully finishing on the web or PC based courses buids self-information and fearlessness and urges understudies to assume liability for their learning.

Disadvantages of E-Learning in Distance Education

- Unmotivated learners or those with poor study habits may fall behind.
- Lack of familiar structure and routine may take getting used to
- Students may feel isolated or miss social interaction thus the need to understanding different learning styles and individual learners needs.
- Instructor may not always be available on demand.
- Slow or unreliable internet connections can be frustrating.
- Managing learning software can involve a learning curve.
- Some courses such as traditional hands-on courses can be difficult to simulate.

Conclusion

E-learning has been very famous. The ascent in web clients and the progressive changes that have occurred in training have made a fruitful domain for e-figuring out how to develop. The substance of advanced education has encountered an ocean change throughout the decades. Once described by the conventional homeroom demonstrate, advanced education today has changed into discovering that is moment, on the web, self-propelled and in a hurry. The adventure of advanced education in India has been set apart with countless achievements most as of late, E-learning.

❒

49

Health Education for Prospective Teachers

The primary aim of the National Health Policy, 2017, is to inform, clarify, strengthen and prioritize the role of the Government in shaping health systems in all its dimensions- investments in health, organization of healthcare services, prevention of diseases and promotion of good health through cross sectoral actions, access to technologies, developing human resources, encouraging medical pluralism, building knowledge base, developing better financial protection strategies, strengthening regulation and health assurance. The policy supports voluntary service in rural and under-served areas on pro-bono basis by recognized healthcare professionals under a giving back to society initiative.

The policy lays greater emphasis on investment and action in school health by incorporating health education as part of the curriculum, promoting hygiene and safe health practices within the school environs and by acting as a site of primary health care. Promotion of healthy living and prevention strategies from AYUSH systems and Yoga at the work-place, in the schools and in the community would also be an important form of health promotion that has a special appeal and acceptability in the Indian context.

Every school day provides more number of students to opportunity to learn the importance of healthy lifestyles and skills necessary to engage in healthy behaviors. Not only do schools provide critical outlets to reach millions of children and adolescents to promote lifelong healthy behaviors, they also provide a place for students to engage in these behaviors, such as eating healthy and participating in physical activity. Health education programs in schools can contribute directly to a student's ability to successfully adopt and practice behaviors that protect and promote health and avoid or reduce health risk. The American Cancer Society, the American Diabetes Association, and the American Heart Association believe that quality health education programs delivered in the nation's schools can improve the well-being and health of their children and youth. According to the U.S. Centers for Disease Control and Prevention's (CDC) Healthy Youth initiative and the Carnegie Council on Adolescent Development, schools can play a vital role in establishing healthy behavior patterns among young people that carry into adulthood.

Health Education for Prospective Teachers

Health education is the profession of educating people about health. It promotes good care in terms of environmental health, physical health, social health, emotional health, intellectual health, and spiritual health and to take precautionary action for the individuals' well being. The Joint Committee on Health Education and Promotion Technology of 2001 defined Health Education as "any combination of planned learning experiences based on sound theories that provide individuals, groups, and communities the opportunity to acquire information and the skills needed to make quality health decisions." The World Health Organization defined Health Education as "comprising of consciously constructed opportunities for learning involving some form of communication designed to improve health literacy, including improving knowledge, and developing life skills which are conductive to individual and community health."

The focus on developing teacher competencies has its roots in the middle of the 20th century, when competency-based (i.e. performance-based) teacher education models became popular. Some decades later, a more humanistic approach was adopted to highlight the need to focus on the process of becoming a teacher, on the teacher as a person and not merely on the lists of skills that teachers require. Nevertheless, "teaching professionals now face unprecedented challenges; the demands that society places on them are constantly evolving at the same time as our understanding of what makes for effective learning". This necessitates renewed understanding of the competencies teachers should have, to be able to react to these new demands. Core competencies can give coherence to the practice of teaching health. Core competencies are defined as the minimum set of competencies that constitute a common baseline for all health promotion roles. They are what all practitioners are expected to be capable of doing in order to work efficiently and effectively. It is important that all teachers are equipped with strong, professional competencies. In order for health promotion actions to be sustainable in schools, teachers need to be capable, competent and skilled health educators. This is particularly so because they are uniquely positioned to contribute to a nation's health gain through the provision of health education to future adults. Many teachers face considerable challenges in placing health education as a priority on the school agenda.

Teachers Competency in Health Education

The health and well-being of our nation's young people is not a matter of luck. It is not a chance or random event. It must be a planned outcome. Improved health status is of economic value to Indian citizens. While funding for health, education and sanitation programmes in budget 2018-19 appears to be the highest over the last three years – a 13 percent rise from the previous year- the money set aside has declined from actual allocations of 2017-18, The case for well-designed, well-resourced, and sustained health education in the nation's prospective teachers is compelling.

"Teaching is a profession that carries with it a high degree of responsibility and the qualifications and skills of those who take on this responsibility constitute a major factor that affects, be it positively or negatively, any education system". In our National policy state the Health Promotion for Staff—Opportunities for school staff to improve their health status through activities such as health assessments, health education and health-related fitness activities. Improved health status is of economic value to Indian citizens. The economic returns to education are relatively easily understood as the result of the human capital formed in the education process. The health effects of education are much broader in scope, reflecting a much wider set of outcomes with an equivalently wider set of mechanisms. Human capital is an important channel but other personal resources are also important. Prospective teachers health education programs can reduce health risk behaviors of students such as tobacco use, poor nutrition, lack of physical activity, drug and alcohol use, as well as actions that increase stress, and risk of injury, and violence. Because these behaviors are amenable to change, quality school health education taught by trained prospective health educators provides the best opportunity to promote positive health behavior among children and adolescents.

Conclusion

In conclusion, the potential for prospective teachers' health education to improve health and save lives is significant. If we as a nation want to keep children and adolescents healthy, it is important to find better ways to provide quality school health education. One of excellent way is providing health education for prospective teachers it will enhance the knowledge competency of the teacher and also leads our young buds life in a healthy way. ❐

50

Educational Perspectives in Indian Society

Education gives us knowledge of the world around us and changes it into something better. It develops in United States a perspective of gazing life. It helps United States build opinions and have points of read on things in life. People discussion over the topic of whether or not education is that the solely issue that offers data. "Intelligence and character are the goal of true education." "The main purpose of the American school is to supply for the fullest potential development of every learner for living morally, creatively, and fruitfully in a very democratic society." Education edges entire countries additionally. .. each on personal and national level, education has been shown to extend economic process and stability. One of the foremost necessary edges of education is however it improves personal lives and helps societies run swimmingly.

Relationship between Educational Perspectives in Indian Society

Drawing on Durkheim's ideas, Talcott Parsons argues that after primary socialisation within the family, the school takes over as the 'focal socialising agency'. In school, the child must interact with other members of the school in terms of fixed set of rules. School acts a bridge between the family and society as a whole, preparing the child for his adult role. Within the family, the child is judged and treated largely in terms of 'particularistic' standards

By reflecting the operation of society as a whole, the school prepares young people for their adult roles. Universalistic standards and achieved status of adult society. As part of this process, schools socialise young people into the basic values of society. These values have important functions in society as a whole.

Finally, Parsons sees the educational system as an important mechanism for the selection of individuals for their future role in society. In his words, it "functions to allocate these human resources within the role structure of adult society". Thus, schools, by testing and evaluating students, match their talents, skills and capacities to the jobs for which they are best suited. The school is therefore seen as the major mechanism for role allocation.

Education Plays Major role in Modern Society

Education brings awareness in folks and keeps them aloof from irrational beliefs. It provides absolute best settlement not solely in Bharat however conjointly in several western countries. Education can direct the person to maneuver in right path in the least times in life. An extremely educated person will perpetually manage things severally. Educated people will junction rectifier his life with several comforts. Education makes students physically and mentally strong. Education is that the best investments for the folks as a result of well educated folks have additional opportunities to urge employment which provides them satisfaction. Educated people are going to be perpetually revered in any a part of world and his talent can award and rewarded. Education also makes the person to be positive. Sometimes folks scarify their enjoyment and work flat out day and night, because they realize that education is their passport for the further. Literacy rate depend on education. All the advancement in technology is because of education. Education is the ultimate factor that provides employment, so it plays a vital role in development of the country and also in raising the per ca pita income of the country. Education is the best weapon to eradicate poverty. Education promotes knowledge and understanding in rural communities. Education keeps the people away from superstitions beliefs. Educated person will be health conscious. Education is simply pathway to take care of success in life. It increases the ethical values of the person. Education isn't solely learning concerning books however conjointly learning concerning life. It rapidly increases your skill and awareness. Educated person can establish the distinction between sensible and dangerous. Education provides food at all times. In life if education is there with US, there's everything in life. It is best source to raise the economy.

Education as Medium of Cultural Reproduction, Indoctrination

The enduring operate of education is that the cultural copy. It has been recognised to be its main role. It is by education that the newborn is initiated within the social ways that. It transmits culture to him. At the first stages the aim is to introduce the kid to the normative order of his cluster. In the ancient society kin worked for the kid to the current finish. In advanced fashionable industrial society of the West, this work is undertaken by specialised agencies like college.

In ancient society, cultural copy could present itself by oral teaching of heritage and culture; history and legend and during a sensible approach by collaborating within the celebration of festivals. One may at a successive stage be introduced to culture through books. Yet one might not be during a position to understand it. It is solely once one has been initiated and driven that one gets cultivated within the cultural ways that. As indicated on top of it's a womb-to-tomb instructional method.But in present time's family, college and academics aren't any longer the sole establishments that influence the growing generations. The movies, radio, record trade, and the television are strong instruments to impart education. Their appeal is direct. But these aren't absolute to any normative customary. Their basic standard is the marketability. The cultivated morality is challenged; established values are disregarded; mockery is created of humility and decency.

With the irrespective of the standard values, the growing children find themselves like the waves in the boundless sea, and the older feel to have been left high and dry. "Perhaps nothing disturbs the fundamental operate of cultural transmission by the establishment of education as will this growth of a mass media that's not normatively regulated, and indeed that has not been consciously allotted such a operate among the society. Conclusion

The role of education as associate degree agent of the transmission of culture is so decreasing. It is becoming a specialized process. Education specifically the teaching of history provides this link between the individual and society. If the history of his society is brought alive to the kid, he will come to see that he is a part of something larger than himself, he will develop a way of commitment to the group.

❐

51

Explorative Study on Awareness of S.B. Learning among D.El.Ed Students of Na.D

This paper describes an explorative study on awareness of Smart board among primary teacher training students i.e., diploma in elementary education (D.El.Ed). In this competitive world, there exists a tremendous focus on having e-learning and e-technology in a variety of departments. According to the Merriam-Webster dictionary, learning is knowledge or skills acquired by instruction, study or experience. Using smart board learning, we can provide the quality education to remote and rural regions with the help of modern technologies like satellite, internet, and etc.

Smart board learning is entirely different from the traditional way of teaching by writing on black boards. Smart board learning can be defined as the improved way of education in which teachers teach and students learn in colleges or universities with advanced and significant use of technology. Student teachers are able to learn and understand difficult concepts and understand the complex problems by watching highly effective audio visuals and animations. By using these we can make learning a fun for the student teacher which will definitely improve their overall performance. Smart board classroom also enables faculties to rapidly evaluate the learning by their students in class. Smart board class rooms are also supposed to be environmental friendly, so that they can provide good environmental practice for the student teachers as well as faculties and instructors.

Review of Related Studies

Anurag Chaudhary (2014) This paper is about the much growing technology “SMART CLASS and E-LEARNING”. The usage of smart teaching techniques is now more prevalent in school as well as other colleges and institutes. It was generated back in 1980s and is growing since then. This new technology helps the students with the benefit of learning with a different experience. The methods of e-learning make the classroom more interactive and interesting. It has also created a greater impact on our society as well as on education system. The government has also started implementing this idea of e-learning in the schools. There are several examples available in the market that encourage the idea and work for its betterment. The smart classes have their own merits and demerits but this new technology s welcomed by the society in a great manner.

Mehedi Masud (2016) The large number of reasonably priced computers, Internet broadband connectivity and rich education content has created a global phenomenon by which information and communication technology (ICT) has used to remodel education. E-learning can be explained as the use of available information, computational and communication technologies to assist learning practice. In the modern world, education has become more universal, and people are looking for learning with simplicity and interest. Students are looking for more interactive and attractive learning style rather than old traditional style. Using technological learning, we can enhance the education system. We can deliver quality education to students as well as we can ease and uniform the process of education by using the modern technologies and methods.

Statement of the Problem

The problem of the study is stated as, “Explorative study on awareness of smart board learning among D.El.Ed students of Nagapattinam district”

Definitions of Terms Used in the Study.

Smart Board Learning

Smart board learning classrooms aim at offering distinguished educational environment which can enhance the collaborative learning environment and providing diverse knowledge sources through many interactive tools. In literature, smart board classroom concept has evolved from broader concept that was the distance education system which utilized Internet as a medium in order to transform a conventional classroom into an intelligent space, equipped with several hardware and software components. It is also defined as a teaching and learning environment where participants can interact, communicate, view and discuss presentations, and engage with learning resources while working in groups, all in an online setting.

Significance of the Study

Education is the driving force of economic and social development in any country. Hence, it is necessary to find ways to make education of good quality, accessible and affordable to all, using the latest technology available. From last two decades ICT has been used and its usage has caused a revolutionary change in the development of society. Computer mediated learning is being carried out by student teacher's in teacher education for their competency and other general activities. Every human being lives in the web and social world. It provides lot of facilities for the teacher educations, particularly smart virtual classroom learning. It helps with new platforms come new forums for training students to discuss, video conferencing, etc., It becomes highly attractive tool in our teacher education program to develop teaching competency. Hence, it is concluded that the smart board learning of the study is focused on improvement of learning outcomes through smart board classroom among teacher training students of Nagapattinam district.

Objectives of the Study

To find out awareness of smart board class room learning among teacher training students in terms of

- Gender
- Locality

Hypotheses of the Study

- There is no significant difference in an awareness of smart board class room learning among teacher training students with reference to their gender.
- There is no significant difference in an awareness of smart board class room learning among teacher training students with reference to their locality.

Methodology

The investigator used the survey method in this study. The survey method is aimed at finding out an awareness of smart board class room learning among teacher training students. In the simplest way, the research is a plan structure and strategy of investigation in order to answer the research question. The investigator has planned structured strategy to gather data for their study.

Sampling Technique

The research work using the stratified random sampling technique. After selecting institutions 100 teacher training students were selected randomly selected from teacher training institute.

Tools Used for the Study

The tool used for the present investigation was on the basis of Likert attitude scales. The tool used in study to assess the smart virtual class room learning of tool developed by Ernet India engineers and teacher educator. This tool measures the awareness of smart board class room learning consisting 5 areas dealt within the scales

Procedure

The investigator personally visited all the selected teacher training institute and met the teacher training students for explaining the purpose of study and instructed them as how to respond to the questionnaire.

Scoring Procedure

The questionnaire was prepared on the bases of five point likert type scale. The responses to the tool were comforted on a 5 point scale strongly agree, agree, undecided, disagree and strongly disagree. The responses were given the weight age of 5, 4, 3, 2 and 1 for positive statement and 1,2,3,4 and 5 for negative statement. The range of score is from 40 to 200.

Statistical Techniques Used tor the Present Study

Descriptive and differential statistics were used for analysis data, teacher training students 't' test was employed to find out the difference in various aspects from the level of awareness of smart board classroom learning including gender and locality of students.

Delimitation

The present study has selected teacher training students Nagapattinam District only.

Analysis and Interpretation of Data

For analysis and interpretations of data, the relevant input and analytical finding and inferences derived have been presented in different tables and their discussion provided after the table;

Hypothesis - 1

There is no significant difference in an awareness of smart board class room learning among teacher training students with reference to their gender.

Variables	No	Mean	S.D	't' Value
Male students	20	119.55	39.90	0.91
Female students	80	128.325	31.56	

From the above table, it is observed that the mean of awareness of smart boardclass room learning score for teacher training students of male and female are 119.55 and 128.325 respectively. The calculated't' value is 0.91. It is not significant at 0.01 levels. Therefore, the formulated null hypothesis "There is no significant difference in an awareness of smart board class room learning among teacher training students with reference to their gender" is accepted.

Hypothesis-2

There is no significant difference in an awareness of smart board class room learning among teacher training students with reference to their locality.

Variables	No	Mean	S.D	't' Value
Urban students	38	129.632	28.2789	0.76
Rural students	62	124.694	36.2177	

From the above table, it is observed that the mean of awareness of smart board class room learning score for teacher training students of urban and rural are 129.632 and 124.694 respectively. It is not significant at 0.01 levels. Therefore, the formulated null hypothesis "There is no significant difference in an awareness of smart board class room learning among teacher training students with reference to their locality" is accepted.

Findings

- The male and female teacher training students have similar awareness of smart board class room learning.
- The urban and rural teacher training students l have similar awareness of smart board class room learning

Implications of the Study

- These findings of the study will be of immense use of understanding the awareness of smart board classroom learning.
- Areas tor Further Research
- The present study was confined to the teacher training institute only. This study can be done in various type teacher education departments like B.Ed college, Universities etc.
- This work can be done in comparative study of different colleges, universities, districts etc.

Conclusion

It is fact that smart board class rooms, i.e., Information and Communication Technology are playing a vital role in improvement of teacher education platform. Smart virtual class room is designed to help faculties and teacher trainees to compete with new challenges and developing teaching competency and performance. They can interact directly without any hesitations. Smart class has many benefits to the students and faculties. It is very clear that innovation in technology is impacting everywhere and bringing new opportunities for schools, universities and educationalists. We can help students, student teacher as well educators by using advanced technologies to make the future bright.

52

Past, Present and Future of Teacher Education

Education is a symbol of development. The development of any nation depends mainly on the standards of its educational institutions. The standard of its educational institutions depends mainly on the standards of its teachers and teacher education programmes. Teacher has a pivotal role in the process of development. In India, the position of teacher is above the god after mother and father. Education is a key for both national and individual development. In the 21st century the scope of education is more. We are living in the globalized, modernized, scientific, technological and digital world. The expectations of an individual are changing from time to time. The needs of a society are also changing day by day. Planning or policy is very important for development of any nation. The policy document shows the direction where we want to move, how much time we required to reach our destination, how to solve any problems if arise and where we are. Teacher education programmes are the main source to visualize the type of educational system we need for our development for healthy and wealthy nation for the betterment of all.

Teacher Education

NCTE has defined Teacher education as – A programme of education, research and training of persons to teach from pre-primary to higher education level. Teacher education is a programme that is related to the development of teacher proficiency and competence that would enable and empower the teacher to meet the requirements of the profession and face the challenges therein. According to Good Dictionary of Education Teacher education means, "all the formal and non-formal activities and experiences that help to quality a person to assume responsibilities of a member of the educational profession or to discharge his responsibilities more effectively". The American Commission on Teacher Education rightly observes: *"The quality of a nation depends upon the quality of its citizens. The quality of its citizens depends not exclusively, but in critical measure upon the quality of their education, the quality of their education depends more than upon any single factor, upon the quality of their teacher"*. It is common knowledge that the academic and professional standards of teachers constitute a critical component of the essential learning conditions for achieving the educational goals of a nation.

Revision of the Centrally Sponsored Scheme of Teacher Education

The Department has initiated the process of revision of the Teacher Education Scheme. The revised Scheme is guided by the following factors:

- To integrate teacher education with overall education development in the States;
- The need for expansion of capacity of teacher education institutions, especially in some of the deficit States of East and North-Eastern Region;
- Address the problem of large number of untrained teachers and the possibility of large number of persons being recruited (because of the Pupil Teacher Ratio (PTR) specified in the RTE Act) without possessing the prescribed professional qualification;
- Expanding institutional capacity to provide in-service training for secondary school teachers in light of the Rashtriya Madhyamik Shiksha Abhiyan (RMSA);
- Strengthening the decentralized structures of BRCs and CRCs to provide adequate institutional support for professional development of school teachers on a continuous basis;
- To link elementary teacher education with the higher education system
- To develop and put in place a mechanism to monitor the implementation of the Scheme on various physical and financial parameters with pre-defined outcomes for improving the overall quality of various activities of the teacher education institutions.

National Curriculum Framework on Teacher Education

The National Council of Teacher Education (NCTE) has prepared the National Curriculum Framework of Teacher Education, which was circulated in March 2009. This Framework has been prepared in the background of the

NCF, 2005 and the principles laid down in the Right of Children to Free and Compulsory Education Act, 2009 which necessitated an altered framework on Teacher Education which would be consistent with the changed philosophy of school curriculum recommended in the NCF, 2005.

While articulating the vision of teacher education, the Framework has some important dimensions of the new approach to teacher education, as under.

- Reflective practice to be the central aim of teacher education
- Student-teachers should be provided opportunities for self-learning, reflection, assimilation and articulation of new ideas;
- Developing capacities for self-directed learning and ability to think, be critical and to work in groups.
- Providing opportunities to student-teachers to observe and engage with children, communicate with and relate to children.

Reforms in Regulatory Framework

The National Council for Teacher Education (NCTE) was constituted under the National Council for Teacher Education Act, 1993 for achieving planning and coordinated development of teacher education in the country, for regulation and proper maintenance of norms and standards in the teacher education system. In the recent past the NCTE has undertaken various steps for systemic improvements in its functioning and in improving the teacher education system, as under:

1. Based on the study of demand and supply of teachers and teacher educators of the various states, the NCTE has decided not to receive further applications for several teacher education courses in respect of 13 States. This has led to substantial rationalisation in the demand-supply situation across States;
2. The Regulations for grant of recognition and norms and standards for various teacher education courses were revised and notified on 31st August, 2009. The applications for grant of recognition are now processed strictly in chronological order. The new Regulations make the system more transparent, expedient and time bound, with reduction in discretionary powers of the Regional Committees;
3. E-Governance system has been introduced by way of providing online facility for furnishing of applications and online payment of fees. MIS has been developed to streamline the process of recognition;
4. The National Curriculum Framework for Teacher Education has been developed keeping in view NCF, 2005;

5. Academic support is being provided through preparation of Manual for the teacher education institutions and publication and dissemination of Thematic Papers on Teacher Education.
6. Various quality control mechanisms have been developed, including re-composition of the Visiting Teams, periodical monitoring of the teacher education institutions and de-recognition of institutions not conforming to the Norms and Standards prescribed by the NCTE.

Teacher Education in the Present (12th FYP-2012-17):

There are large numbers of teacher vacancies in the school system. An estimated 12.58 lakh (5.64 lakh old and 6.94 lakh newly sanctioned under SSA) vacancies exist at the elementary level. These are mainly accounted for by six States: UP (3.12 lakh), Bihar (2.62 lakh), West Bengal (1.81 lakh), MP (0.89 lakh), Chhattisgarh (0.62 lakh) and Rajasthan (0.51 lakh). Several States in the North, East and North-Eastern regions have an acute problem of untrained teachers. Therefore, pre-service and in-service training of teachers needs to be mounted on a mission mode during the Twelfth Plan. In particular, modular teacher training programmes should be developed so that para-teachers can attend training courses during the summer and winter vacations and get formally qualified over a three- to five-year period. In-service training using technology and innovative delivery methods could address the problem of poor quality of existing teachers.

Justice Verma Commission submitted their report on August 2012 to the government. The commission has suggested valuable suggestions to government for quality teacher education programmes in India. Because of Verma Commission report the NCTE has given directions to all the state governments to implement new curricula along with new duration of the different courses. The UPA-II government has given more importance for teacher education India. The present NDA government also is giving first priority for teacher education. The UGC has issued a notice to all the central universities to start teacher education department at the earliest.

Teacher Education in the Future:

The future of the teacher education of India depends on the past and the present of teacher education. Based on the existing system of teacher education programmes in India, the performance of teacher educators is not up to the mark. The whole system of teacher education is facing problems regarding quality and quantity. The present NDA government is going to launch New Education Policy soon. The future of teacher education depends mainly on the New Education Policy. Hope that, the New Education Policy will look all the issues which mentioned in the past and the present of teacher education in India.

Suggestions

By keeping the problems which mentioned earlier the investigators are suggested the following suggestions for quality teacher education in India with special reference to New Education Policy. The suggestions are:

- For quality teacher education it is the duty of government to encourage teacher education colleges to apply for NAAC.
- The public/people participation in teacher education is lagging. There is a need to strengthen this participation for effective implementation of teacher education programmes.
- The performance of private teacher education colleges (not all) is not up to the mark. It is better to take over these colleges by government/s for the interest of nation.
- It is good to pay salaries which collected from private college managements to teacher educators of private colleges through government treasuries.
- It is not good to continue recognition of teacher education colleges which are not conducting classes regularly.
- The list of teacher educators is not available in the website of NCTE. NCTE should be maintained and update the information regarding teacher educators in the NCTE website.
- NCTE wants to take necessary steps to strengthen the quality of teacher education by providing necessary teaching-learning materials to all the teacher education colleges in India.
- There is an urgent need to establish NCTE regional offices at different regions of India.
- Government should be taken steps to stop or minimize corruption in teacher education programmes.
- There is a need to establish a separate grievance cell to solve the problems of teacher educators and student-teachers.
- It is important to organize orientation programme and refresher course at Human Resource Development Centres for better examination and evolution reforms of teacher education programmes.
- Government should be taken necessary steps to link teacher education programme with employment opportunities.

Conclusion

The present situation of teacher education programmes in India is not up to the mark. The quality of teacher education is coming down day by day. The private college managements (not all) are not taking necessary steps to strengthen the quality of teacher education. The main motto of private college managements of teacher education colleges is profit. In the field of teacher education in India, the LPG concept was not supported positively. There are so many un-solved problems in the field of teacher education in India. Without solving the present problems, it is difficult and impossible to provide quality teacher education for the welfare of nation. There are so many committees and commission on teacher education in India and many organizations are also working for the teacher education at national and state levels. When compared to developed countries, India is still at an initial stage to provide all the necessary things to teacher education programmes. The upcoming New Education Policy may take care to strengthen teacher education in India. Without strengthening the teacher education programmes, it is not possible to provide quality education for all the students in the country. Under Hon'ble Prime Minister of India, Mr. Narendra Modi the New Education Policy will take necessary steps to strengthen the existing teacher education with quantity wise and quality wise.

❐

53

Problems and Prospective in Distance Education in India in the 21^Ist^ Century

The term distance education received a formal recognition in 1982 when the four decades old international council for correspondence education was renamed as the international council for distance education. The old concept of distance education was exclusively associated with print materials, whereas the new concept of distance education includes supplementary material being used through non-print media such as radio, television, computers, laptops, recorded lectures in mpeg and AVI formats in CDs and DVDs and self learning materials (SLM) through projectors, video conferencing and interactive sessions between students and synchronous and a synchronous are the two types of distance education. Synchronous method requires face to face participation of the student. The interaction is done in "real time" and has immediacy whereas asynchronous does not require simultaneous participation.

The objective of correspondence education is to provide an alternative method of education to enable a large number of persons with necessary aptitude to acquire further knowledge and improve their professional competence. correspondence courses are thus intended to cater for (a) students who had to discontinue their formal education owing to pecuniary and other circumstances; (b) students in geographically remote areas; (c) students who had to discontinue education because of lack of aptitude and motivation but who may later on become motivated; (d) students who cannot find a seat or do not wish to join a regular college or university department although they have the necessary qualifications to pursue higher education; and (e) individuals who look upon education as a life -time activity and may either like to refresh their knowledge in an existing discipline or to acquire knowledge in a new area.

Advantages of Distance Education

- It saves a lot of time, money and energy by cutting down on travel. The time saved can be judiciously used for personal and professional life.
- You can work at your own convenience: since all the classes are asynchronous, you have the liberty to review your assignments or do your homework during off- hours or at home.
- Videos a lot of flexibility to professionals, especially if they have a travelling job.
- It's easily accessible to all through online classes, online resources, virtual class- rooms, video conferencing with the particular subject lecturer, study materials provided at the right time and so on the increased use of the internet has facilitated distance education in more than one way.

Disadvantages of Distance Education

- You have to juggle between job and studies.
- It does not offer immediate feedback from the learners and instructors.
- It leads to social isolation: most often you'll be studying alone.
- Students pursuing distance education tend to be less seriousness.
- There its lack of interaction and motivation.

Problem of Research

The distance education is analyzed as a problematic conception in social reality. Because of the educational facts, it has been realized many radical changes in modern era that could be rated as revaluation. New technologies develop continuously distance education models, so it must be expected new revolutions become reality. However, rapid change in social reality causes to lose structural balances and to prevent benefits of distance education.

Distance education and technology are contributing to this general fact. Interactions between people and society make education institutionalized and develop technology. The most important factor in new knowledge society is to use new technologies in education. It speeds up the process of social mobility, and condenses socialization. In conclusion, researches in the field of distance education should cover all social units in which socialization is in question.

In order to describe the technologies used in distance education, we have selected "the 4-square map of Groupware options" that was developed by

Johansen et al. (1991) which is based on recent research in groupware (see fig.1). This model seemed most suitable to our purpose, because we see distance education moving from highly individualized forms of instruction, as in correspondence education, to formats that encourage teaching students as a group and collaborative learning among peers. The "4-square map of groupware option" model is premised on two basic configurations that teams must cope with as they work: time and place. Teams or groups of people who work together on a common goal deal with their work in the same place at the same time as in face-to-face meetings, and sometimes they must work apart in different places and at different times, as in the use of asynchronous computer conferencing. They also need to handle two other variations: being in different places at the same time, as in the use of telephones for an audio teleconference, and at the same place at different times, as in workplaces, study centres, or laboratories.

Distance education in India had its genesis in the early 1960s. it started as correspondence education - a supplementary method of education to meet the growing demand for higher education. Since then it has expanded rapidly, particularly over the last two decades. In 2005, there were 12 open universities [including the Indira Gandhi National Open University - (IGNOU)] and 106 dual mode university distance education institutes / centres in the country, catering to over 2.8 million students. At present, there are 13 state open universities, 127 dual mode universities and 9 institutions conducting distance education programmes of which IGNOU has the lion's share of enrolment of 2.5 million students so far. Each year, nearly 1.3 million students register for various courses in these universities and institutions. This is an economical and a quick way of increasing enrolment in higher education. The present research is carried out scientifically to suggest why the enrolment and passed out ratio has decreased tremendously for the last three years and to give positive recommendations to implement the system.

Methodology of Research

General Background of Research

Based on their operations, popularity of courses and study centres the distance education institutes analyses the following parameters.

- Resources' & Reach
- Learning & experience

As of now the available data of 10 distance education institutes are taken into consideration based on their enrolment, study materials efficiency, personal contact programmes and Learning technology.

1. **Resources' & Reach**
   The parameters used in this involves number of faculties/total students admitted, number of academic counsellors / total students admitted, number of study centres or student support centres / total students admitted, number of courses offered, current enrolment, and active enrolment / years in existence.
2. **Learning & Experience**
   In learning and experience the parameters considered are the quality of course material in SLM format (self-learning material), e-learning platform, quality of e-learning platform (verifying by testing), telephone counselling availability (include effective tool-free nos.), quantum of audio visual study materials created, exam schedule, responsiveness (student friendliness & forthcoming), and personal contact programmes (PCP).
3. **Result & Efficiency**
   The parameters used in result & efficiency are: pass ratio, transparency, unique features/ special projects/seminar, validity of course certificates, and job opportunities.

Sample of Research

Out of 149 institutes which vary in size, reach, quality and efficiency and with different curriculum and syllabus the data of 10 selected institutes has been taken based on the quantitative and qualitative parameters as explained earlier. (Refer Table 2).

Data Analysis

The HRD ministry annual report reveals the following student's data. We have taken these data for a comparative study.

TABLE. 53.1: Progress Overview During 2009-10

Total Enrolment in Universities and Colleges	136.42 lakhs
University Departments	16.69 lakhs (12.24%)
Affiliated Colleges	119.73 lakhs (87.76%)
Enrolment in Distance learning	30 lakhs
Enrolment of Women	65.49 lakhs
Intake in Technical Education Degree Diploma	14.10 lakhs & 5.09 lakhs
Institutions in Technical education Degree level Diploma level	7272 & 2324
Number of Universities	504
Number of Colleges	25,951
Faculty	5.89 lakhs

Academic Staff Colleges	66
National Assessment and Accreditation Council as on 28 March 2010, assessed	4094 Colleges and 159 Universities

Source: Annual Report, MHRD, 2009-10

TABLE. 53.2: Student's Enrolment Data from Various Distance Education Universities & Institutes.

S. No.	Name of the University/Institutes	Total Enrolment up to Dec.2010
1.	Indira Gandhi National OpenUniversity, New Delhi	3200000
2.	YCM Open University, Nasik	2432000
3.	Dr.B.R.Ambedkar Open University, Hyderabad	465000
4.	Delhi University, Delhi	322000
5.	Tamil Nadu Open University,Chennai	250000
6.	M.P. Bhoj University, Bhopal	205000
7.	Sikkim Manipal University, Gangtok	185000
8.	Annamalai University,Annamalai Nagar	179000
9.	Maulana Azad National Urudu University Hyderbad	169000
10.	University of Madras	15000

Source: Rrom the Respective Websites of the Universities & Institutes.

TABLE. 53.3: Top 9 Courses in Distance Education Mode in India

S.No	Name of the Course	Duration	Institute/University
1.	BA in Applied Sign Language Studies	3 Years	IGNOU,New Delhi
2.	M.Com in Business Policy and Corporate Governance	2 Years	IGNOU, New Delhi
3.	MA in Participatory Development	2 Years	IGNOU, New Delhi
4.	MSc in Dietetics and Food Service Management (DFSM)	2 Years	IGNOU,New Delhi
5.	M.Sc in Geoinformatics	2 Years	Annamalai University
6.	BSc in Visual Communication	3 Years	Annamalai University
7.	Certificate Course in Employability Skills	2 Years	IMT Jodhpur
8.	MS in Cyber Law and Security	91 Hours	IGNOU,New Delhi
9.	MBA in Shipping and Logistics	2 Years	TNOU,Chennai

Source: Careers360 Magazine of OUTLOOK

Discussion

India is the pioneer in the innovative course in the distance education mode. As seen in table 3 the innovative courses offered in India through distance education mode is most welcome irrespective of fees. For example: the general fee for MBA programme in all universities is Rs.10, 000(220 USD) per year. But, for MBA in shipping and logistics it costs about Rs.30, 000(660 USD) per year because of its industrial orientated curriculum and job assurity. Moreover country's biggest management B Schools offer distance education at a cost of Rs.20, 000(440 USD) to Rs.60, 000(1320 USD) per year.

According to the national Knowledge commission the achievement of target of 15% of GER (General enrolment ratio) by the end of the 11th five year plan and 20% by the end of the 12th five year plan. Thus, many trends in higher education will influence the future of distance learning. Student enrolments are growing to surpass the capacity of traditional infrastructures. Learner profiles are changing, and students are shopping for education that meets their needs.

Conclusion

In response to these trends, distance learning may rise to meet student needs and overcome funding challenges that traditional institutions cannot. Distance education administrators must resolve concerns with faculty and university administrators to ensure adequate support, as well as to develop the needed course management systems and teaching strategies. Technological advances and increased fluency will continue to open opportunities for distance education. Although higher education institutions are changing to favour distance education, the complexities of major transformations will require patience.

❐

54

Role of Distance Education in Society

By the development of the technology, every styles of life and human being action face with changes. Fast, global and remarkable time come to be considerable. People can reach fast, useful information through the computer based system. Social, global, cultural, educational competitiveness have been changed by the implication of the technology. Therefore; these changes also affect the learning styles, duration and method of individuals. People start to search for fast, accountable, home atmosphere knowledge learning instead of the classical learning in class rooms. Distance Education refers the interactive, educational process between two people, student and teacher, separated by the physical distance . Distance Education requires to be interested in learner's individual differences and in the way students reacts to the media.

The Role of the Distance Education in Twenty-One Century

Therefore; in learning process also personality features, intellectual abilities, cognitive and learning styles are important concern in distance education (Harry et al., 1993). The role of the distance education in twenty-one century can be summarized as that distance education programs catch the huge popularity in the educational world with having and spreading discussible sides. Therefore; the concrete questions come to mind of us what distance education is. From the teacher-centered campus, students reach immediate course application through the internet that there can be huge distance among the students and teacher interaction by distance education. If the main concepts are the science and technology today's context, these concepts leads all fields to be fast, global implementation. The educational fields should catch the new effective tool of the world with the existence of distance education.

The development of the learning through distance learning-education based on the individualistic learning process which means that learner reach the knowledge by research on computer assisted programmes under the fast, comfortable conditions individually for catching stable learning rather than lecturing method. Distance Education is really related by the discovery of truth for gaining antithesis sides of the thoughts to get the exact knowledge (Willis, 2002). Distance educators refer to three distinct applications of computer to the home study environment. These applications are Computer Managed Instruction, Computer Aided Learning and Computer Conferencing. Computer Managed Instruction is management that facilitates the administration of learning process. It can provide electronic counselling of students, on-line registration, institutional record keeping, tracking of student progress. Computer Aided Learning includes software applications to teach students through pre-structured and programmed materials, different subjects, and concepts matter. This courseware either replaces or supplements material which students are expected to get through other media (print, television, audio cassette). This falls into two categories like tutorials and simulation. Computer Conferencing is the name given to an electronic network that enables individuals to communicate via computers in delayed synchronic time either as a group or between two individuals or with database. In its simplest form, distance educators to allow speedy and effective two-way communication between instructor and student have used electronic mail. This provides discussion atmosphere to clarify problems. People who have roles in distance education can be categorized in four subtitles; a-Students:

Teacher has role to guide the students.c-Designer Groups: These responsibilities are the real establishers of process in the distance education whatever they are not in the visual representation of distance education. They are the responsible to design material, cyber and digital environment for the effective teaching-learning atmosphere. d- Directors: In the all institutes, there are people who plan this kind of education and implementers the education process

Importance Roles of Students and Teachers

Distance Education, or earning a degree online is a rapidly growing industry already slated to be worth billions. While many people waste countless hours surfing on the net looking at nothing more than garbage, many people are investing their time into new ways of improving their education. Many people and institutes of higher education are embracing this new revolution. When the aim of the research considered, it can be noticed that roles of teacher and students are really defined and effectiveness of them are evaluated in distance education by the related required researches. In that subject what are the roles of teachers and students in learning through distance education makes us to evaluate role and effectiveness on learning and training. Distance Education also requires professionalism on any subject training to individualism.

Therefore; it supports individual learning by dealing the education with different subjects, fields to qualified people or to do qualified people. Distance Education is the new revolution of education that eliminates distance, time and financial accounts on education. This subject requires considering on exchanging information, arguing, commending, expanding data between student and teacher for reaching stable learning.

Findings and Comments

Distance Education requires individualistic learning process that learner can reach knowledge from the computer-assisted programs. With the development of the high technology, people look for fast, easy, no time, space extension education opportunities to catch educational standards based on the global worldwide. Distance Education comes to today's' education view as an alternative. Through the distance education, roles of the students and teachers are the main considerations with the parallel thinks with the classical education standards. It is assumed that Internet based technology have great power on permanent learning, education can be easier than classical learning through distance education by emphasizing self-learning than teaching, self-responsibility should be occurred whatever there is distance and there is no face to face communication. Distance Education regards particular fee, Distance Education automatically creates concrete rules and roles for communicators.

According to findings and comments of the research, it can be carried to the conclusion that students and teachers reflect their roles as self-responsible, individualistic communicators and self-evaluators on their actual performance that can come up with some kind of communicational barriers. Learning in high technological, global world presents many roles and responsibilities for both teacher and learner. In addition to this; there is a radical change in construction and delivery of course content. The use of interaction between and among learners, teachers, content promises to increase opportunities and experience of deep and meaningful learning. There should be constructivist transaction between learning teaching that student-teacher roles are so important in distance education. Isman (1999) requires constructivist approach on learning for being interactive within teaching learning transaction. Constructivist approach also relate with self-development of students beside the learning and teaching activities. Students should search and design their activities according to their selfexperience on the subject and construct all activities under the sense of evaluation (Isman, 1997).

In the constructivist approach, student is the centre of the instruction to be an active role in learning by the support of the technology. For making learning easy and making learning products permanent, technology is the main concern. Technology requires increasing the attention of the students to the subjects and enhancing motivational cues, helping to remember the subjects. Constructivist Approach that includes the technology support requires learning by doing philosophy of learning for students. The technology, self development of students and learning by searching through the technological implementation carry us to think constructivist approach as a part of the distance education.

Teacher Role in Distance Education Based on Constructivist Approach

1. **Teacher should be in Consciousness of learner Autonomy:** Teachers should inform be aware of the individual differences of them.
2. **Teacher should use Real and Current Information to Transmit knowledge:** In other words, teacher should be well educated and on going researcher in order to reflect information and give concrete update examples and summarizes about subjects for the permanent learning of the students.
3. **Teachers should give the Importance of thoughts of Students:** They should posses the research environment to the students in order to search and evaluate their experiences on content under the sense of self-regulation.
4. Teachers should be aware on the individual differences of the students and design course materials based on this consciousness.
5. Teachers should know the students prerequisite skills on the content to build new knowledge construction. In addition to this; teacher should know the how learner can learn based on strategies.
6. Teachers are the main communicators to establish interaction between the teacher and students. Teacher should have technological, communicational skills to implement distance education effectively.

Student Role in Distance Education Based on Constructivist Approach

1. Students should be in interaction between teacher in order to get proper feedback on their self-directed subjects and consult to teacher for correctness and evaluation. Students can be in collaborative learning with their class members through the technological support.
2. **Students are Self-Responsible on their learning:** They should decide what they want to learn and make individual study on their subject.
3. Students should come to the solutions for problems with data through the research instead of implementing available data. Therefore they should be researcher.
4. **Students should be Problem Solver:** They should implement what they learn on problems and set solutions strategies with using relevance information.
5. Students should be well informed from the technology to not face with communicational barriers because of technology. In addition to this; they should use technology to construct the learning with rich materials.

❐

55

Major Principles for Curriculum Planning

Teaching-learning of any subject depends upon its curriculum. Curriculum is a Latin word which means the 'race course' or a 'run-way', which one takes to reach a goal. Thus, a curriculum is the instructional and educative programme through which the pupils achieve their goals, ideals and aspirations of life. Cunningham says, "Curriculum is a tool in the hands of the artist (the teacher) to mould his material (the pupil) in accordance with his ideals in his studio (the schools)" (qtd. in Kochhar 66). The curriculum however cannot be considered synonymous with courses of study, although they form an important part of curriculum. The Syllabus and Curriculum are central to any course of study. Different people look for different outcomes from this.

Principles of Curriculum Planning

1. A good curriculum is one that helps in the harmonious development of personality. There should be provision of a large number of activities which have their impact on the personality of the individual.
2. Curriculum should be based on the interest, needs and requirements of the learners. It has to be broad based and not narrowly conceived one. It should be of flexible type. Any amendment or change should be adopted.

3. It should suit to the learner's entry level as well as the desired terminal level of learning. It involves the selection and gradation of linguistic items like vocabulary, structures, and functions.
4. Curricula are divided into various stages like primary, secondary, tertiary and so on. Each stage of learning is assigned a specific period of time. For instance, in some parts of India primary education is for five years; secondary for another five years and higher secondary for two years. Each stage is visualised in relation to the other stages.
5. As children learn new things, they tend to forget what they learnt already. It is therefore necessary to consolidate earlier and arrive at a blend of the old and the new. Such consolidation ensures revision and reinforcement of what has been learnt earlier. Learning is thus envisaged as a cycle.
6. Curriculum must have correlation, this is also known as horizontal integration, and involves the simultaneous handling of various aspects of learning, for example, the skills of listening, speaking, reading and writing. What is taught in the speaking lesson may have to be related to the writing lesson, so that learners are able to view the learning phenomenon as a complete experience rather than as a number of isolated parts.
7. It should make provision for flexibility within a framework of acceptable principles and values. It must be socially and personally relevant to the reader. It is necessary that it is flexible and dynamic and able to keep pace with the rapidly expanding frontiers of knowledge in science and technology and the changing socio-economic conditions of our society.
8. Curriculum should be related to the life needs and aspirations of the people. It will become an instrument of social change if it is related to national integration, social justice, and productivity, modernisation of the society and cultivation of normal and spiritual values.
9. Curriculum should be able to develop a rational outlook. Subjects like Science and Mathematics can go a long way in giving children modern knowledge, developing their curiosity, teaching them the scientific method of participation in a changing society and culture. These will develop a rational outlook among the pupils.
10. Curriculum should lay emphasis on learning to live rather than on living to learn. It should be useful to act as a source of strength and inspiration to an individual in solving life's problems and meeting life's situations. It must aim at making him fit for life and the world and teach pupils the way to utilize the sources of happiness which nature supplies and to use all these facilities to the greatest advantage to him and others.

11. Curriculum should make provision for socially useful productive work. Socially useful productive work needs to be provided to enable the pupils to develop insight into the material phenomena and human relationships involved in any organised productive work, and develop the attitudes necessary for cooperative accomplishment of talks and discharging of social responsibility within a framework of equality as well as of the freedom of the human spirit.
12. Curriculum should be able to promote social justice, democratic values and national integration. It should be designed to develop tolerance, friendship, cooperation and peace between nations.
13. Curriculum should make adequate provision for the study of languages. Languages need to be taught to the pupils to develop a catholicity of outlook and an appreciation of the basic values.
14. Curriculum should make provision for artistic experience and expression. Ample opportunity must be provided to each one to preserve and develop his originality and creative talents and make use of his gifts, aptitudes and personal form of expression.
15. Curriculum should make provision for physical development. Provision for strengthening the body and developing its skills and capacities, training the muscles and nerves, cultivating the senses and inculcating hygienic and proper dietary habits is to be developed.
16. Curriculum should make provision for character building and human values. It can be framed in a manner to centre round the objective of character building like discovering their potentials, expressing themselves and finding self-fulfilment. It should cultivate the basic qualities of compassion, endurance, courage, decision making, resourcefulness, respect for others, the team spirit, truthfulness, faithfulness, loyalty to duty and the common good.
17. Curriculum should provide both for uniformity and variety. It should help to develop the common as well as the uncommon. It should help to compare and contrast, to get at the truth, to be sceptical of angled; reporting, to resist the sits of the hidden persuaders, to appreciate that racial differences can be explained by history and geography, to be critical of society and to arrive at reasoned judgement.
18. Curriculum should provide for continuity in the whole programme. The continuity must be vertical as well as horizontal. Vertical continuity means using a sequence of subject matter from class one vertically up through class twelve. For horizontal continuity all of the subjects must be correlated. The educational process must be so close that an operating unit is perceived.

19. Curriculum should be well integrated. It is very necessary to enable pupil to correlate their experiences in study, recreation, life and in the realms of the spirit; to cultivate in them single minded ness, as well as like mindedness; to present to them the knowledge of material, moral and spiritual things as one and not as three; to confirm their education with coherence and continuity from subject to subject, from work to plan, from class to class, from school, and from school to school work; to establish an intimate relationship between what is taught and done.
20. Principle of utility is an important aspect of curriculum. The learner has to be benefited. His family, society and nation also should benefit along with him. Therefore, the framer of the curriculum should see to it very carefully that the curriculum is really a useful one.

Conclusion

A good curriculum is the cooperative effort of children and teachers and helps to solve the problems the children face in the school and outside the school. The experiences are suited to the age of the learner, the emotional, physical and intellectual maturity of the learner and his previous experiences and learning. Curriculum for teaching of English need be revolutionised. The above mentioned easy steps could be followed to frame a better Curriculum. It must include practical as well as theoretical aspects of teaching English. Keeping the different aims of teaching English in view, suitable type of programmes is chalked out by language experts.

❐

56

Issues Concerning Gender Inequalities in Education

Education is the most powerful instrument to enhance capabilities of an individual and to achieve the desired objectives for the social and economic development of a country. Education enables individuals to broaden their horizons and provide opportunities to raise voice in decision making. Unfortunately, since independence, women in India remained marginal beneficiaries of the Education system. Gender inequality remains a serious problem for all the developing countries, where majority of women have been sufferers of social, cultural, political and environmental impacts of development. Lack of education is the most vital cause behind these inequalities.

Achieving gender equality in education implies equality of opportunities for women in relation to men, equality in learning process, equality in outcomes as well as equality in external results after leaving education (UNESCO, 2004). Gender equality in education implies that girls and boys are ensured and actually offered the same chance and treatment in access, process and outcomes of an educational system of good quality and which is free from any stereotypes (UNESCO, 2009). Over the past several years, the movement towards gender equality gained momentum in countries throughout the world (Elson, 2002). Worldwide commitment to gender equality in education was reflected in Dakar Framework of Action on 'Education for All' (EFA-2000) and Millennium

Development Goals (MDGs 2000). The two development frameworks under their gender and educational specific related goals insisted on elimination of gender disparities in all levels of education by 2015. But even today, Gender equality remained a dream.

Women Empowerment

Women empowerment is (a result of) a process of women identifying their inner strength, opportunities for growth, and their role in reshaping their own destiny (Saraswathy, et al. 2008). According to Malhotra et al., (2002) women empowerment has frequently been termed as a process of women gaining more access to a steady income and economic power or security. UN WOMEN (2014) defined women empowerment as a bottom up process of transforming gender power relations through individuals or groups developing awareness of women's subordination and building their capacity to challenge it.

Open and Distance Learning (ODL)

Open and Distance Learning is an approach to learning that focuses on freeing learners from constraints of the time, space and place while offering flexible learning opportunities (SADC, 2012). It aims at including greater dimensions of openness and flexibility, whether in terms of access, curriculum or other elements of structure (UNESCO,2002). The first Open University was established in 1969 in United Kingdom in which first students enrolled in 1971. The idea behind was to bring high quality in learning to the people who had not got the opportunities to study in formally set up universities. Open universities provides diplomas & degrees in education through their open enrollment, distance and internet based education programmes. Dr. B.R. Ambedkar University was the first Distance Education University established in 1982 in Hyderabad, India. In the present times, open universities have become an invaluable component of National Education Programmes and policies in both developed and developing countries. Information and Communication Technologies (ICTs) play an important role in empowering women in the developing countries of the world. Distance education has proved as an advantage to women to prove their abilities through acquisition of knowledge, leading towards new ways of thinking and to be autonomous and liberated.

Role of Education in Eempowering Women

Education is a fundamental right for all individuals in the society and all of them should be benefitted equally without any discrimination based on sex, creed or religion. But according to the data based on literacy levels of the whole world, there is a significance difference between men and women. According to UNESCO, literacy rate of women are found very low as compared to the literacy rate of men particularly in South Asia. Government explores the use of distance education to provide education at large scale because of expensive conventional educational methods. This also results in excluding of marginalized groups i.e. women who cannot cope up with regular campus based learning.. According to Malik, Belawati and Baggaley (2005), Distance education has been exercising its influence on education at all levels. Open universities are powerful instruments for equalizing opportunities in higher education and also for eliminating educational imbalances (Plummer, 2000; Satyanarayana and Meduri, 2013). Learning takes place outside the schools, colleges and university campuses in Distance Education and communication is provided through Radio, Television, Print Media, Internet, Whats app, Skype etc. and there is absence of formal lectures (Janaki, 2006). According to Kwapong (2007), Distance mode of study suites women because of their discharging different roles as mothers, housewives and employees in some Government, Quasi-government or private organization. Further the distance mode provides flexible time and prevents them from regular classroom attendance.

Vocational Education Programmes for Empowering Women

A number of Vocational Education Programmes have been designed by various open universities to enhance the knowledge and skills of students for their immediate employment. These programmes are primarily helpful for the under privileged sections of the country, as they have to shoulder many domestic responsibilities. These days Internet has also become a tool of empowerment of women. There is also growing access of Web these days which has resulted in empowering women by using various tools on the internet. Women have begun to access various social networking sites like Facebook, Twitter etc. for Online Activism which has empowered them to organize campaigns and also in voicing their opinions for equality rights. Blogging has also become a powerful tool in recent years for the educational empowerment of women. Electronic Learning (e-learning) has made easy accessibility and affordability for women as they can study from their homes.

Information and Communication Technologies (ICTs) for Gender equality

Information and Communication Technology (ICT) touches all parts of life including education. The impact of ICT in education can be felt strongly by observing the uses of ICT tools, such as multiple media, in teaching. These ICT tools support the predominant print media being used by the ODL system. The current multiple media being used by the ODL system include audio and video cassette tapes, CD-ROM, interactive radio, television, teleconferencing, video-conferencing, online teaching through multimedia and instruction delivery through iPods. Computer Assisted Instruction (CAI) is one of the important distance education approaches.

Conclusion

Apart from the regular stream of Formal education, Open and Distance Learning mode of Education has enabled women to have access of functional training, made them self-reliant and trained them to meet the demand of the social system. Distance Education has great potential to equalize opportunities for women and it is an important milestone in the development of Higher Education. Open and Distance Learning is a way of fulfilling women's educational aspirations to meet obligations of the career and the society. It is, therefore, regarded as a tool that enables women to access education and to overcome the various obstacles. This ultimately results in achieving gender equality in education.

❐

57

Online Professional Development of In-Service Teacher of H.Edu. through Swayam

The term professional development, on the other hand, is usually used to encompass 'all types of learning undertaken by teachers beyond the point of their initial training' (Craft, 2000). The term is used to refer to processes, actions and activities which are designed for the purpose of enhancing the teachers' professional knowledge, teaching skills and attitudes in teaching to improve students' learning (Guskey, 2000). Teacher training usually involves providing training in curriculum subjects to teachers by organizing workshops over periods of time. Cambridge Professional Development Qualifications (2014) recognize the importance of teacher training and professional development by stating that, "The most important factor in the quality of students' learning is the quality of teaching and school leadership. Teachers and leaders need to develop their professional thinking and practice continuously throughout their careers."

Teacher Professional Development

As teachers we all know that learning about educational practice in general and teaching in specific is an ongoing activity. The field of educational practice is ever emerging and hence there is always something new to learn. Most of us start learning about our profession through a formal teacher preparation program. Since, any such preparation is incomplete without practicing the profession, the learning continues even after starting the practice of teaching. Additionally, it is not practical to expect to learn everything through formal learning in an ever emerging field like teaching. Starting from the initial teacher preparation program to ongoing teacher learning activities, teacher professional development can be seen as a continuum. It is in this sense the teacher professional development is defined as follows:

Teacher Professional Development (TPD) is 'a systematized, initial and continuous, coherent and modular process of professional development of educators in accordance with professional competency standards and frameworks'. Teacher professional development would also include training in the adaptation to the evolution of change of the profession of teachers and managers of education systems.

From the definition we understand that it consists of systematic activities with clear purpose. The purposes are concurrent with the needs of teachers that arise from time to time. With the evolution of professional practice, the professional competency standards and frameworks that are to be developed in tune with the philosophies that govern the educational theory and practice. All these would happen on a continuous but in modular process, but always coherent when seen together. The course you are presently studying is an example of your professional development activity.

The teacher professional development is now a developing area in teacher education. There are different models that are in practice for this purpose. One model proposed by Hart J (2010) that speaks of workplace learning looks useful to understand various avenues for teacher professional development in the context of ICT.

Study Webs of Active –Learning for Young Aspiring Minds

SWAYAM is a programme initiated by Government of India and designed to achieve the three cardinal principles of Education Policy viz., access, equity and quality. The objective of this effort is to take the best teaching learning resources to all, including the most disadvantaged. SWAYAM seeks to bridge the digital divide for students who have hitherto remained untouched by the digital revolution and have not been able to join the mainstream of the knowledge economy.

- SWAYAM uses indigenously developed IT platform, facilitating hosting of all courses, taught in classrooms from Class 9 till post-graduation to be accessed by anyone, anywhere at any time.
- SWAYAM aims to provide interactive courses, prepared by best teachers in the country and are available free of cost to the residents in India. Over 1,000 specially chosen teachers from across the country have participated in preparing SWAYAM courses.

- Course format: SWAYAM courses are available on SWAYAM.gov.in website in four quadrants: video lecture, specially-prepared reading material that can be downloaded/printed, self-assessment tests through tests and quizzes and an online discussion forum for clearing the doubts.
- National coordinators: To ensure best quality content, seven national coordinators have been appointed. They are NPTEL for engineering, UGC for post-graduation education, CEC for under-graduate education, NCERT & NIOS for school education, IGNOU for out of the school students and IIMB for management studies.

This is done through an indigenous developed IT platform that facilitates hosting of all the courses, taught in classrooms from 9th class till post-graduation to be accessed by anyone, anywhere at any time. All the courses are interactive, prepared by the best teachers in the country and are available, free of cost to the residents in India. More than 1,000 specially chosen faculty and teachers from across the Country have participated in preparing these courses.

Annual Refresher Programme in Teaching

The Ministry of Human Resource Development, Government of India has invested significant amount of resources towards capacity building and enhancement of professional skills of faculty of higher education institutions under the scheme of Pandit Madan Mohan Malaviya National Mission on Teachers and Teaching (PMMMNMTT). Annual Refresher Programme in Teaching (ARPIT) is one such initiative, launched by MHRD on 13th November, 2018 with the objective of providing online courses in various disciplines for professional development of higher education faculty using the Massive open online courses (Mooc) platform SWAYAM.

For the implementation of ARPIT, 75 discipline-specific National Resource Centres (NRCs) have been identified to prepare online training material with focus on latest developments in the discipline including new & emerging trends, pedagogical improvements and methodologies for transacting revised curriculum.UGC has already granted equivalence to ARPIT courses at par with Refresher Courses for the purpose of Career Advancement Scheme.

Annual Refresher Programme in Teaching (ARPIT), a major and unique initiative of online professional development of 15 lakh higher education faculty using the MOOCs platform SWAYAM. For implementing ARPIT, 75 discipline-specific institutions have been identified and notified as National Resource Centres (NRCs) in the first phase, which are tasked to prepare online training material with focus on latest developments in the discipline, new & emerging trends, pedagogical improvements and methodologies for transacting revised curriculum.

The course is a 40 hour module with 20 hours of video content and 20 hours of non-video content. They are offered in a highly flexible format and can be done at one's own pace and time. There are built-in assessment exercises and activities as part of the academic progression in the course. At the end of the course, they will be a terminal assessment which can be either online or a written examination. All faculties who have successfully completed the online refresher course will be certified. The courses will remain open from 1stNovember, 2018 to 28th February, 2019. Till now, more than 30,000 teachers have enrolled to obtain online professional development training. Necessary regulations will be taken out by UGC, recognising the MOOCs based online refresher training of teachers for the CAS (Career Advancement Scheme).

The production of MOOCs courses by the teachers is also recognised for the CAS. This is expected to be a major incentive for the higher education faculty to undergo training through MOOCs courses and also to produce MOOCs courses.ARPIT will be an ongoing exercise so that every year NRCs will continuously develop new refresher module in their earmarked discipline each year. The training materials will be uploaded and made available through SWAYAM. NRC will publish the list of the faculty who have been certified. The NRCs will revolutionize professional development of faculty by catering to massive numbers by leveraging ICT and online technology platform of SWAYAM.

Conclusion

In an online course, teachers can take advantage of anytime, anywhere access to their instructor and their peers, participating on their own time, whether it is before, during or after working hour. By leveraging the Internet combined with a live teacher, instructors can benefit from high availability regardless of the day of the week or time of day. Online education inherently has a number of benefits that are attractive to teachers; however, not all professional development is created equal. Like anything, educators should choose experienced online learning providers for their professional development needs.

❒

58

ICT in Modern Education System: A Case Study

There is no doubt that technology in this contemporary society is used more and more widely, especially for the purpose of teaching and learning. This is because modern technology offers many tools that can be used in classrooms to improve teaching and learning quality (Bruniges, 2003; Lefebvre, Deaudelin, & Loiselle, 2006; Bingimlas, 2009; Hamidi et al., 2011; Hussain et al., 2011). Rosnaini Mahmud and Mohd Arif (2008) define ICT integration as the process of determining where and how technology fits in the teaching and learning scenario. It is able for everyone can enter the websites from everywhere at any time to use the free information by the internet. Worldwide research has shown that ICT can lead to improve students' learning as well as better pedagogical practices.

In addition, ICT has the potential in preparing students for life in the 21st century. Through learning ICT skills, students are ready to face future challenges based on proper understanding (Grimus, 2000). Bransford, Brown, and Cocking (2000) believe that ICT use can help students to develop the competencies needed for the current globalization. This is because ICT can help students to develop their skills, boost up their motivation and widen their knowledge and information (Grabe & Grabe, 2007; Hussain et al., 2011).

Integrating technology in education is a complex task due to its dynamic nature. Hence planning for ICT integration in education is considered as a key element for improvement and development. Previous research shows that due to the issues and challenges related to the use of learning technologies in the Malaysian education system, ICT integration and implementation is a complex process which requires strategic planning by the policy and decision makers (Hashim, 2007; Ghavifekr & Sufean, 2010; Zellweger, 2006).

ICT Integration in Education

Information and Communications Technologies (ICTs) have become the most basic building block of modern industrial society in a very short time. Mastering information technology and understanding basic skills and concepts of ICT are now highly regarded by many countries (Daniels, 2002; Rampersad, 2011). ICT has been increasing at an amazing rate in instruction among teachers.

The need for development of ICTs is a global resolution and has been a subject of great significance to all mankind (Olaofe, 2005). These technologies have become central to contemporary societies. Whether one is talking on the phone, sending an email, going to the bank, using a library, listening to sports coverage on the radio, watching the news on television, working in an office or in the field, going to the doctor, driving a car or catching a plane, one is using ICTs. These include: competence to make personal use of ICT in instruction, competence to master a range of educational paradigms that make use of ICT in instruction, sufficient competence to make use of ICTs as mind tools, competence to make use of ICT in instruction as a tool for teaching, competence in mastering a range of assessment paradigms which make use of ICT in instruction, competence in understanding the policy dimensions of ICT use in instruction for teaching and learning. The ICTs have the potentials not only in ensuring effectiveness and efficiency in these two areas of teaching and learning; but also in erasing the administrative duties.

Challenges in Implementing ICT

Infrastructure and Access

Infrastructure development remains the biggest constraint for the use of ICT in the education sector. The cost of equipment and bandwidth are barriers to entry for schools and, therefore, students. This is compounded by the major distribution disparity of infrastructure between the urban and rural areas. Schools in rural areas are most disadvantaged; most of the existing infrastructural resources are concentrated in the urban areas.

Lack of Resources

Most schools and even colleges have not factored in ICT development to their organisation's budget. The public schools are entirely dependent on the federal government plans to equip them with the various ICTs and on donations from well-wishers.

Awareness of the benefits of ICT

Lack of awareness of the benefits of ICT is a major hindrance to its adoption, especially within the education sector. Most rural communities in India, which form more than 80% of the population, have not woken up to the issues of the information society.

Language barrier

Unfortunately, a lot of content on the Internet is in English, which creates a barrier to the native language speaking population.

Discussion & Conclusion

The tremendous potential of ICT in promoting the learning outcome with more latest of knowledge without and obstruction on accessibility and distance limitation, and yet straighten students' thinking skills is undeniable (Education Blueprint, 2013). With ICT integration in the classroom, students will be able to engage in interactive tasks with a wider range of information and knowledge during their learning. At the same time, the teachers' beliefs and attitudes will influence them to integrate ICT in their teaching practice (Hatlevik & Arnseth, 2012; Rampersad, 2011). With the full support by Ministry of Education in integrating ICT in teaching, teachers will able to access updates and richer resources to improve their teaching practices. The teaching and learning with ICT specific in internet accessibility will make the teaching and learning knowledge borderless and create a virtual learning environment for both teachers and students.

The findings of this study indicate that most of the teachers in the India are more likely to use ICT applications and resources for educational purposes, such as the Internet, multimedia computer, projector system, PowerPoint presentation, or word processor programs during the teaching and learning process. At the same time, the advanced usage of ICT like build a learning website or creating learning software such as educational games appear to be rarely used in the teaching and learning process or even preparation for educational purposes.

❐

59

Awareness of E-Learning among the H.Sec.S. Students in Trichy District

Education can enable individuals to make personal responsibility for improving their own status and their community and nation. Computer is bringing some exciting innovations to education. It helps the individual to make over the most of the drudgery of schooling. Computer allocates learning resources to individuals and groups. Computer education provides easy access to files of information for reference and guidance. Computer education engages the students in tutorial, interacting and dialogue. E-learning is commonly referred to the intentional use of networked information and communications technology in teaching and learning. A number of other terms are also used to describe this mode of teaching and learning. They include online learning, virtual learning, distributed learning, network and web based learning.

E-Learning

The letter "e" in e-learning stands for the word "electronic", e-learning would incorporate all educational activities that are carried out by individuals or groups working online or offline, and synchronously or asynchronously via networked or standalone computers and other electronic devices. The computer is the gateway to information without frontiers, and the catalyst for teacher and student dialogs beyond the walls of a single class or school. Today, when a major effort is being invested in the transformation of the classroom, moving away from frontal, expository, didactic presentations to environments where learners are active discoverers and builders of knowledge, the computer is the tool with the potential to help in reaching these goals.

Need and Significance of the Study

Accepting the new things help the human being to develop their attitude on that field and helps them to succeed in the future needs. Day by day our technology improved a lot. Lot of drastic change occurs every day. We have to accept the change and live according to the situation. In order to bring effective improvement in the quality of education, it is necessary to focus attention on the new technologies. One such recent and most dominating technology is Computer Technology. Computer plays great revolution in every walk of life. But when we think about its development in the field of education, it is only in an infant stage. Now many people start thinking to add computer education curriculum at all possible ways. Hence it is important to study the awareness of E-Learning among Higher Secondary School Students. Hence the investigator made an attempt to study the e-learning awareness of Higher Secondary School Students.

Statement of the Problem

Awareness of E-Learning among the Higher Secondary School Students in Trichy District

Objectives of the Study

1. To find out the E-learning awareness among the higher secondary students.
2. To find out significant difference between the Higher Secondary School Students with respect to e-Learning Awareness based on their Gender.
3. To find out significant difference between the Higher Secondary School Students with respect to e-Learning Awareness based on their Location.
4. To find out significant difference between the Higher Secondary School Students with respect to e-Learning Awareness based on their Medium of study.
5. To find out significant difference between the Higher Secondary School Students with respect to e-Learning Awareness based on their Type of Management.

Hypothesis of the Study

1. There is no significant difference between the E-learning awareness among Higher Secondary School Students with respect to their Gender.
2. There is no significant difference between the E-learning awareness among Higher Secondary School Students with respect to their Location.

3. There is no significant difference between the E-learning awareness among Higher Secondary School Students with respect to their Medium of study.
4. There is no significant difference between the E-learning awareness among -Higher Secondary School Students with respect to their Type of management.
5. The awareness of E-learning among the higher secondary students is low.

Description of the Tool

Sample for the Study

The focus of this study is on Higher Secondary School Students in Trichy district. A simple random sampling technique was adopted for the selection of sample. The schools selected for this study are divided into different demographic variable as gender, location, medium of study and type of management. The sample size of this study is 300 students.

Level of E-Learning Awareness

Level	Score Range	Percentage
Low	0 – 40	18.33%
Average	41 – 80	62.24%
High	81- 120	19.43%

From the above table, the awareness level of E-learning among the higher secondary students is Average.

Hypothesis Testing

Null Hypothesis – 1

There is no significant difference between the e-learning awareness among Higher Secondary School Students with respect to their Gender.

TABLE. 59.1: The mean Scores of E-learning Awareness among the Higher Secondary School based on their Gender

Gender	N	Mean	S.D	't' Value	Level of Significance
Male	150	14.10	9.265	1.337	NS
Female	150	15.47	8.505		

From the above table, it is inferred that t- value (1.337) is less than the table value (1.96) at 0.05 level. Hence there is no significance difference between the Male and Female Higher Secondary School Students on their e-Learning Awareness. Therefore the above hypothesis is accepted.

Null Hypothesis – 2

There is no significant difference between the e-learning awareness among Higher Secondary School Students with respect to their Location.

TABLE. 59.2: The mean Scores of E-learning Awareness among the Higher Secondary School based on their Location

Location	N	Mean	S.D	't' Value	Level of Significance
Rural	180	13.38	8.96	3.42	S
Urban	120	16.89	8.43		

From the above table, it is inferred that t- value (3.42) is greater than the table value (1.96) at 0.05 level. Hence there is a significance difference between the Rural and urban area Higher Secondary School Students on their e-Learning Awareness. Therefore the above hypothesis is rejected.

Null Hypothesis – 3

There is no significant difference between the e-learning awareness among Higher Secondary School Students with respect to their Medium of study.

TABLE. 59.3: The mean Scores of E-learning Awareness among the Higher Secondary School based on their Medium of Study

Medium of Study	N	Mean	S.D	't' Value	Level of Significance
Tamil	150	30.28	7.23	2.95	S
English	150	40.35	9.56		

From the above table, it is inferred that t- value (2.95) is greater than the table value (1.96) at 0.05 level. Hence there is a significance difference between the Tamil and English medium Higher Secondary School Students on their e-Learning Awareness. Therefore the above hypothesis is rejected.

Null Hypothesis – 4

There is no significant difference between the e-learning awareness among Higher Secondary School Students with respect to their Type of Management.

TABLE. 59.4: The mean Scores of E-learning Awareness among the Higher Secondary School based on their Type of Management

Variable	Sum of Squares	DF	Mean Squares	'F' Value	Level of Significance	
E-Learning Awareness	Between Groups	64722.231	2	31574.721	10.591	S
	Within Groups	89432.450	297	2981.235		

From the above table, it is inferred that t- value (10.591) is greater than the table value (1.96) at 0.05 level. Hence there is a significance difference among the Government, Government Aided and Private Higher Secondary School Students on their e-Learning Awareness. Therefore the above hypothesis is rejected. Therefore it is considered for the further analysis.

TABLE. 59.4 (a). The Significance Difference of Type of Management of Higher Secondary School Students for E-Learning Awareness

Variable	Type of Management	N	Mean	SD	't' value	Level of Significance
E-Learning Awareness	Govt.	100	32.05	7.02	7.204	S
	Aided	100	55.23	24.25		
	Govt.	100	31.54	7.25	18.246	S
	Private	100	62.35	14.25		
	Aided	100	55.25	24.26	1.852	S
	Private	100	62.25	13.25		

From the above table, the t- value is found to be significant difference in the E-learning awareness of Higher Secondary School Students with respect to Government, Aided and Private Higher Secondary School Students at 0.05 level. Hence the Null hypothesis is rejected.

Findings

1. It is found that there exist no significance difference between the Male and Female Higher Secondary School Students on their E-Learning Awareness.
2. It is found that there exist is a significance difference between the Rural and Urban area Higher Secondary School Students on their E-Learning Awareness.
3. It is found that there exist is a significance difference between the Tamil and English medium Higher Secondary School Students on their e-Learning Awareness.
4. It is found that there exist is a significance difference among the Government, Government Aided and Private Higher Secondary School Students on their e-Learning Awareness.
5. The awareness level of E-learning among the higher secondary students is Average.

Suggestions for Further Research

The investigator has suggested the following topics for the future studies

1. Teacher Educators' Attitude towards Computer.
2. Investigating Pre-Service Early Childhood Teachers' Attitudes towards the Computer Based Education in Science Activities.

3. The Effects of Organizational Learning Environment Factors on E-Learning Acceptance.
4. The Effects of Education Compatibility and Technological Expectancy on E- Learning Acceptance.
5. Implementing Computer-Based Assessment Web-Based Mock Examination Changes Attitudes.

Conclusion

Computer technology has become so much a part of our lives that even imagining a day without it is now out of question. Even our enjoyment is being controlled by the computer technology. It can be regarded as the greatest contribution of science, a realization of the dream, "global village". Unfortunately, computers are used all too often in ways that are developmentally inappropriate. Young children are comfortable clicking various options to see what is going to happen next. Teachers may want to intervene when children appear frustrated or when nothing seems to be happening. Providing children with minimal help teaches them they can operate the computer successfully. In addition, by observing what children are doing, the teacher can ask probing questions or propose problems to enhance and expand children's computer experiences. The feature of the Nation depends upon the quality of Education. This will lead to bring the future students with deep knowledge in computers and make our nation.

❐

60

Communication Preferences among Distance Education Students

Education is the basic need of every human being and today's technology has a big part in every sphere of life. In fact, Education is the most important investment by countries,societies, families and individuals for the future. A communication network has become an essential tool in today's educationa environment than ever before. Today's society is said to have entered into the age of a new social revolution, i.e. 'Information revolution'.

What is ICT

Stands for "Information and Communication Technologies." ICT refers to technologies that provide access to information through Telecommunication. It is similar to Information Technology (IT), but focuses primarily on communication technologies. This includes the Internet, wireless networks, cell phones, and other communication mediums.

Distance Education

Distance education is defined as the practice of using correspondence, either written or virtual, to learn. With this practice, a teacher in New York could provide instruction to students all over the United States and the world. This helps students access teachers who may live geographically too far away to attend a class; it also assists students who cannot take classes during traditional hours because of work or other responsibilities.

Uses of in ICT Distance Education

ICT are a potentially powerful tool for extending educational opportunities, formal and non formal. ICTs also facilitate access to experts, resource persons, researcher, professionals, mentors, business leader, and peers- all over the world. For developing countries ICT have the potential for increasing access to and improving the relevance and quality of education. ICTs stand for information and communication technologies are defined, for the purpose of this primer, as a "diverse set of technological tools and resources used to communicate, and to create, disseminate, store and manage information."

Technology has become a part of our life on campus, at home, and modern technologies used in open and distance learning are telephone tutoring, teleconferencing, audio graphics, video conferencing, computer conferencing drill and practice, fiber optics, and videotext, multimedia and hypermedia CAI, e-books, the "Internet", the World Wide Web (WWW), or the "Information Super Highway" on-line database, on line discussion, call-in course- on demand, satellite, talk-back TV etc. All of these technologies should have a place in the knowledge base of expert teachers.

In the concept of new technology, distance learning provides multimedia- based education content to the student utilizing standard data networking, protocols and infrastructure. The main advantages of using technologies in distance education are cost effectiveness, independence of time and place, quality of education access resulting from the mass production of course materials, teaching a lot of students simultaneously, and finding a lot of educational resources.

Haddad and Draxler (2002) identify at least five levels of technology use education: presentation, demonstration, drill and practice, interaction, and collaboration. Each of the different ICT sprint, audio/video cassettes, radio and TV broadcasts, computers or the Internet—may be use for presentation and demonstration, the most basic of the five levels. Except for video technologies, drill and practice may likewise be performed using the whole range of technologies.

These include factors such as affordability, availability, access and the unique pedagogical characteristics of the particular technological application, instructional objectives financial resources available at the institution and student personal resources. The appropriate use of media and technology has provided information access to all students in remote, rural and urban areas as well as across nations.

Synchronous learning

Examples of synchronous e-learning are online chat and videoconferencing. Any learning tool that is in real-time, such as instant messaging that allows students and teachers to ask and answer questions immediately, is synchronous. Rather than learning on their own, students who participate in synchronous learning courses are able to interact with other students and their teachers during the lesson.

Asynchronous learning

Asynchronous learning, on the other hand, can be carried out even when the student or teacher is offline. Coursework and communications delivered via web, email, and messages posted on community forums are perfect examples of asynchronous e-learning. In these instances, students will typically complete the lessons on their own and merely use the internet as a support tool rather than venturing online solely for interactive classes.

Conclusion

Rapid advances in information and communication technology pose new opportunities as well as challenges for every society. In the education sector, ICT has enormous potential to help countries address issues of access to learning, quality of the teaching-learning process and management of education systems. In order to ensure the quality of education, the distance education institutions must be careful about the use of proper technologies and media. So We have to think the uses of media and technology in regard to appropriateness and acceptability in the society as well as on the ability of the institution offering the program.

❒

Bibliography

1. Law of the Republic of Uzbekistan on education, № 464-1, 29.08.1997
2. National program on Personnel Training in Uzbekistan, 29.08.1997
3. Data of the Ministry of higher and secondary specialized education of the Republic of Uzbekistan http://edu.uz/en
4. Data of the Ministry for Development of Information Technologies and Communications of the Republic of Uzbekistan http://mitc.uz/en/
5. Al Infande EdD (2013). A Dozen Strategies for Improving Online Student Retention. Faculty Focus 8th July, 2013.
6. Kim E. Dooley & Jane, Magill (2002). Faculty perception and participation in distance education: Pick fruit from the low hanging branches. In Ricxhard Discenza, Caroline Howard & Karen Schenk (Eds). The Design and Management of Effective Distance learning program. IRM Press. PA, USA.

7 Moore, M. G. (1991). Distance Education Theory. The American Journal of Distance Education.5(3).http://www.ajde.com/Contents/vol5_3.htm#editorial.

8. Visser, Lya (2012). Obstacles and opportunities of Distance Higher Education inInternational Settings. In Visser, Lya, Yusra, Visser Ray Amirault and MichaelSimonson (Eds). Trends and Issues in Distance Education. International perspectives.2nd edition. Information Age Publishing, Inc. North Carolina.
9. Aggarwal J.C, "Principles, Methods &Techniques of Teaching", Vikas Publishing House Pvt. Ltd., 2009.
10. "LR Educational evaluation and measurement Competencies for analysis and Application.," Ed.2.

11. Guilbert, J. J., "Educational Handbook for Health Personnel, World Health Organization," Geneva, 1982.
12. O, Connor, Andrea B; "Nursing Staff Development and Continuing Education," Little Brown Company, Bonston, 1986.
13. Sanatombi Elsa, "Manipal Manual of Nursing Education", CBS Publishers & Distributors, NewDelhi, 1st Ed., 2006.
14. ArulSekar, J.M. and Thiyagu, K. (2007). *Information and Communication technology in Educational.* Tiruchirappalli: Prophet Publishers.
15. Dewey and John (1917). *Democracy and Education.* New York: The MacMillan Company.
16. Dignmatri Bhaskara Rao (2001). *Information Technology.* New Delhi: Publishing Home.
17. Dikshit, E. (2005). *Statistic in Education and Psychology.* New Delhi: Paragon International Publishers.
18. Ediger and Marlow (2003), *Teacher Involvement to Evaluate Achievement.* Education, 124(1).
19. John W. Best and James V. Kahn (2002). *Research in Education.* New Delhi: Prentice Hall of India Private Limited.
20. Aupperle, K.D., Carroll, A.B. & Hatfield, J.D. (1985). An Empirical Investigation of the Relationship between Corporate Social Responsibility and Profitability. *Academy of Management Journal,* 28, 446–463.
21. Lee. M. (2011), Configuration of External Influences: The Combined Effects of Institutions and Stakeholders on Corporate Social Responsibility Strategies, *Journal of Business Ethics.*
22. Marquina, P. (2010), The Influence of Corporate Social Responsibility on Peruvian´s Consumers Purchasing Behavior, *Journal of Leadership,* Accountability and Ethics, Vol. 8 (2).
23. Stanaland, A.J.S., Lwin, M.O, & Murphy, P.E. (2011), Consumer Perceptions of the Antecedents and Consequences of Corporate Social Responsibility, *Journal of Business Ethics.*
24. Timane, R. & Tele, T. (2012), A Study of Corporate Social Responsibility in India, International Journal of Research in IT & Management, Volume 2, Issue 12, December.
25. Ghosh, S. M. (2015). Job satisfaction among government and private school teachers of Ranchi. The International Journal of Indian Psychology, 2(2), 88-93.
26. Suki, N. M., & Suki, N. M. (2011). Job satisfaction and organizational commitment: The effect of gender. International journal of psychology research, 6(5), 1-15.

27. Teh, P. L., & Laosirihongthong, T. (2011, September). Job involvement, job satisfaction, and organizational commitment: Predicting propensity to leave a job among skilled employee. In Quality and Reliability (ICQR), 2011 IEEE International Conference on (pp. 1-5). IEEE
28. Bozeman, W. C. (1999). Educational technology: Best practices from American schools. Larchmont, NY: Eye in Education.
29. Lawless, K.A., & Pellegrino, J.W. (2007). Professional development in integrating technology into teaching and learning: Knowns, unknowns, and ways to pursue better questions and answers. *Review of Educational Research,* 77(4), 575-614.
30. Fulton, K., Glenn, A., & Valdez, G. (2003). Three preservice programs preparing tomorrow's teachers to use technology: A study in partnerships. (http://www.ncrel.org/tech/preservice). Verified on 16/02/2011.
31. Hughes, J. (2004). Technology learning principles for preservice and in-service teacher education. Contemporary Issues in Technology and Teacher Education, 4(3), 345-362.
32. neither can traditional classroom teaching.
33. ICTs for education and building human capital, http://www.itu.int/visions.
34. Victoria L. Tinio, ICT in Education, http://www.apdip.net.
35. Jonassen, D. H. Peck. K. L., and Wilson, B.G (1999). Learning with Technologies; A Constructivist Perspective, New Jersey: Merrill/Prentice Hall.
36. Agarwal, J.C. (1995) Essential of Educational Technology: Teaching Learning Innovations in Education. Delhi: Vikas Publishing House (P) Ltd.
37. Clark (Ed.) Learning from Media: Arguments, Analyses and Evidence, Greenwich, CT: Information Age Publishing.
38. Dziuban, C.D., Hartman, J.L. & Moskal, P.D. (2004), Blended Learning, Edu-cause Center for Applied Research, Research Bulletin, 7, retrieved January 15, 2008, from htt://www.educause.edu/ir/library.
39. Alexander, B. (2006). Web 2.0: A new wave of innovation for teaching and learning?Retrieved October 8, 2011, fromhttps://net.educause.edu/ir/library/pdf/erm0621.pdf.
40. Bryan Alexander. (2006). Web 2.0: A new wave of innovation for teaching and learning?October 8, 2011,retrieved fromhttps://net.educause.edu/ir/library/pdf.
41. Coyer, K., Dowmunt, T., & Fountain, A. (2007). The alternative media handbook. London: Routledge.

42. Datt, R. (1993). India. In H. Katō & S. Wong (Eds.), Distance education in Asia andthe Pacific: Country papers (pp. 57-95).
43. Jan Hylen. (2007). Open educational resources: Opportunities and challenges.Retrieved from OECD website: http://www.oecd.org/edu/ceri/37351085.pdf.
44. Abel, R. (2005). Implementing Best Practices in online learning. EduCause Quarterly, 28(3)
45. Akkoyunlu, B., & Soylu, M. Y. (2008). A Study of Student's Perceptions in a Blended Learning Environment Based on Different Learning Styles. Educational Technology & Society, 11 (1), 183-193.
46. Bath, d. & Bourke, J. (2010) Getting Started with Blended Learning. Retrieved August 27, 2015
47. from Blended Learning 101 handbook. (2013). Blended Learning: Steps to Success. Retrieved August 16, 2015 from aspirepublicschools.org.
48. Berge, Z., & Huang, Y. (2004). A model for sustainable student retention: A holistic perspective on the student dropout problem with special attention to e-learning. Deosnews, 13(5). Retrieved from: http://www.ed.psu.edu/acsde/deos/*deosnews*/deosnews13_5.pdf
49. Yousefi, F., Redzuan. M., Mariani, B., Juhari, R.B., and Talib, M.A. (2014). The effects of family income on Test-anxiety and academic achievement among Iranian high school students. *Asian Social Science,* 6 (6), 74-79.
50. Zinta, R.L. (2008). Effectiveness of guided mastery treatment for reducing Test-anxiety among self-efficacious students. *Journal of the Indian Academy of Applied Psychology,* 34(2), 233-239.
51. Zoller, U., & Ben-Chain, D. (1990). Gender differences in examination type, test anxiety, and academic achievement in college science: a case study. *Science education,* 74(6), 597-608.
52. Nongkynrih B, Anand K, Kusuma YS, Rai SK, Misra P, Goswami K. Linking undergraduate medical education to primary health care. Indian J Public Health. 2008;52:28-32.
53. Negandhi H, Sharma K, Zodpey SP. How can departments of community medicine shape the future of public health education in India? Indian J Public Health. 2010;54:184-9.
54. Ananthakrishnan N. Medical education in India: is it still possible to reverse the downhill trend? Natl Med J India. 2010;23:156-60.
55. Kotwal A. Innovations in teaching/learning methods for medical students: research with mentoring. Indian J Public Health. 2013;57:144-6.
56. Belanger, F., & Jordan, D. H. (2004). Evaluation and implementation of distance learning: Technologies,

57. tools and techniques. Hershey, PA: Idea Group Publishing.
58. Brown, G., & Wack, M. (1999). The difference frenzy and matching buckshot with buchshot. The Technology
59. Honeyman, M; Miller, G (December 1993). "Agriculture distance education: A valid alternative for higher education?" (PDF). Proceedings of the 20th Annual National Agricultural Education Research Meeting: 67–73.
60. Distance Education Accrediting Commission. "CHEA-Recognized Scope of Accreditation." "Archived copy". Archived from the original on 24 December 2016. Retrieved 4 November 2015.. April 2013.
62. Rengarajan, P. & Senthilnathan. S (2012), *Teacher Educators Attitude towards E-Learning.* Edutracks. 12 (1). 34-37.
63. International Journal for Research and Development, journal for the social science (2017, Sep/Oct). *Attitude towards electronic courseware in learning history among the high school students. 5* (3).36-39.
64. JagannathMohanty, 1982,Indian Education in the Emerging Society, Sterling Publishers
65. Private Limited, New Delhi.
66. S.D.Khanna, V.K. Saxena, T.P.Lamba, V.Murthy, Education in the Emerging Indian Society and the Teacher.
67. G.R. Madan, 1966, Indian Social Problems, Allied Publishers Private Limited, Bombay
68. S.K.Nanda , 1982, Indian Education and its Problems, Kalyani Publishers, New Delhi.
69. S.Lakshmi, 1989, Challenges in Indian Education, Sterling Publishers Private Limited, New Delhi.
70. Ahmad, I. and Bokhari, M.U. (2011). Distance Education: From Asynchronous to Synchronous E-Learning. CPMR-IJT.
71. Chowdhury, M.H. and Khatun, Amina. (2013). Modeling E-Learning Assisted Distance Education System for Bangladesh. International Journal of Advanced Science and Technology.
73. Killedar, M. (2001). Distance Education Through Internet Based. Indian Journal of Open Learning, 8-79.
74. Kim, W. and Shih, T.K. (2003). Distance Education: The Status and Challenges. Journal of Object Technology.
75. Nagy, A. (2005). The Impact of E-Learning. E-Content: Technologies and Perspectives for the European Market (pp. 79-96). Berline: Springer-Verlag.
76. Kawatra, P. S., & Singh, N. K. (2006). E-learning in LIS education in India. In C. Khoo, D. Singh & A.S.Chaudhry (Eds.), Proceedings of

the Asia-Pacific Conference on Library & Information Education & Practice 2006 (A-LIEP 2006), Singapore, 3-6 April 2006 (pp. 605-611). Singapore: School of Communication & Information, Nanyang Technological University.

77. Agarwal D.D (2004) 'Modern methods of teaching biology' Sarup and Sons, New Delhi.
78. Maya .S (2016) 'Teaching of biology', APH publishing corporation, New Delhi.
79. Edward William Benjamin. A. (2013) 'Effectiveness of e-Learning Modules in science at higher secondary school level in India' Indian Journal of applied research, Vol 3, Issue 4, Page 29- 31.
80. https://distancelearning.louisiana.edu/Curriculum
81. Dr. AR. Saravanakumar & Dr.S.Subbiah, (2011), "Teacher Education Programme Through Distance Mode – A Technological Approach", Indian Journal of Applied Research, India, Vol.1, Iss 3.
82. Dr.AR.Saravanakumar (2019), 'Distance Mode (DM) Teacher Education Programme (TEP) in India: An Integrated Approach (IA)', Journal of Emerging Technologies and Innovative Research (JETIR) , December 2018, Volume 5, Issue 12, www.jetir.org.
83. Saravanakumar, AR & Dr.S.Subbiah , Multidimensional Practices in Teacher Education (TE) Through Distance Education (DE), Indian Streams Research Journal, Vol.1, Issue XII, 2012.
84. Noriko Fujioka-Ito (2013), "Designing a Curriculum for a Distance Learning Class: An Example of a First-year Japanese Course",Theory and Practice in Language Studies, Vol. 3, No. 10, pp. 1717-1725.
86. M.Chinnappan & Dr.A.Edward William Benjamin (November 2017). Effectiveness of E-Modules in learning history among the high school students. International Journal of multidisciplinary Researches.ISSN NO:2249-8684
87. R.Selvaganapathy & T.Ganesh (2017). Teaching and learning of Tamil language. International Conference on Tamil Language, Literature, Teaching and Learning.
88. https://chemsense.sri.com/about/papers/ozmaRussellMultimedia2004.pdf
89. Bibliography=87
90. Fisher, R. Teaching children to think. London: Nelson Thornes, 2005.
91. Lamb, S. M. Pathways of the brain: The neurocognitive basis of language. Amsterdam: J. Benjamins Publishing Co, 1999.
92. Muñoz A P. "A usage-based and neurocognitive approach to the learning of English as a foreign language with deaf and hard of hearing students: A Case Study." US-China Foreign Language, 14, No. 9, (2016): 630-643

93. Ahmad, I. and Bokhari, M.U. (2011). Distance Education: From Asynchronous to Synchronous E-Learning. CPMR-IJT.
94. Chowdhury, M.H. and Khatun, Amina. (2013). Modeling E-Learning Assisted Distance Education System for Bangladesh. International Journal of Advanced Science and Technology.
95. Killedar, M. (2001). Distance Education Through Internet Based. Indian Journal of Open Learning, 8-79.
96. Baytiyeh, Hoda (2018) Students' Use of Mobile Technologies: Motivational Factors International Journal of Information and Communication Technology Education, v14 n1 Article 6 p73-85 EJ1167915.
97. Guha A.S & IsagahahLawrniang (2018) Use of Social Site Networks in Distance Education Learning to Learn University News 56(02) Jan 08-14 pp.29-31.
98. Akkoyunlu, B. & Soylu, M. Y. (2006). "A Study on Students' Views About Blended
99. Learning Environment". *Turkish Online Journal of Distance Education-TOJDE, 7* (3).
100. Azizan, F.Z. (2010). Blended Learning in Higher Education Institution in Malaysia.
101. *Proceedings of Regional Conference on Knowledge Integration in ICT.*
102. Badawi, M.F. (2009). Using Blended Learning for Enhancing EFL Prospective Teachers'
103. Pedagogical Knowledge and Performance. *Conference paper: Learning & Language - The Spirit of the Age.* Retrieved from: http://eric.ed.gov.
104. Chen, C.C., & Jones, K.T. (2007). "Blended Learning vs. Traditional Classroom Settings:
105. Assessing Effectiveness and Student Perceptions in an MBA Accounting Course". *The Journal of Educators Online,* 4 (1).
106. Davis, H.C. & Fill, K. (2007). "Embedding blended learning in a university's teaching culture: Experiences and reflections". *British Journal of Educational Technology,* 38 (5).
107. Jayaram, N, (2008) School-Community Relations in India: Some Theoretical and Methodological Considerations, Paper presented at National Seminar on Community and School Linkages: Principles and Practices (March 17- 19, 2008), NUEPA, New Delhi
108. Kantha V. Vinay& Daisy Narain (2003) Dynamics of Community Mobilisation
109. SarvaShikshaAbhiyan: framework for Implementation(based on the RTE 2009), Ministry of Human Resource Development,Department of school education and Literacy

110. KhannaKailash (2007) Evolution of Policies in India in MukhopadhyayMarmar&MadhuParhar (ed) Education in India, Shipra, New Delhi. MitsueUemura(1999) Community Participation in Education
111. Avery, L. M., & Kassam, K. A. (2011). Phronesis: Children's local rural knowledge of science and engineering. Journal of Research in Rural Education,.
112. Betageri, G. (2013). Impact of English language teaching on the communication skills of rural students. International Journal on English Language and Literature .
113. Moulton, J. (2001). Improving education in rural areas: Guidance for rural development specialists. For Charles Maguire: The World Bank
114. Aungwatanakun, S., "English Teaching Methodology", (2nd edn.), Bangkok: Chulalongkorn University Press, 1994.
115. alentina Arkorful, Nelly Abaidoo. (2014). The role of e-learning, the advantages and disadvantages of its adoption in Higher Education, International Journal of Education and Research, 2(12), 397-410
116. OECD (2005). E-learning in tertiary education [Online]. Available at http://www.cumex.org. (Accessed 27 /02/ 2014).
117. Wentling T.L, Waight C, Gallagher J, La Fleur J, Wang C, Kanfer A. (2000). E-learning - a review of literature. Knowledge and Learning Systems Group NCSA 9.1–73.
118. https://www.talentlms.com/ebook/elearning/history-of-elearning
119. Traxler, J. Mobile Learning: The Philosophical Challenges, Problems and Implications of Defining and Theorising. S. Afr. J. Open Distance Learn. Pract.2017, 39.
120. Moore, J.L.; Dickson-Deane, C.; Galyen, K. e-Learning, online learning, and distance learning environments: Are they the same? Int. Higher Educ. 2011, 14, 129–135.
121. Valentine, D. Distance learning: Promises, problems, and possibilities. OnlineJ.DistanceLearn. Adm. 2002, 5, 1–11.
122. Folkestad, G. Formal and informal learning situations or practices vs. formal and informal ways of learning. Br. J. Music Educ. 2006, 23, 135–145.
123. Malcolm, J.; Hodkinson, P.; Colley, H. The interrelationships between informal and formal learning. J. Workplace Learn. 2003, 15, 313–318.
124. James K. Luiselli (2002), Behavioral Psychology in the Schools, Child & Family behavior therapy, Volume 24,USA.
125. John F.Davidio (2006), The Psychology of Helping and Altruism: Problems & Puzzles, Lawrence Erlbaum Associates, New Jersey.

126. John F.Davidio(2006), The Social Psychology of Pro social Behavior, Lawrence Erlbaum Associates, New Jersey.
127. Oxford University Press, South Africa.
128. Kirk Jackie e.d. , (2008), Women Teaching in South Asia, SAGE, New Delhi
129. Srivastava Gouri, (2012), Gender and Peace in Textbooks and Schooling Processes, Concept Publishing Company Pvt. Ltd, New Delhi
130. Srivastava Gouri, Yadav Mona, (2013), Training Material for Teacher Educators on Gender Equality and Empowerment, Vol.I, II and III, NCERT, New Delhi
131. Distance Education Accrediting Commission. "CHEA-recognized scope of Accreditation." "Archieved copy". Archieved from the original on 24 December 2016. Retrieved 4 November 2015.. April 2013.
132. Alan Twit. " Reflection on student support in open and distance learning ". The international review of research in open distance learning.
133. IAP. Distance learning... a magazine for leaders volume 2 number 6.
134. Burns, Mary. Distance Education for teacher training: Modes, Models and Methods. Retrieved 10 September 2012.
135. Clark R. C., Mayer R. (2008), E-Learning and the Science of Instruction, Proven Guidelines for Consumers and Designers of Multimedia Learning, Pfeiffer, San Francisco, 8.(1)
136. Madey J., Rudak L. (2009), E-learning versus t-learning, De Gruyter, Warszawa, 103.(2)
137. Rudak L. (2008), E-learning - non-discovered territory (a course on studying by the Internet), accepted for the International Conference "Student Mobility and ICT: can ELEARNING overcome barriers of Life-Long learning?", Maastricht, Netherlands, 21.(3)
138. Rosenberg M. (2011), E-Learning: Strategies for Delivering Knowledge in the Digital Age, Educational Technology & Society, 43.(10)
139. Retrieved May 23, 2009 from: http://www.coe.int/T/E/Com/Files/Themes/e-voting/definition.asp Gronlund, A. (2001).
140. Democracy in an IT-famed society. Communications of the ACM, 44(1), 23-26. Haricombe, I. J. (1998).
141. Literacy in an Information Age (p. 43). [S.l.]: International Visual Literacy Association. Cooper, R., & Dompsey, P. R. (1998).
142. Biswas AB, Roy AK, Sen AK, Biswas R (1990). A study of the impact of health education imparted to school children on their knowledge, attitude and practices in regard to personal hygiene.*Ind. J Pub Health*, 34(2).

143. Dongre AR,Deshmukh PR, Garg BR (2006).The impact of school health education programme on personal hygiene and related morbidities in tribal school children of wardha district. *Ind J of Comm Med,* 31(2).
144. Bundy, D., Shaeffer, S., Jukes, M., Beegle, K., Gillespie, A., Drake, L. et al. (2006) School-based health and nutrition programs. In Jamison, D., Breman, J., Measham, A., Alleyne, G., Claeson, M., Evans, D. et al. (eds), Disease Control Priorities in Developing Countries, 2nd edition. Oxford University Press and the World Bank, New York.
145. Alhawiti, M.M.F.(2014). A proposed model for evaluating the quality of online programs and courses: The case of the university of Tabuk, Education Journal, 3(2): 57-70.
146. Beck, J. K., &Kacirek, K. (2011). Using qualitative methods to evaluate distance education: a case study. In V. Wang (Ed.), Encyclopedia of Information Communication Technologies and Adult Education Integration , 337- 359.
147. Denzin, N. K., & Lincoln, Y. S. (Eds.). (1998). The landscape of qualitative research: Theories and issues. Thousand Oaks: Sage Publications.
148. Guba, E.G.,& Lincoln, Y.S. (1981). Effective evaluation. San Francisco: Jossey.Bass .
149. Kaya ,Z ., &Tan,Ş.(2015). New trends of measurement and assessme
150. Archer, J. (2006). Cross-cultural differences in physcial aggression between partners: A social-role analysis. *Personality and social psychology review,* 10(2), 1331-1353.
151. Bradley, K., & Khor, D. (1993). Toward an integration of theory and research on the status of women.*Gender and Society,* 7(3), 3473-3478.
152. Fanslow, J., Robinson, E., Crengle, S., & Perese, L. (2010). Juxtaposing beliefs and reality: Prevalence rates of intimate partner violence and attitudes to violence and gender roles reported by New Zealand women. *Violence against Women,* 16(7), 8128-8131.
153. Flood, M., Fergus, L., & Heenan, M. (2009). *Respectful relationships education: Violence prevention and respectful relationships in Victorian Schools.* Melbourne: Department of Education and Early Childhood Development.
154. Bibliography-134
155. Arroba, T. (1977). 'Styles of Decision Making and their Use: an Empirical Study', 50-52
156. Baxter Magolda,(1988). Assessing intellectual development: The link between theory and practice. Alexadria, VA: American College Personnel Association. 16-17

157. O'Brien, T. P. (1991). Construct validation of the Gregorc style delineator: An application of LISRAEL 7 [Electronic version]. Educational and Psychological Measurement, 50(3), 631-636.
158. Perry, William G., Jr.(1970). Forms of Intellectual and Ethical Development in the College Years: A Scheme (New York: Holt, Rinehart, and Winston); reprinted November 1998;Jossey-Bass;ISBN:0787941182
159. Sproles, G.B. and Kendall, E.L. (1986). "A methodology for profiling consumers' decision-making styles", Journal of Consumer Affairs,Vol. 20 (2), pp. 267-279.
160. Beringer, V. (2009, Oct 20) For kids, pen's mightier than keyboard. Futurity.org. Retrieved February 25th 2013 from http://www.futurity.org/society-culture/for-kids-pens-mightier-than-keyboard/#more-4909.
161. Branford, J., Brown, A., & Cocking, R. (2000). How people learn: Brain, mind, experience, and school. Washington, DC: National Academic Press.
162. Brill, J. M., & Galloway, C. (2007). Perils and promises: University instructors' integration of technology in classroom-based practices. British Journal of Educational Technology. 38(1), 95-105.
163. Roschelle, J., Pea, R., Hoadley, C., Gordin, D., & Means, B. (2000). Future of children, 10(2), 76-101.
164. Shah (2011, July 16) Why does writing make us smart? huffingpost.com. Retrieved February 25th 2013 from http://www.huffingtonpost.com/2011/07/16/why- does-writing-make-us _n_900638.html
165. Jaiswal, V. (2013). Current Status E-learning In Indian Higher Education: A Case Study Of U.P., available at SSRN: http://ssrn.com/abstract=2231910. http://dx.doi.org/10.2139/ssrn.2231910.
166. Kalaivani, A. (2014, November). Role of E-learning in the Quality Improvement of Higher Education, IOSR Journal of Humanities And Social Science (IOSR-JHSS) P-ISSN:2279-0845 e-ISSN:2279-0837 vol 19, no.11,pp 15-17,www.iosrjournals.org.
167. National Health Policy, 2017, Ministry of Health and family welfare, government of India
168. Saravanakumar, AR & Dr.S.Subbiah , Multidimensional Practices in Teacher Education (TE) Through Distance Education (DE), Indian Streams Research Journal, Vol.1, Issue XII, 2012.
169. Saravanakumar AR, Present Scenario And Future Prospects Of Higher Education In India, Proceeding of the Social Sciences Research ICSSR,p- 9-10, Kota Kinabalu, Sabah, MALAYSIA. Organized by http://WorldConferences.net, 2014.

170. Villegas-Reimers, E. (2003). Teacher Professional Development: an international review of the literature (Paris: UNESCO Publishing).
171. Lokesh koul. (2008). Methodology of educational research (3rd revised ed., pp.111-125) Vikas Publishing house (P) limited, Noida (UP).
172. Radha Mohan. (2010) Research methods in education (2nd ed., pp.35-44) Neelkamal Publications (P) limited, Hyderabad.
173. Vanaja, M. (2005). Educational technology (1st ed., pp.10-20) Neelkamal Publications (P) limited, Hyderabad.
174. ERNET India, Training manual for smart virtual classroom project, DeitY, Government of India.
175. Anurag Chaudhary., Gaurav Agrawal., & Meghna Jharia (2014). A Review on Applications of Smart Class and E-Learning. International Journal of Scientific Engineering and Research, Volume 2 Issue 3, (pp.77-80) March 2014.
176. Amareswaran, N. and Kikon, A.E. (2016, January 29th -30th). ICT in Teacher Education with Special Reference to Nagaland. Paper presented at a National Seminar on Enriching Quality by Integrating ICT in Higher Education: Challenges and Prospects, Salem, Tamil Nadu.
177 Amareswaran, N. and Kikon, A.E. (2016, May 21st). *Employability Skills for Teacher Educators in the 21st Century.* Paper presented at a National Seminar on Preparing Best Teachers: Road Map for Quality Teacher Education, Salem, Tamil Nadu.
178. Amareswaran, N. and Kikon, A.E.(2015, December 22nd -23rd). *Skills for Teachers in the 21st Century with Special Reference to Nagaland.* Paper presented at a National Seminar on Skilling India: Status, Contours and Strategies, Tirupati, Andhra Pradesh.
179. Annual report 2009-2010. (2010). published by ministry of human resource development, Government of India.
180. Education consultants India 1td. (sep 1985). Project rerport: Indira Gandhi national open University,p.27-28.
181. Howell, scott I., Williams, peter B., Iindsay, nathan K. (2003). Thirty-two trends affecting distance education: an informed foundation for strategic planning. *Online Journal of Distance Learning Admin- istration,* Vol.6,no.3.
182. Dominguez, Paula (2001) "Assessing Distance Education Course and Discipline Differences in Their Effectiveness" http://www.findarticles.com/cf_0/m0FCG/1_28/73535502/print.jhtml
183. Harry, Keith, John Magnus, Keegan, Desmond (1993) "Distance Education: New Perspectives" Routledge in London and New York.

184. Holmberg, Borje (1995) "Theory and Practice of Distance Education" Routledge in New York. Huebner, Mary Kathleen and Wiener, R. William (2001) "Distance Education in 2001" http://www.afb.org/jvib/JVIB950902.asp

185. Barnett, M. (2002, April). *Issues and trends concerning electronic networking technologies for teacher professional development:* A critical review of the literature. Paper presented at the annual meeting of American Educational Research Association, New Orleans.

186. Batane, T. (2004).Inservice teacher training and technology: A case of Botswana. *Journal of Technology and Teacher Education,* 12(3), 387–410.

187. Guskey, T. R. (2000). Practical Guidelines for evaluating professionaldevelopment.In T. R. Guskey (Ed.), Evaluating professional development,Chapter 4. Corwin Press.

188. Harasim, L. (1990). On-line education: An environment for collaboration and

189. intellectual amplification in on-line education: Perspectives on a newenvironment. New York: Praeger.

190. Abas, Z. W. (2009). E-Learning in Malaysia: Moving Forward in Open Distance Learning. InternationalJournal of E-Learning, 8(4), 527-537.

191. Barker, K. (2002). Canadian Recommended E-learning Guidelines. Vancouver, BC: Future Ed and Canadian Association for Community Education. Retrieved from http://www.col.org/newsrelease/CanREGs%20Eng.pdf

192. Bhuasiri, Wannasiri; Xaymoungkhoun, Oudone; Zo, Hangjung; Rho, Jae Jeung; Ciganek, Andrew P. (2016) Critical Success Factors for E-Learning in Developing Countries: A Comparative Analysis between ICT Experts and Faculty . Computers & Education, v58 n2 p843-855 Feb 2016.

193 Caminotti, Enzo; Gray, Jeremy (2012) The Effectiveness of Storytelling on Adult Learning. Journal of Workplace Learning, v24 n6 p430-438 2012.

194. Pernas, Ana Marilza; Diaz, Alicia; Motz, Regina; de Oliveira, Jose Palazzo Moreira (2012) Enriching Adaptation in E-Learning Systems through a Situation-Aware Ontology Network . Interactive Technology and Smart Education, v9 n2 p60-73 2012.

195. Broadley, T., J. Downie and D. Gibson. (2015). "Evolving learning paradigms: Re-setting the

196. baselines and collection methods of information and communication technology in education statistics post-2015". Montreal: UNESCO Institute for Statistics.

197. European Commission (2013). "Survey of Schools: ICT in Education. Benchmarking Access, Use and Attitudes to Technology in Europe's Schools" Belgium: European Commission.
198. Barden, R. A. (1996). "The case for linear instructional design and development: A commentary on models, challenges and myths" Educational Technology 2;5-23.

❑❑❑

Index

❑❑❑